X-O MANOWAR

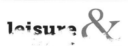

HERO

MATT KINDT | TOMÁS GIORELLO | DIEGO RODRIGUEZ | DAVE SHARPE

CONTENTS

Collection Cover Art: Kenneth Rocafort

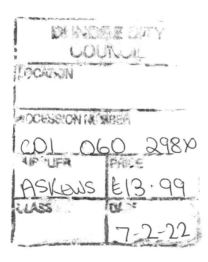
Associate Editor: David Menchel
Senior Editor: Karl Bollers

VALIANT.

X-O Manowar® (2017): Hero. Published by Valiant Entertainment
LLC. Office of Publication: 350 Seventh Avenue, New York, NY
10001. Compilation copyright © 2019 Valiant Entertainment LLC. All
rights reserved. Contains materials originally published in single
magazine form as X-O Manowar (2017) #23-26. Copyright © 2019
Valiant Entertainment LLC. All rights reserved. All characters, their
distinctive likeness and related indicia featured in this publication
are trademarks of Valiant Entertainment LLC. The stories,
characters, and incidents featured in this publication are entirely
fictional. Valiant Entertainment does not read or accept unsolicited
submissions of ideas, stories, or artwork. Printed in the U.S.A.
First Printing. ISBN: 9781682153185.

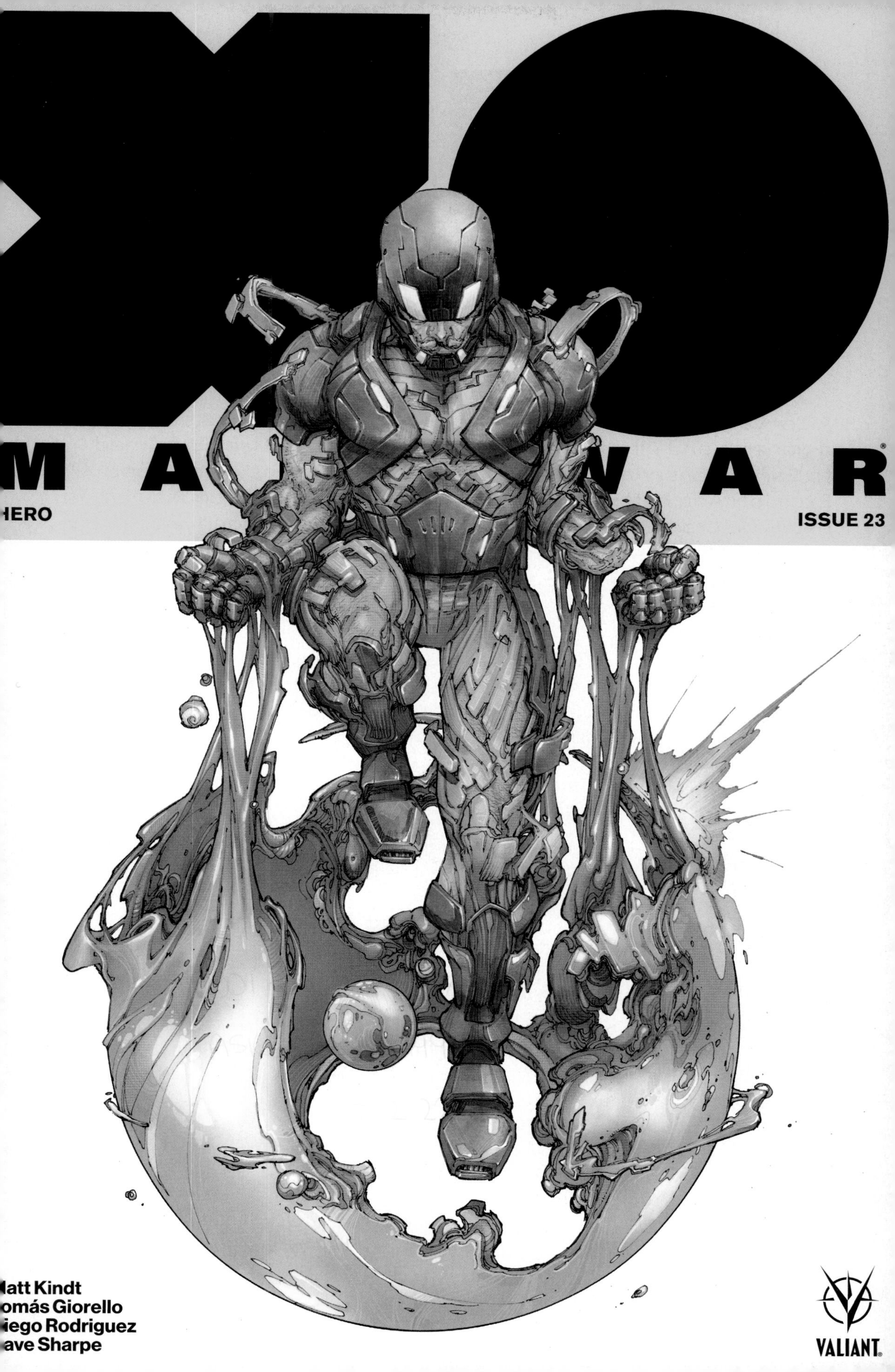

M A W A R
HERO
ISSUE 23
latt Kindt
omás Giorello
iego Rodriguez
ave Sharpe
VALIANT

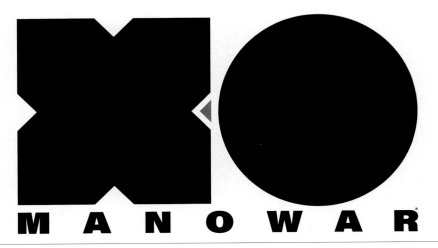

X-O MANOWAR

After years of adventure on planet Gorin, serving as a soldier, a general, and ultimately as an emperor, Aric of Dacia returned to Earth. Conscripted by G.A.T.E., the Global Agency for Threat Excision, Aric battled earthlings and aliens alike for causes he had little stake in. Now, he enjoys some much-needed rest while a threat from his past looms on the horizon...

ARIC OF DACIA

Aric of Dacia is X-O Manowar, Earth's most powerful warrior. He spent some time away on a planet called Gorin, but has returned to Earth, where he was once again called into action by Jamie Capshaw. His last mission completed, Aric hopes to wash his hands of G.A.T.E.'s machinations once and for all.

SHANHARA

The source of Aric's incredible power. Shanhara is a sentient suit of armor from an alien world, who has chosen Aric as her bearer.

JAMIE CAPSHAW

Brigadier General Jamie Capshaw is the leader of G.A.T.E., the Global Agency for Threat Excision. Relying on alien technology stolen during her last mission with Aric, Capshaw aims to restore G.A.T.E. to its full power.

THE PROCESSORS

A team of ruthless intergalactic mercenaries who will do anything for the right price. After suffering a crushing defeat at the hands of Aric, the Processors are headed to Earth to exact their revenge...

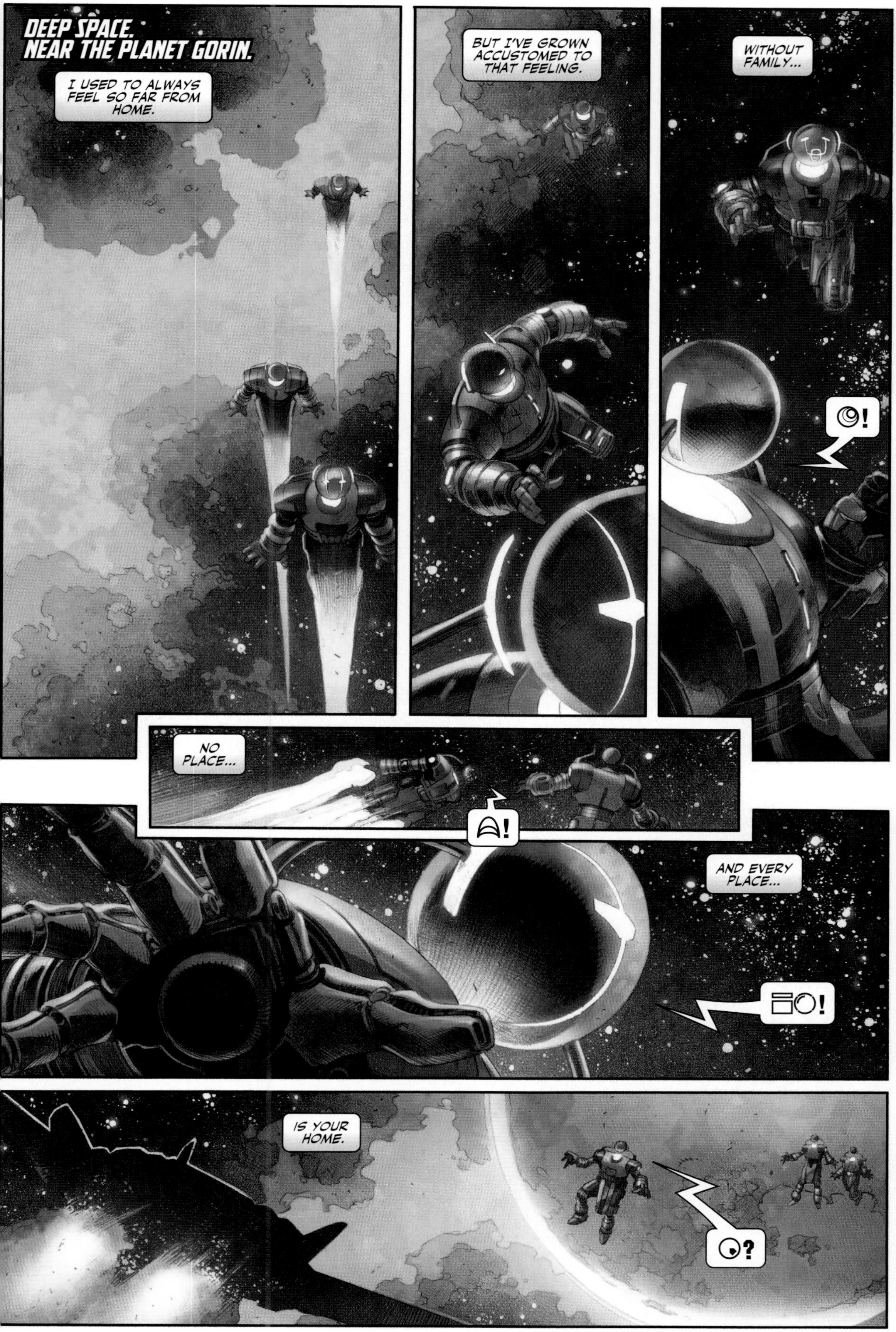
DEEP SPACE.
NEAR THE PLANET GORIN.
I USED TO ALWAYS FEEL SO FAR FROM HOME.
BUT I'VE GROWN ACCUSTOMED TO THAT FEELING.
WITHOUT FAMILY...
NO PLACE...
AND EVERY PLACE...
IS YOUR HOME.

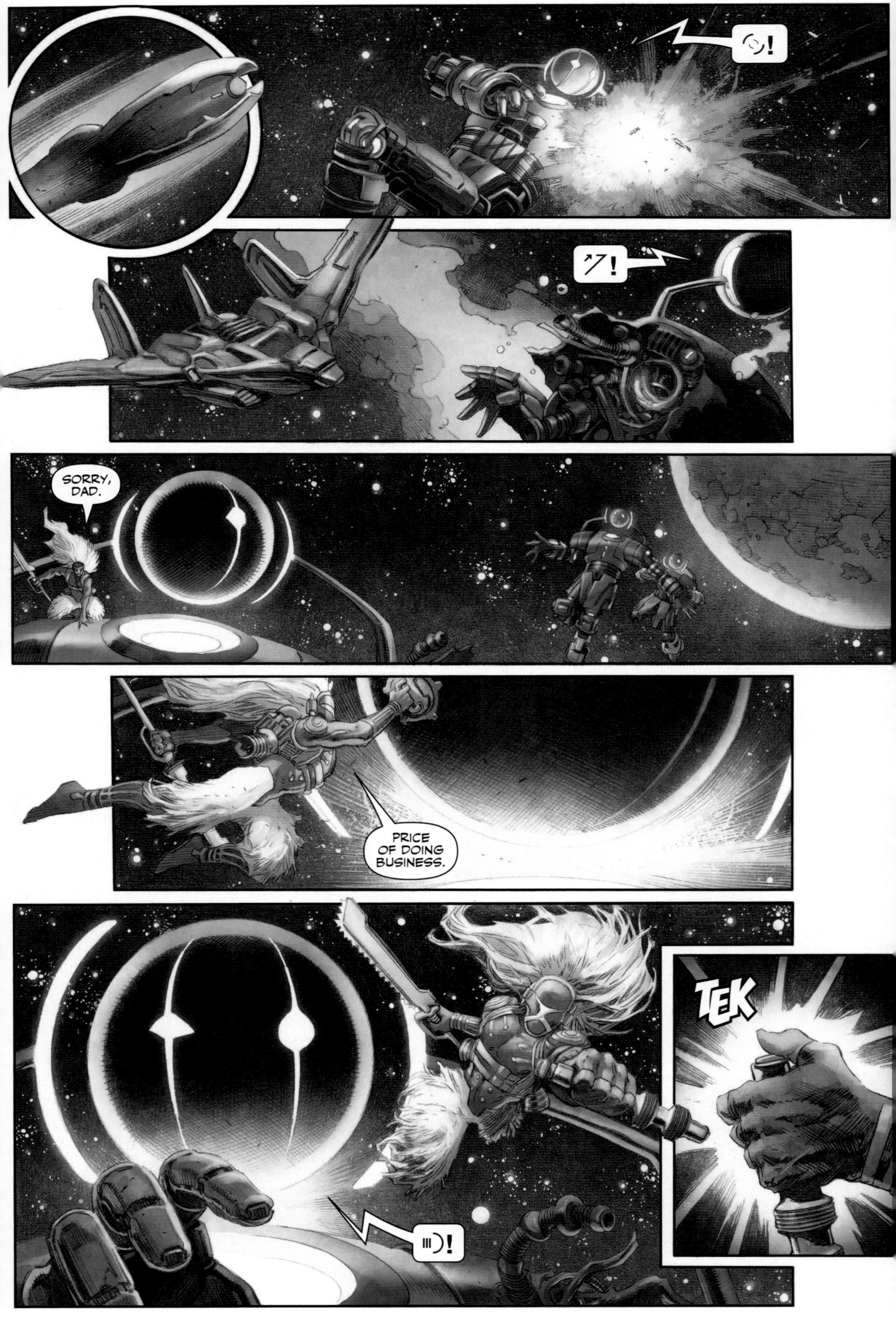

SORRY, DAD.
PRICE OF DOING BUSINESS.
TEK

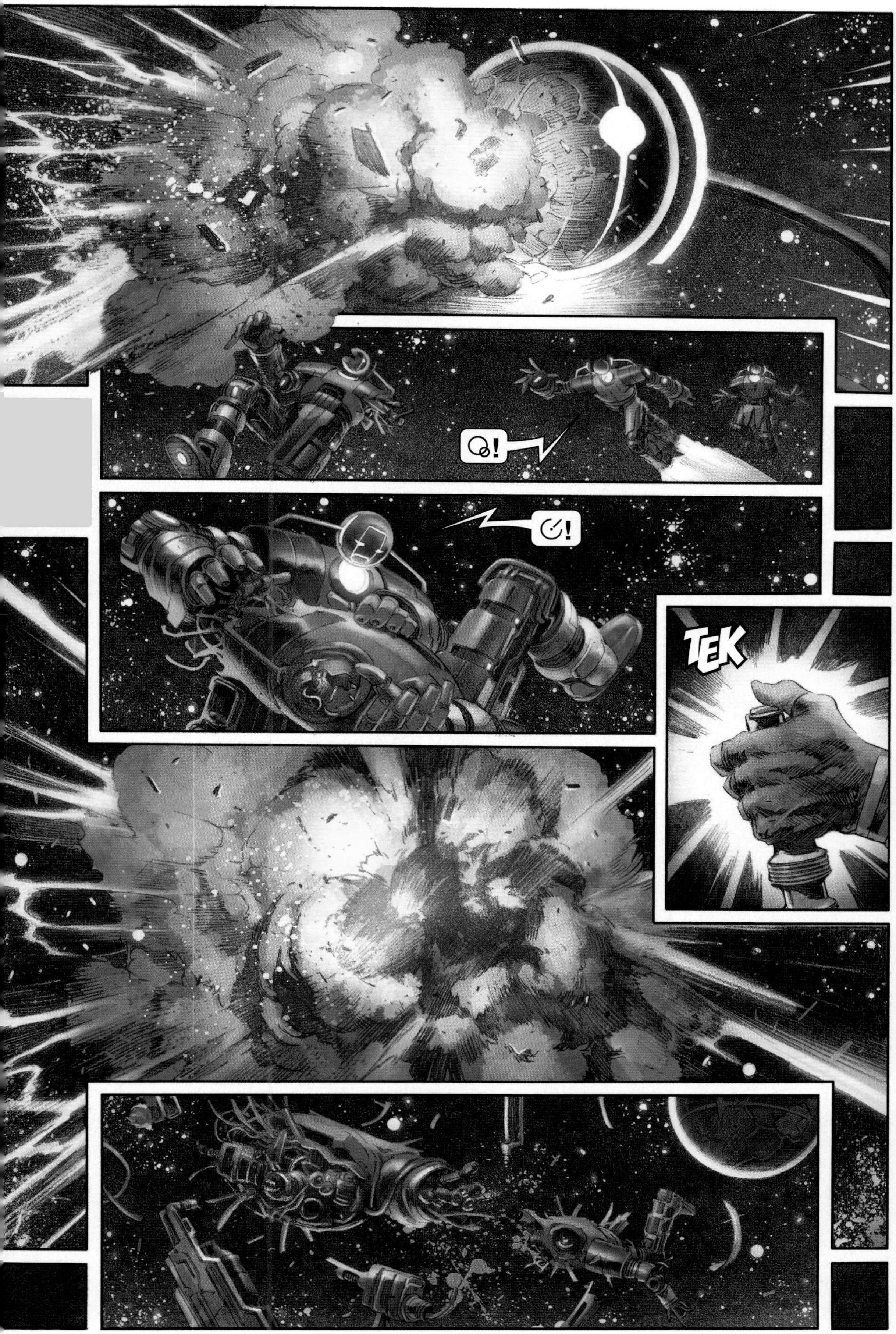

TEK

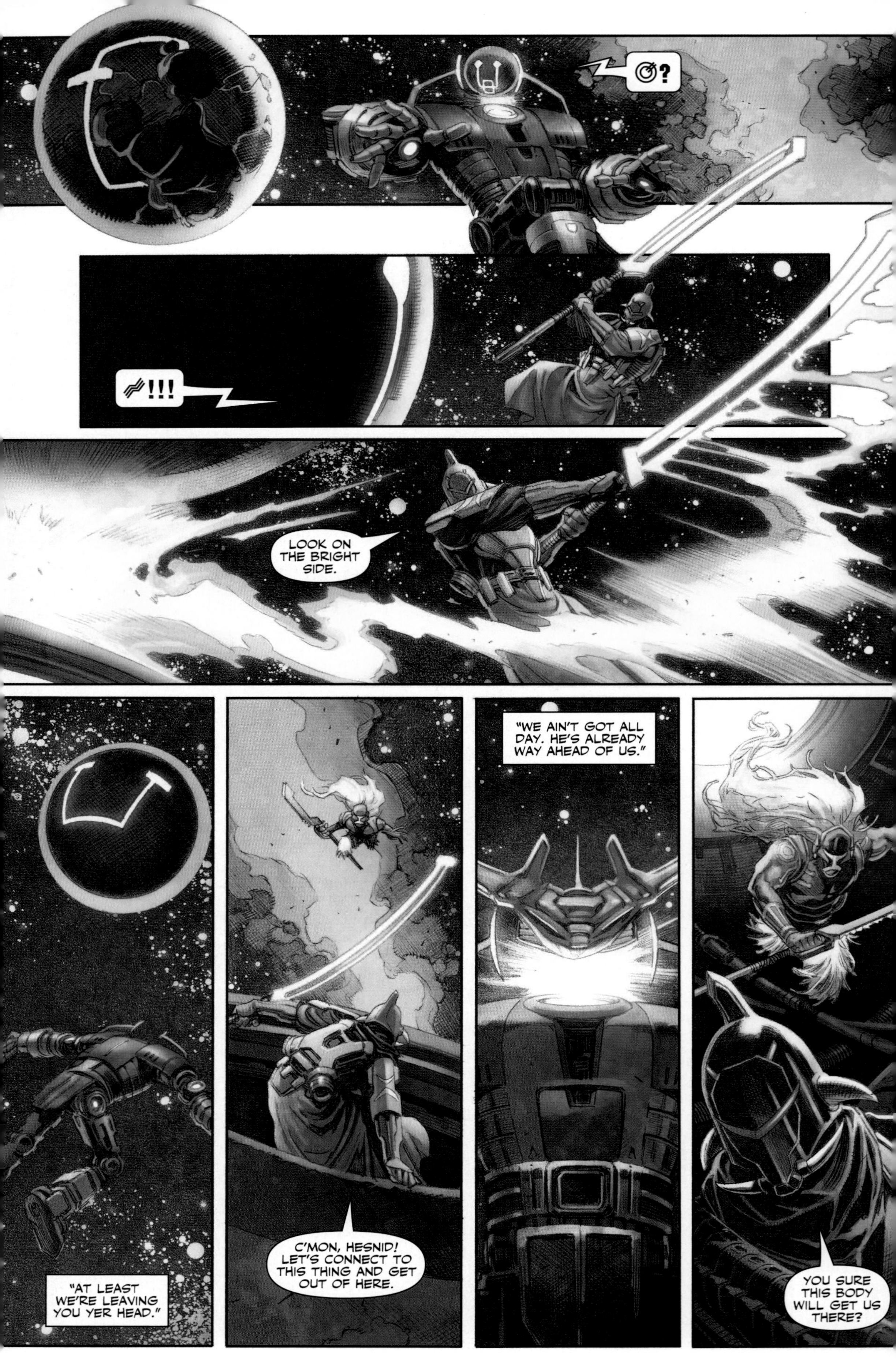
?
!!!
LOOK ON THE BRIGHT SIDE.
"AT LEAST WE'RE LEAVING YOU YER HEAD."
C'MON, HESNID! LET'S CONNECT TO THIS THING AND GET OUT OF HERE.
"WE AIN'T GOT ALL DAY. HE'S ALREADY WAY AHEAD OF US."
YOU SURE THIS BODY WILL GET US THERE?

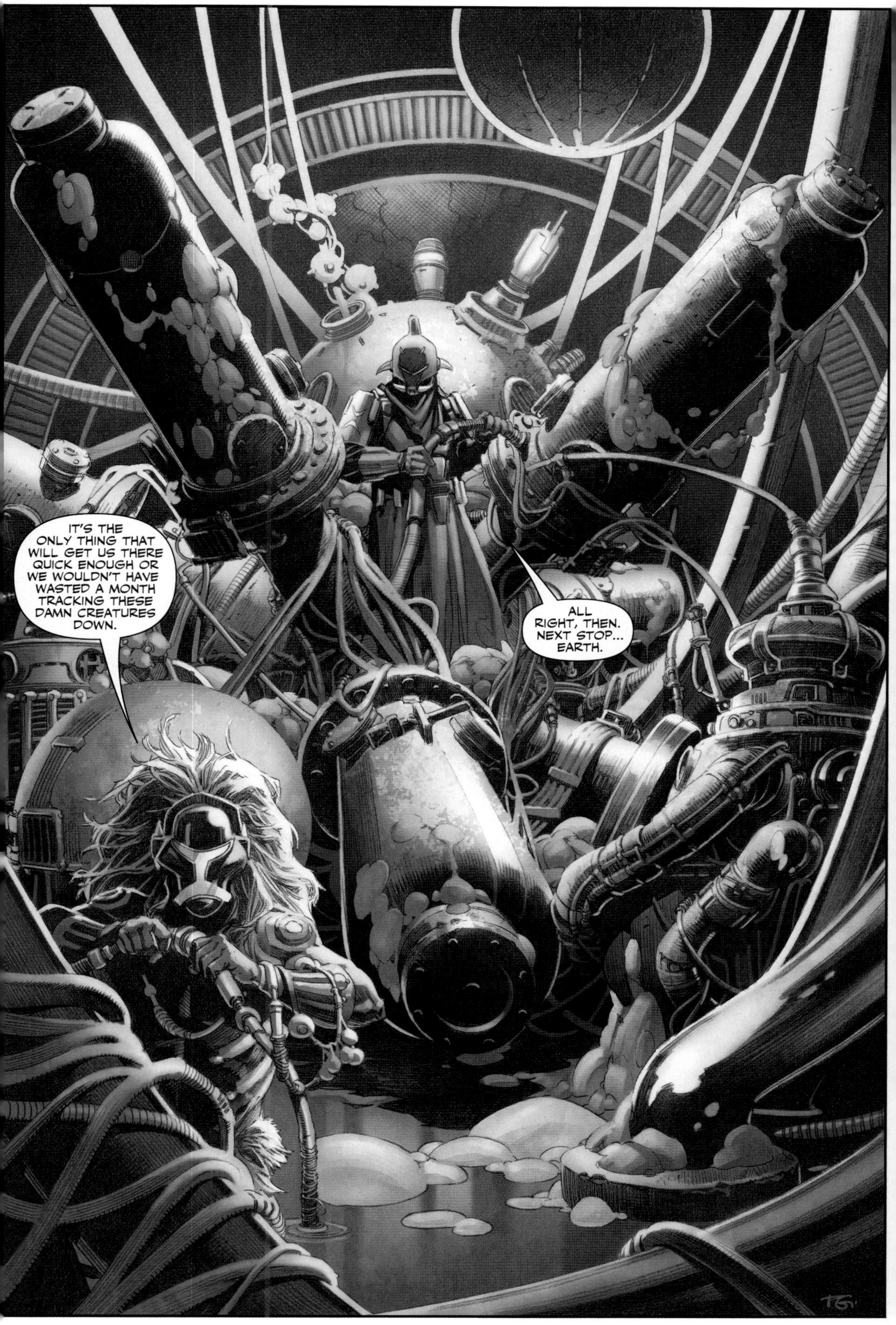
IT'S THE ONLY THING THAT WILL GET US THERE QUICK ENOUGH OR WE WOULDN'T HAVE WASTED A MONTH TRACKING THESE DAMN CREATURES DOWN.
ALL RIGHT, THEN. NEXT STOP... EARTH.

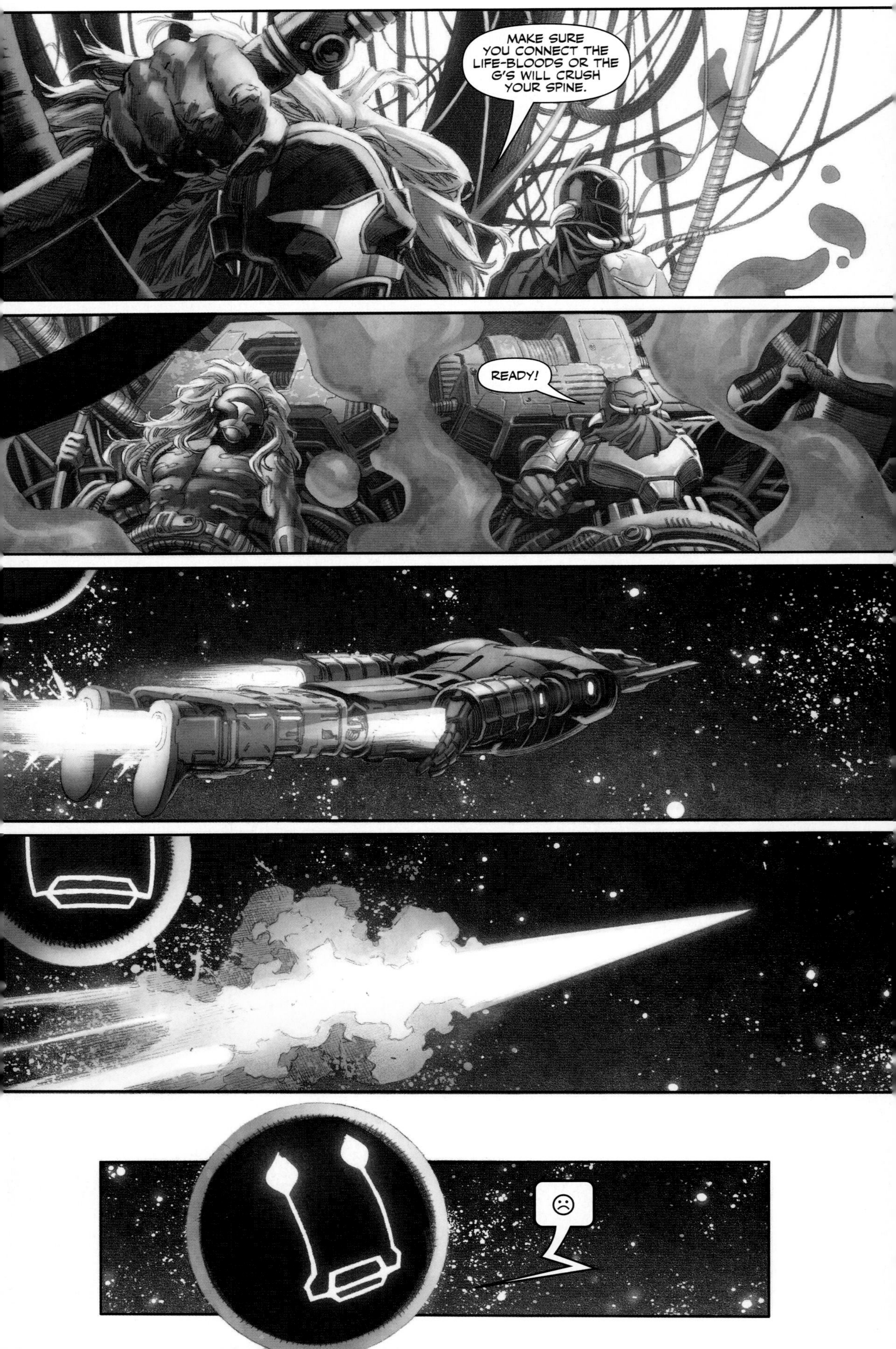
MAKE SURE YOU CONNECT THE LIFE-BLOODS OR THE G'S WILL CRUSH YOUR SPINE.
READY!
☹

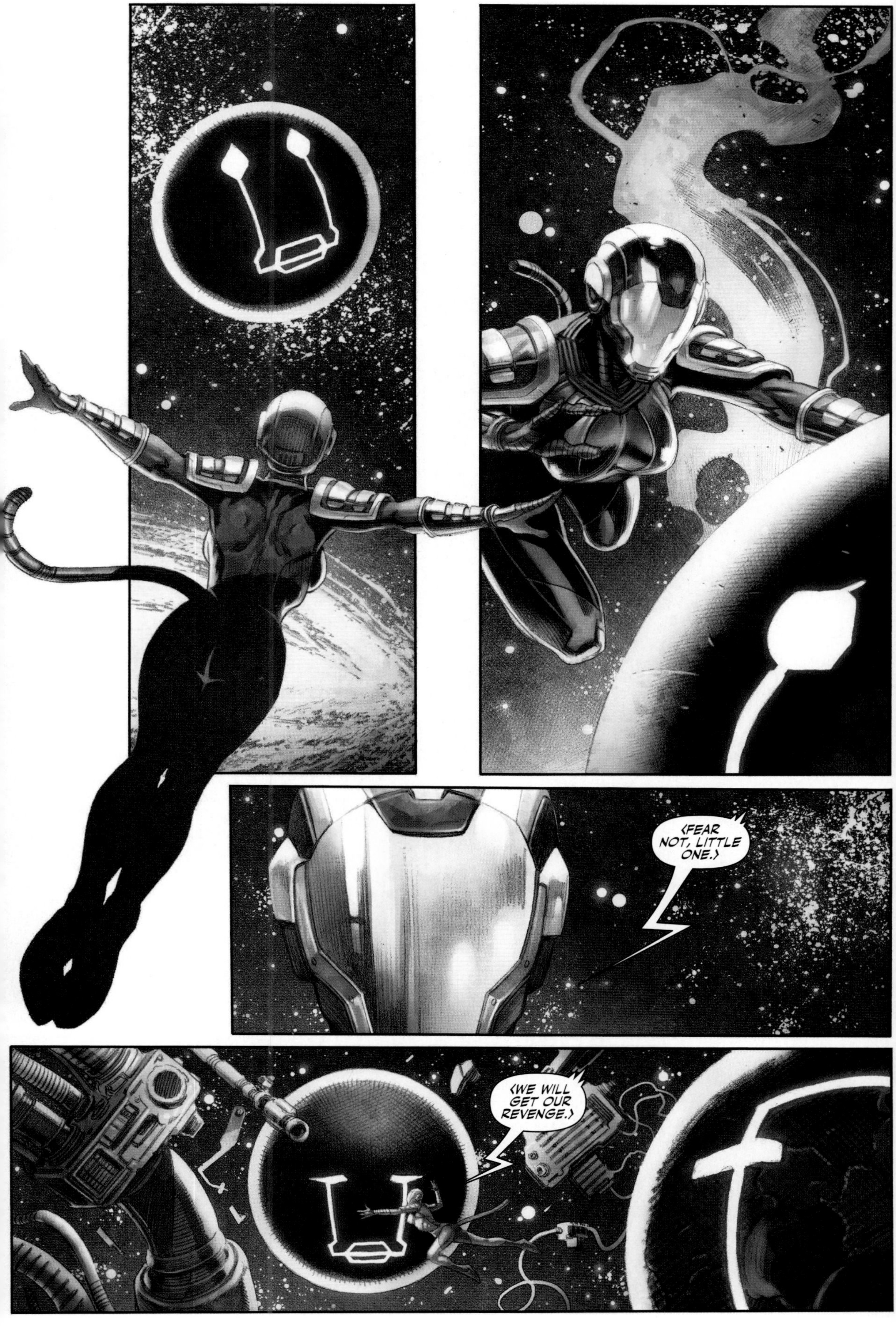
‹FEAR NOT, LITTLE ONE.›
‹WE WILL GET OUR REVENGE.›

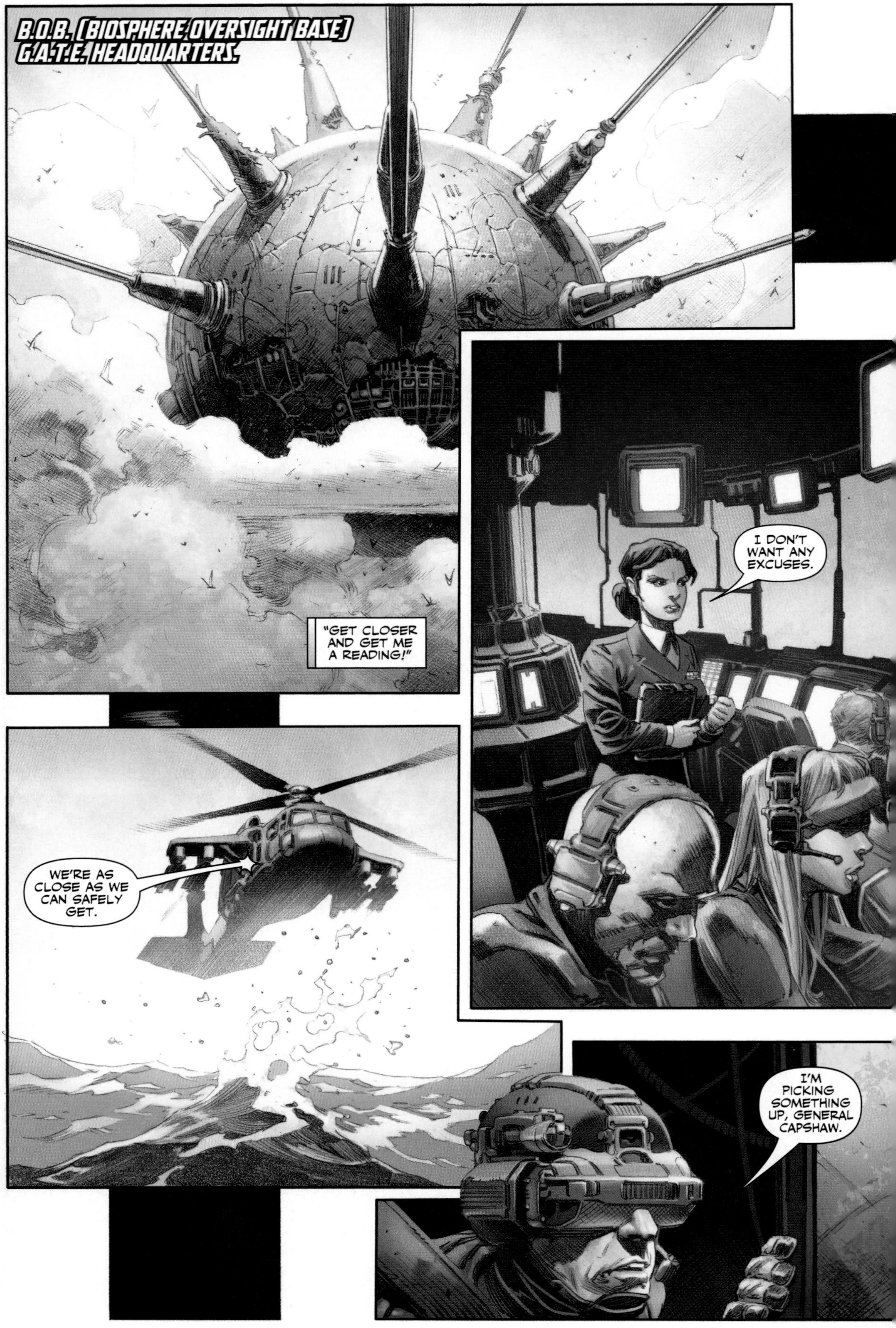
B.O.B. (BIOSPHERE OVERSIGHT BASE)
G.A.T.E. HEADQUARTERS.
"GET CLOSER AND GET ME A READING!"
I DON'T WANT ANY EXCUSES.
WE'RE AS CLOSE AS WE CAN SAFELY GET.
I'M PICKING SOMETHING UP, GENERAL CAPSHAW.

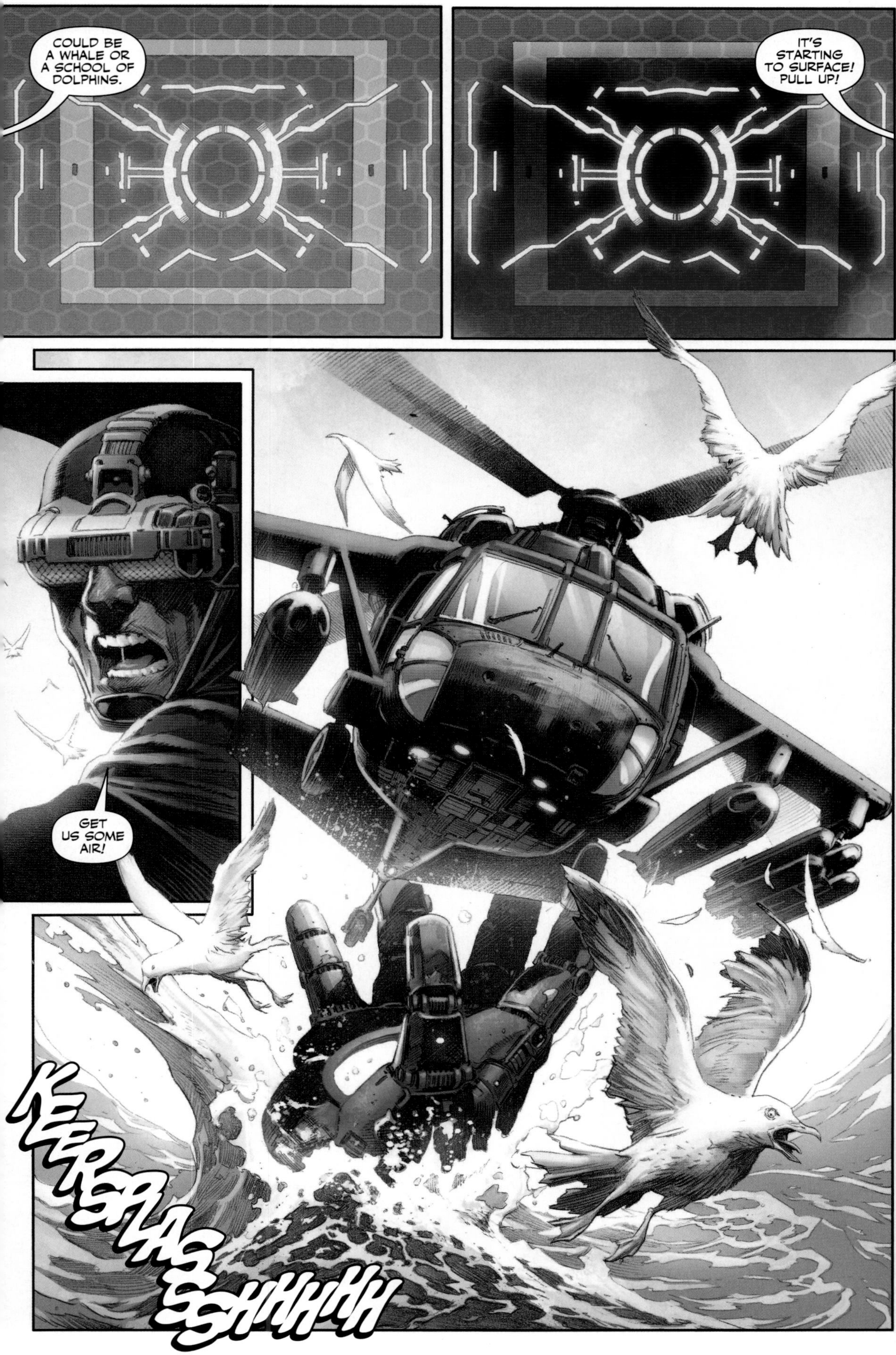
COULD BE A WHALE OR A SCHOOL OF DOLPHINS.
IT'S STARTING TO SURFACE! PULL UP!
GET US SOME AIR!
KEERSPLASSSHHHHH

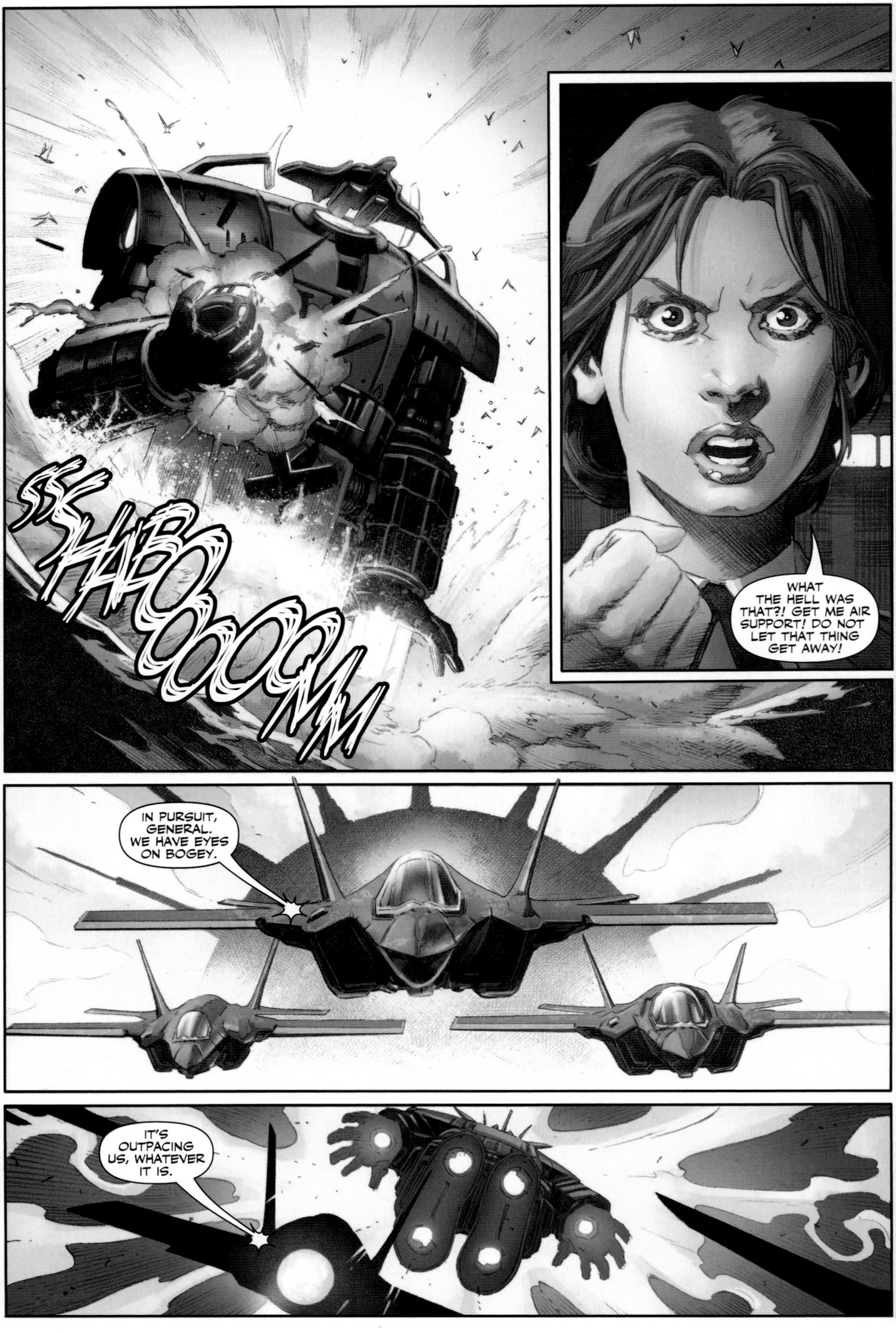
SSHABOOOOMM
WHAT THE HELL WAS THAT?! GET ME AIR SUPPORT! DO NOT LET THAT THING GET AWAY!
IN PURSUIT, GENERAL. WE HAVE EYES ON BOGEY.
IT'S OUTPACING US, WHATEVER IT IS.

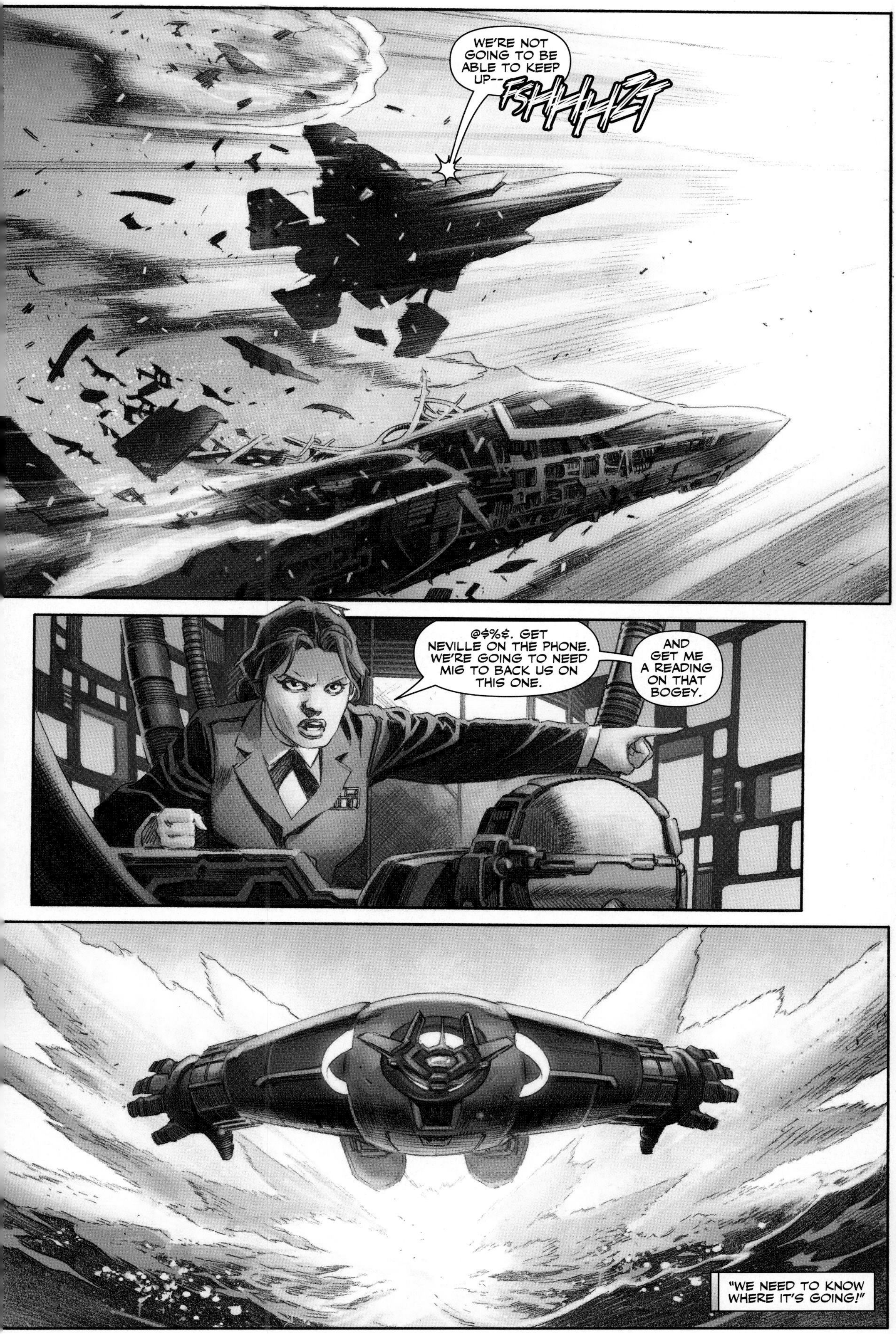

WE'RE NOT GOING TO BE ABLE TO KEEP UP--
FSHHHZT
@$%¢. GET NEVILLE ON THE PHONE. WE'RE GOING TO NEED MI6 TO BACK US ON THIS ONE.
AND GET ME A READING ON THAT BOGEY.
"WE NEED TO KNOW WHERE IT'S GOING!"

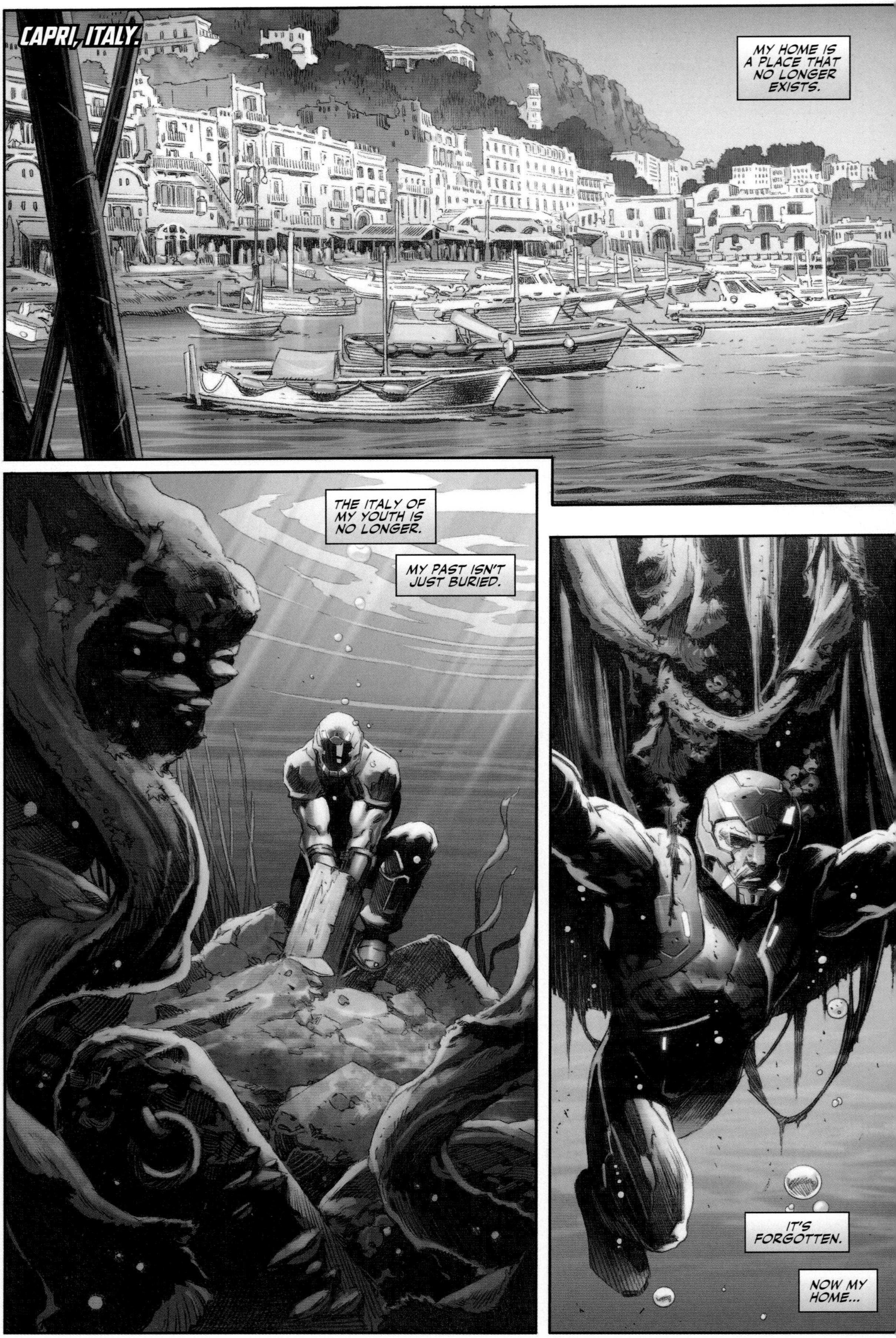
CAPRI, ITALY.
MY HOME IS A PLACE THAT NO LONGER EXISTS.
THE ITALY OF MY YOUTH IS NO LONGER.
MY PAST ISN'T JUST BURIED.
IT'S FORGOTTEN.
NOW MY HOME...

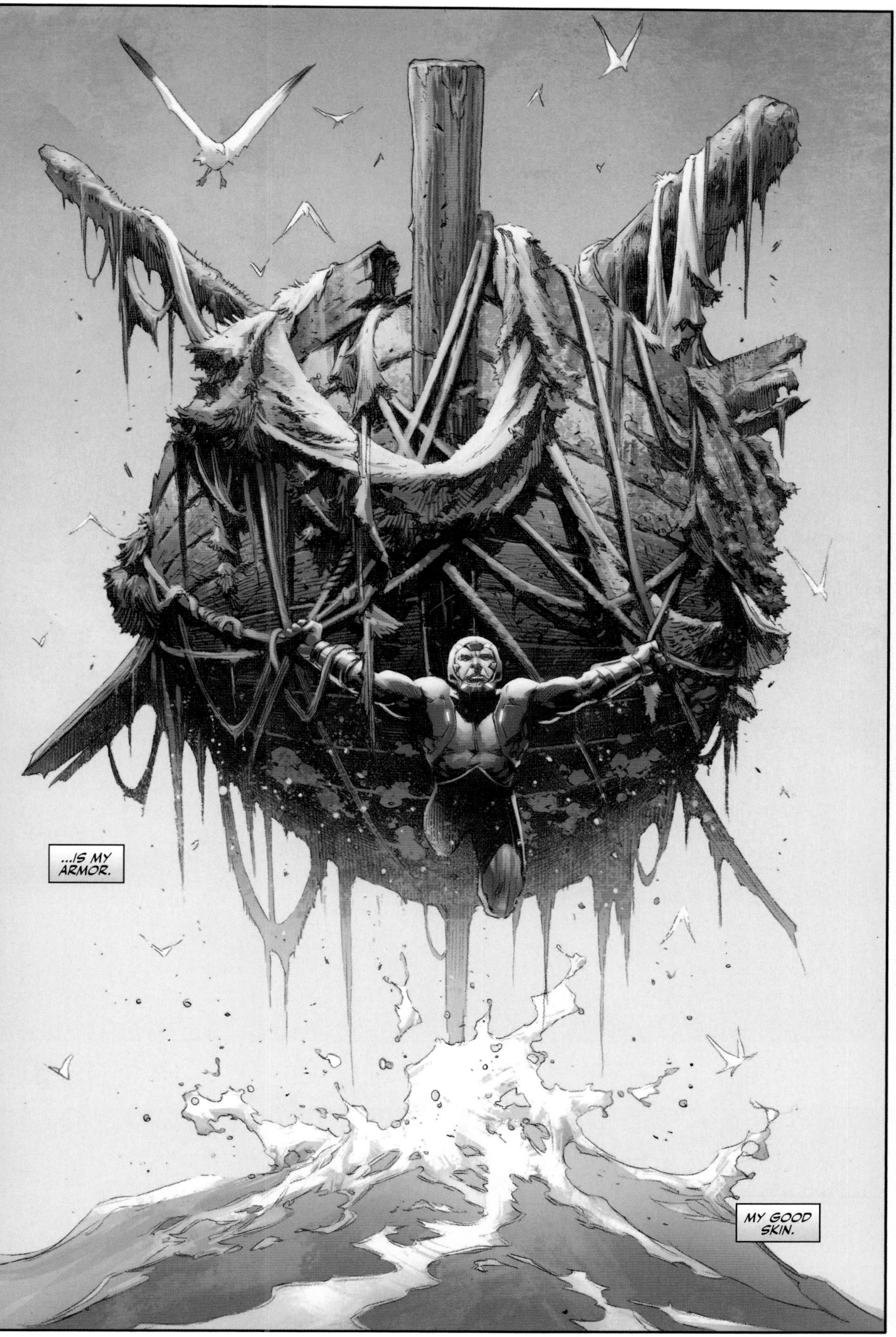
...IS MY ARMOR.
MY GOOD SKIN.

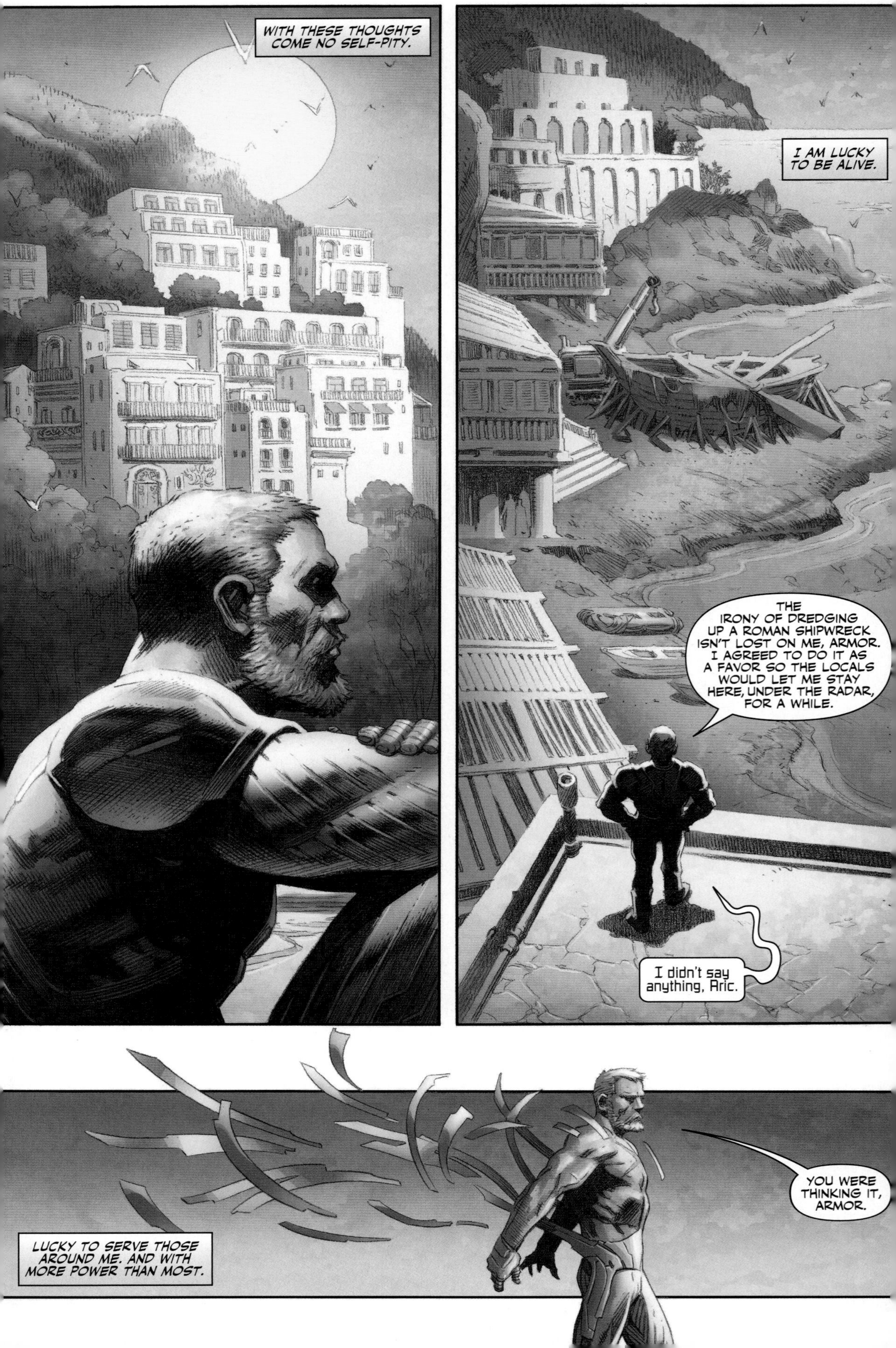
WITH THESE THOUGHTS COME NO SELF-PITY.
I AM LUCKY TO BE ALIVE.
THE IRONY OF DREDGING UP A ROMAN SHIPWRECK ISN'T LOST ON ME, ARMOR. I AGREED TO DO IT AS A FAVOR SO THE LOCALS WOULD LET ME STAY HERE, UNDER THE RADAR, FOR A WHILE.
I didn't say anything, Aric.
LUCKY TO SERVE THOSE AROUND ME. AND WITH MORE POWER THAN MOST.
YOU WERE THINKING IT, ARMOR.

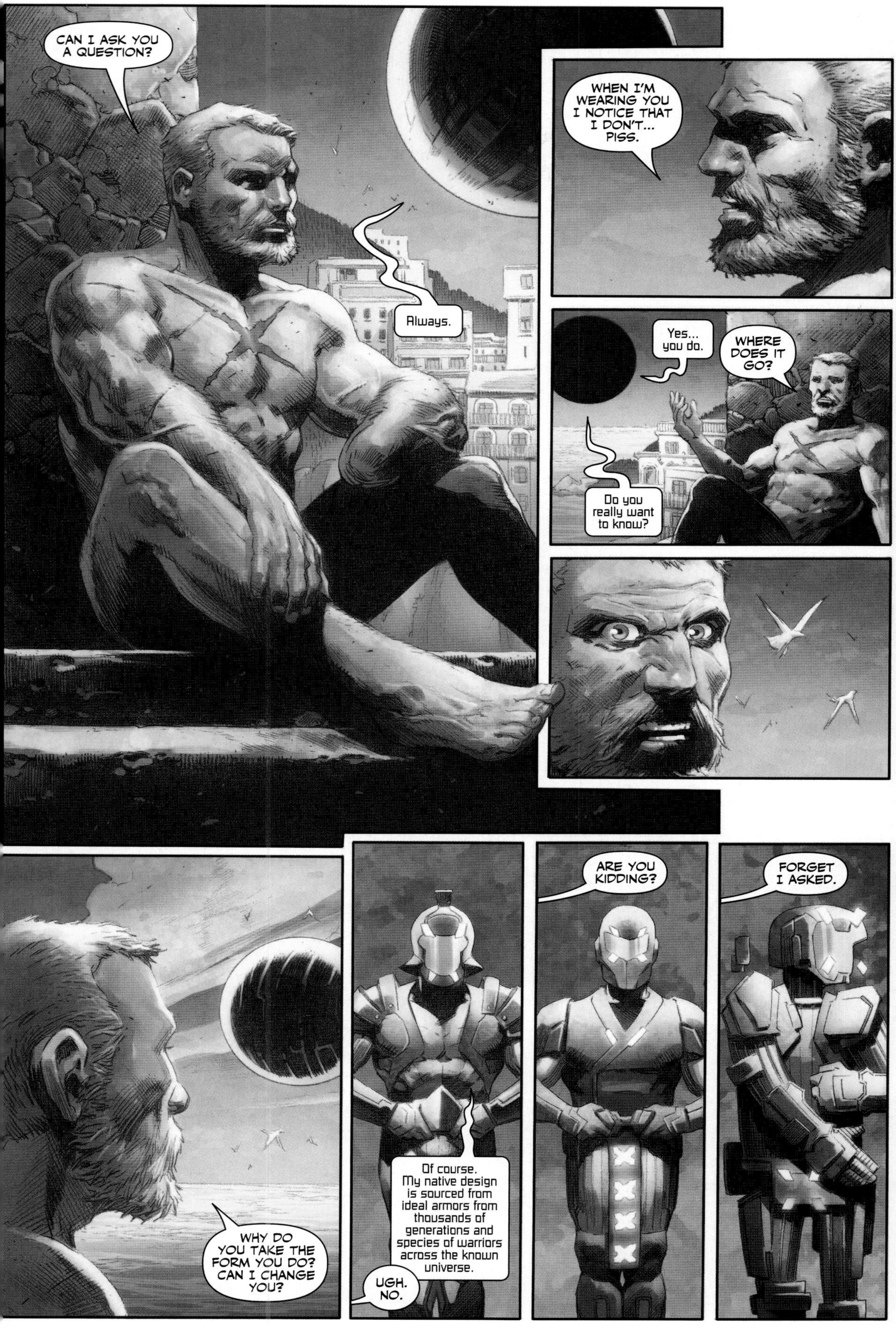
CAN I ASK YOU A QUESTION?
Always.
WHEN I'M WEARING YOU I NOTICE THAT I DON'T... PISS.
Yes... you do.
WHERE DOES IT GO?
Do you really want to know?
WHY DO YOU TAKE THE FORM YOU DO? CAN I CHANGE YOU?
Of course. My native design is sourced from ideal armors from thousands of generations and species of warriors across the known universe.
UGH. NO.
ARE YOU KIDDING?
FORGET I ASKED.

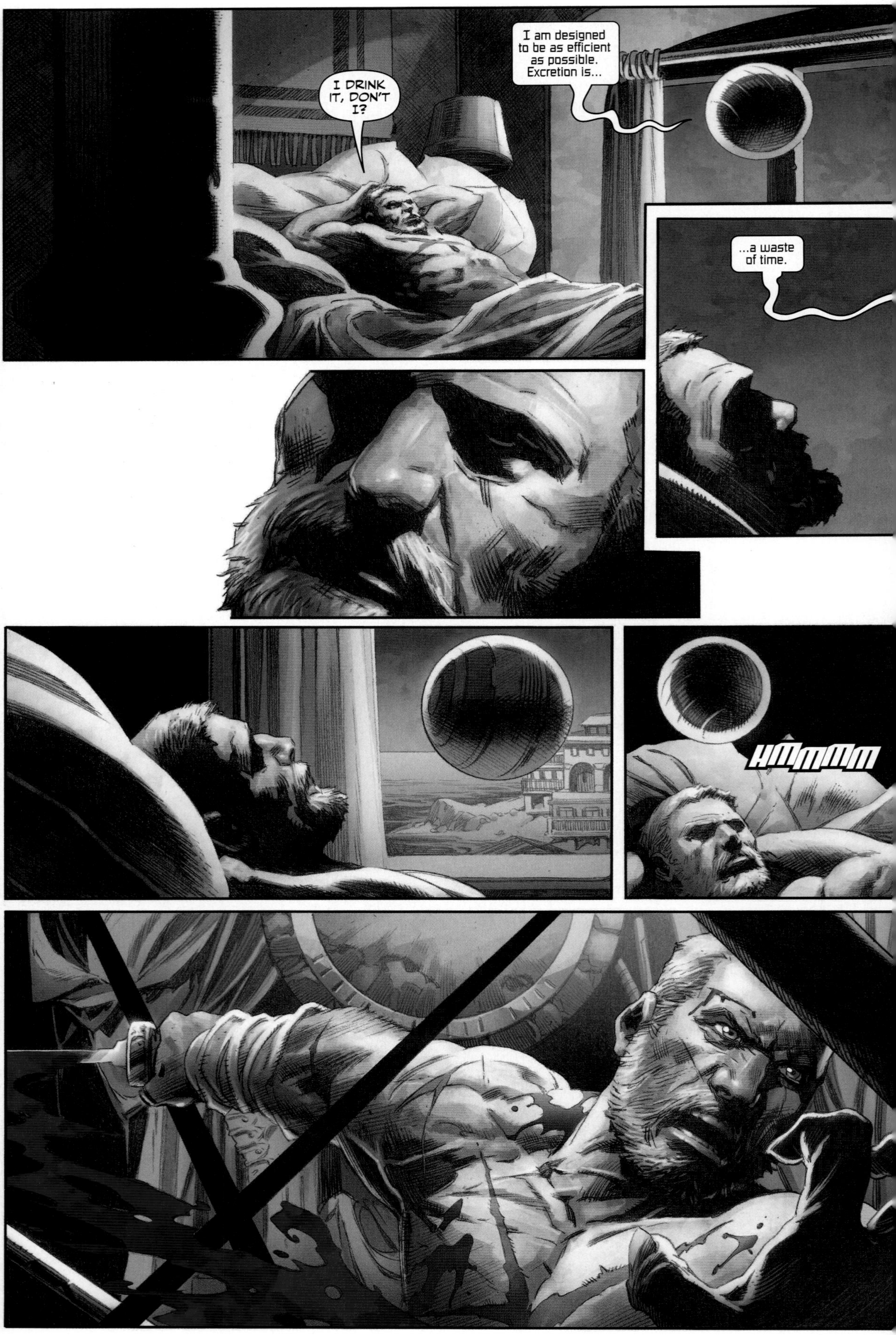
I DRINK IT, DON'T I?
I am designed to be as efficient as possible. Excretion is...
...a waste of time.
HMMMM

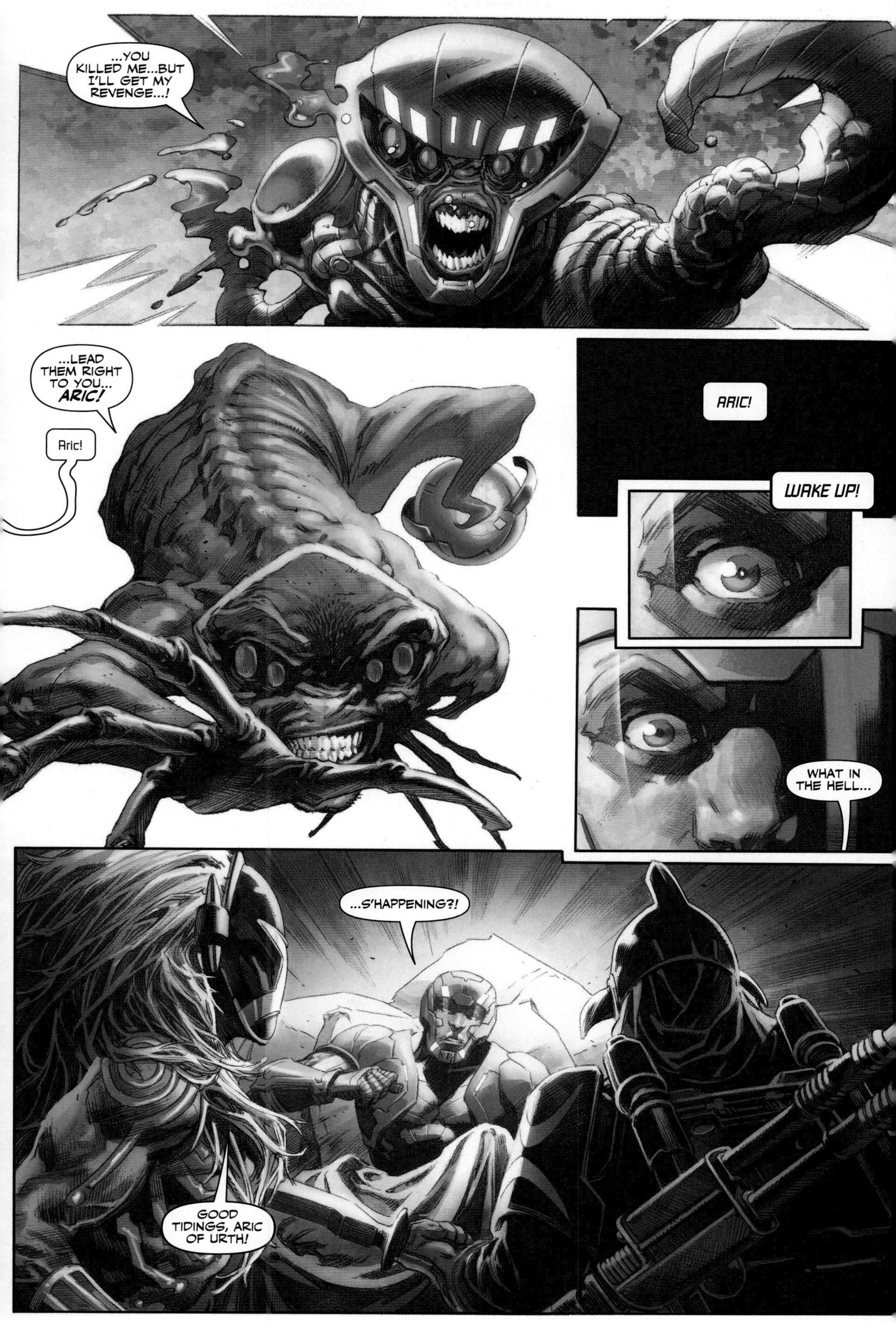
...YOU KILLED ME...BUT I'LL GET MY REVENGE...!
...LEAD THEM RIGHT TO YOU... ARIC!
Aric!
ARIC!
WAKE UP!
WHAT IN THE HELL...
...S'HAPPENING?!
GOOD TIDINGS, ARIC OF URTH!

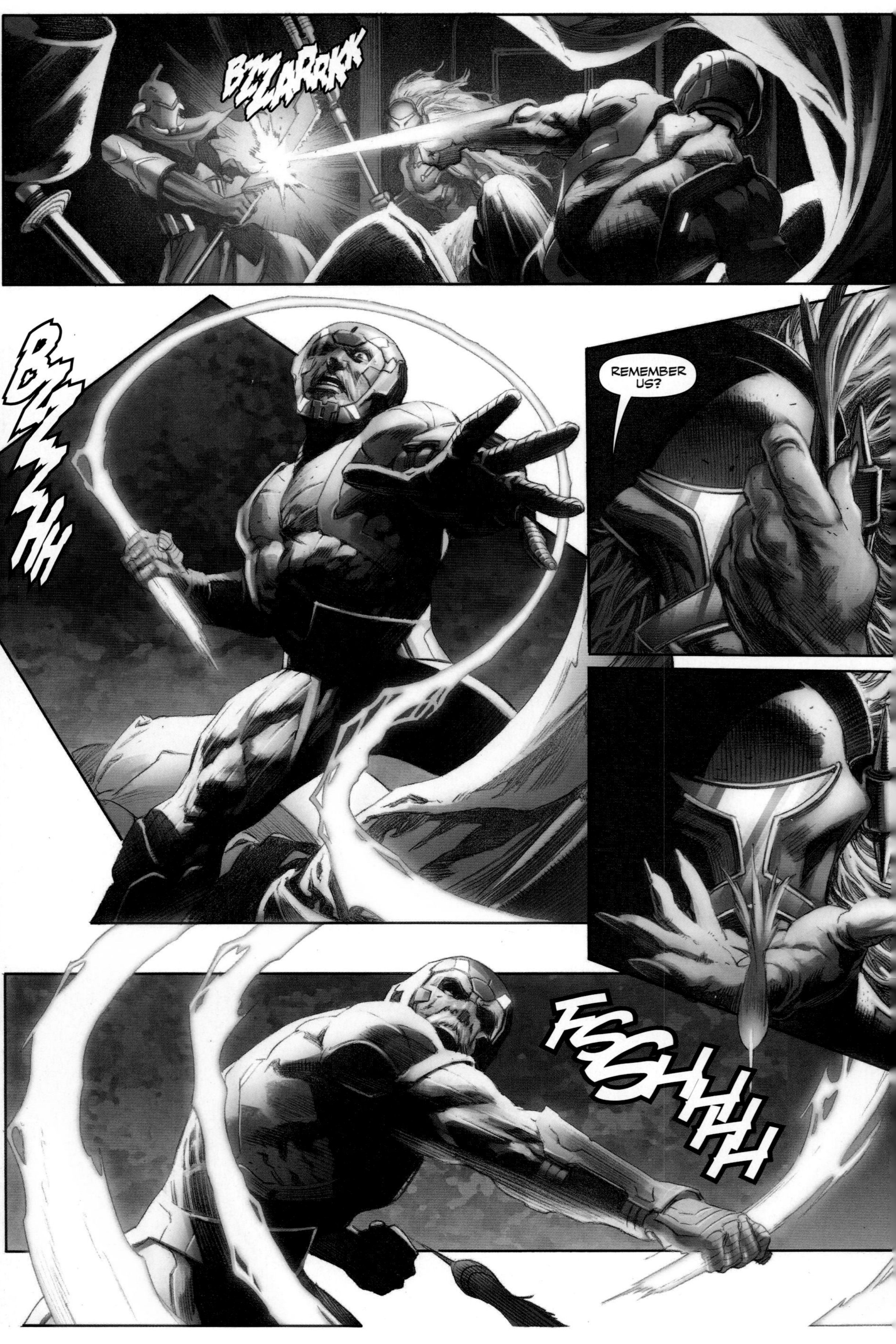

BZZARRKK
BZZHHH
REMEMBER US?
FSSHHHH

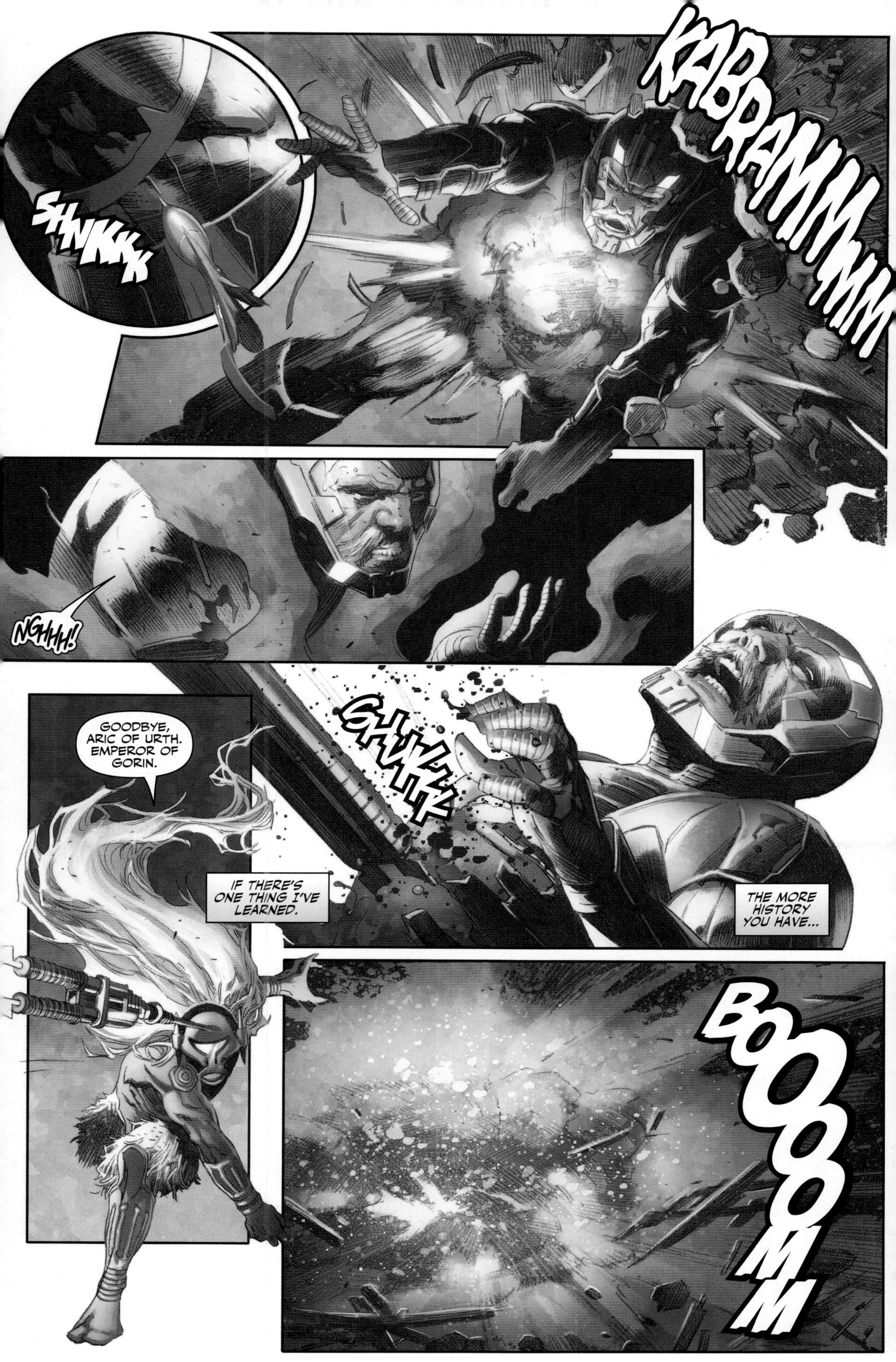

SHNKKK
KABRAMMMMM
NGHHH!
GOODBYE, ARIC OF URTH. EMPEROR OF GORIN.
SHUKK
IF THERE'S ONE THING I'VE LEARNED.
THE MORE HISTORY YOU HAVE...
BOOOOOMM

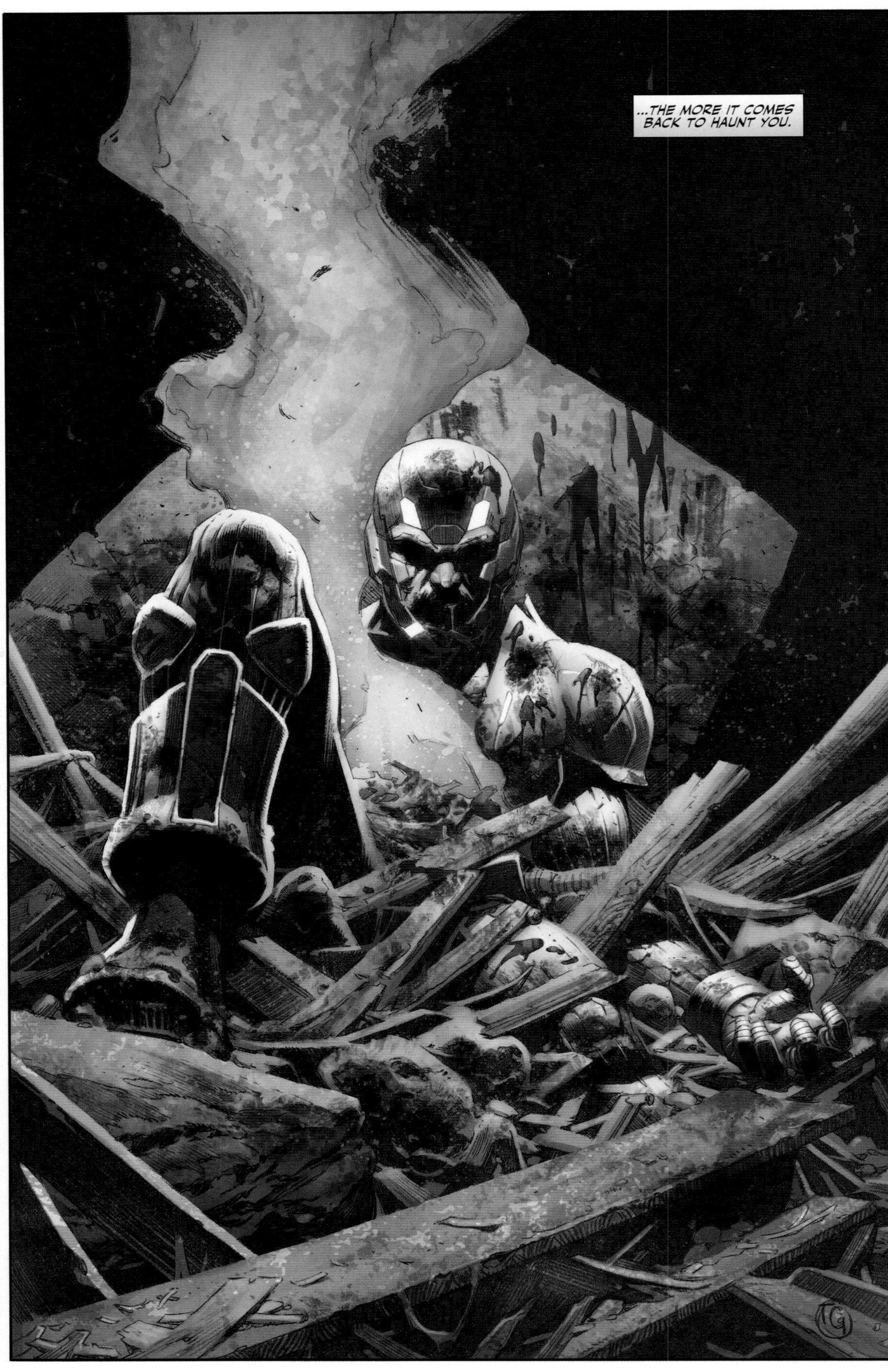
...THE MORE IT COMES BACK TO HAUNT YOU.

X-O MANOWAR

ERO

ISSUE 24

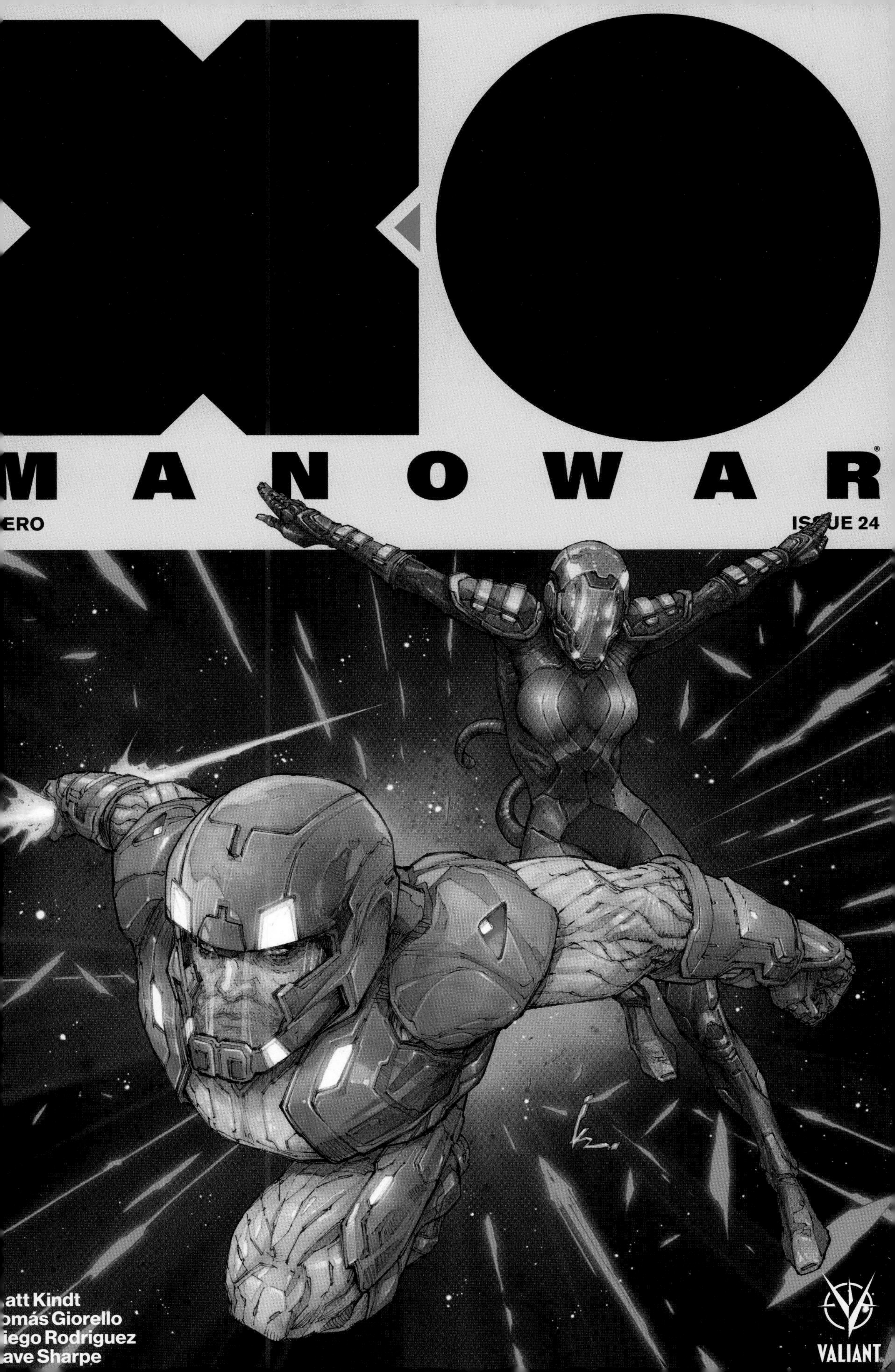

att Kindt
omás Giorello
iego Rodriguez
ave Sharpe
VALIANT

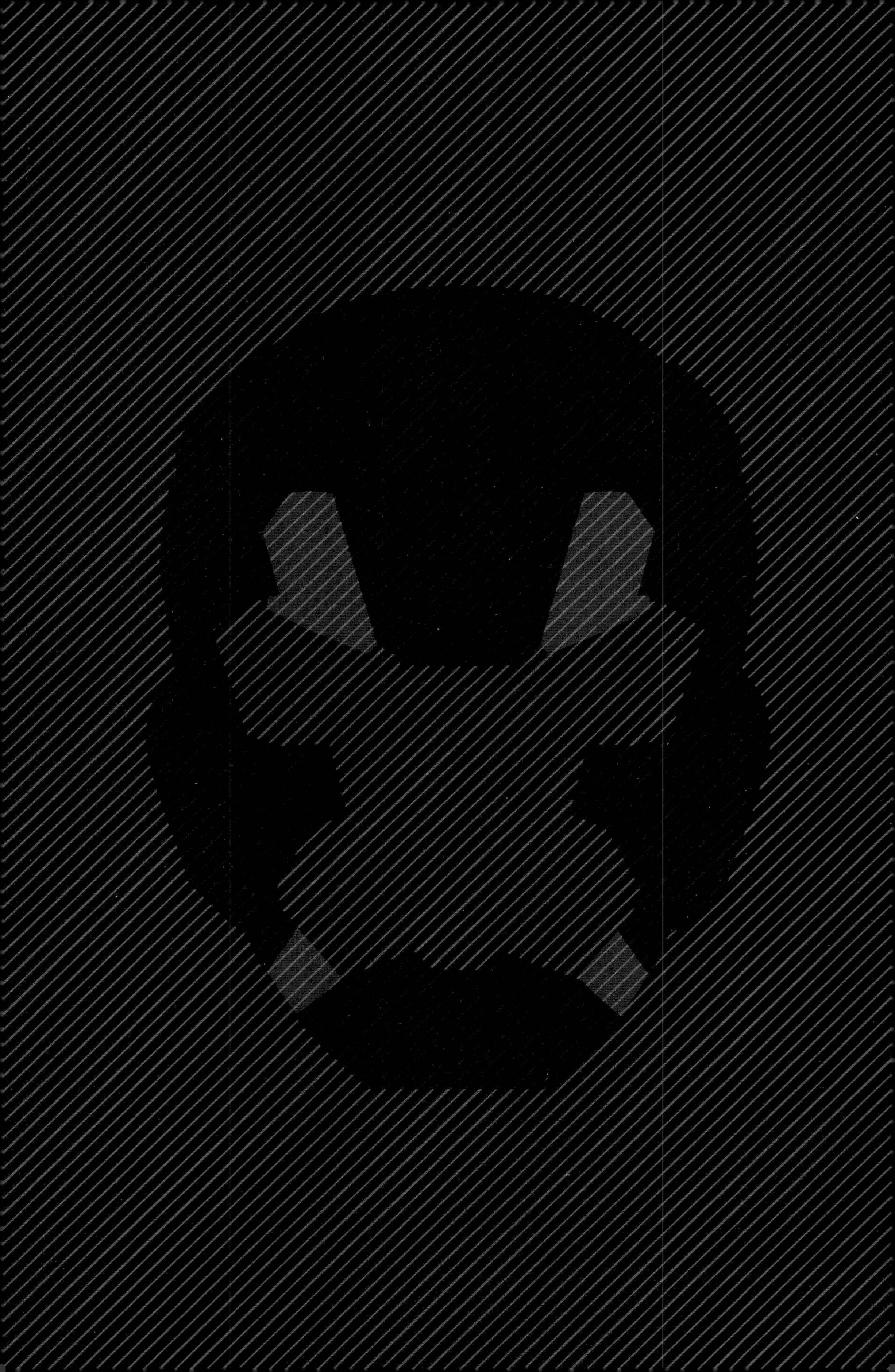

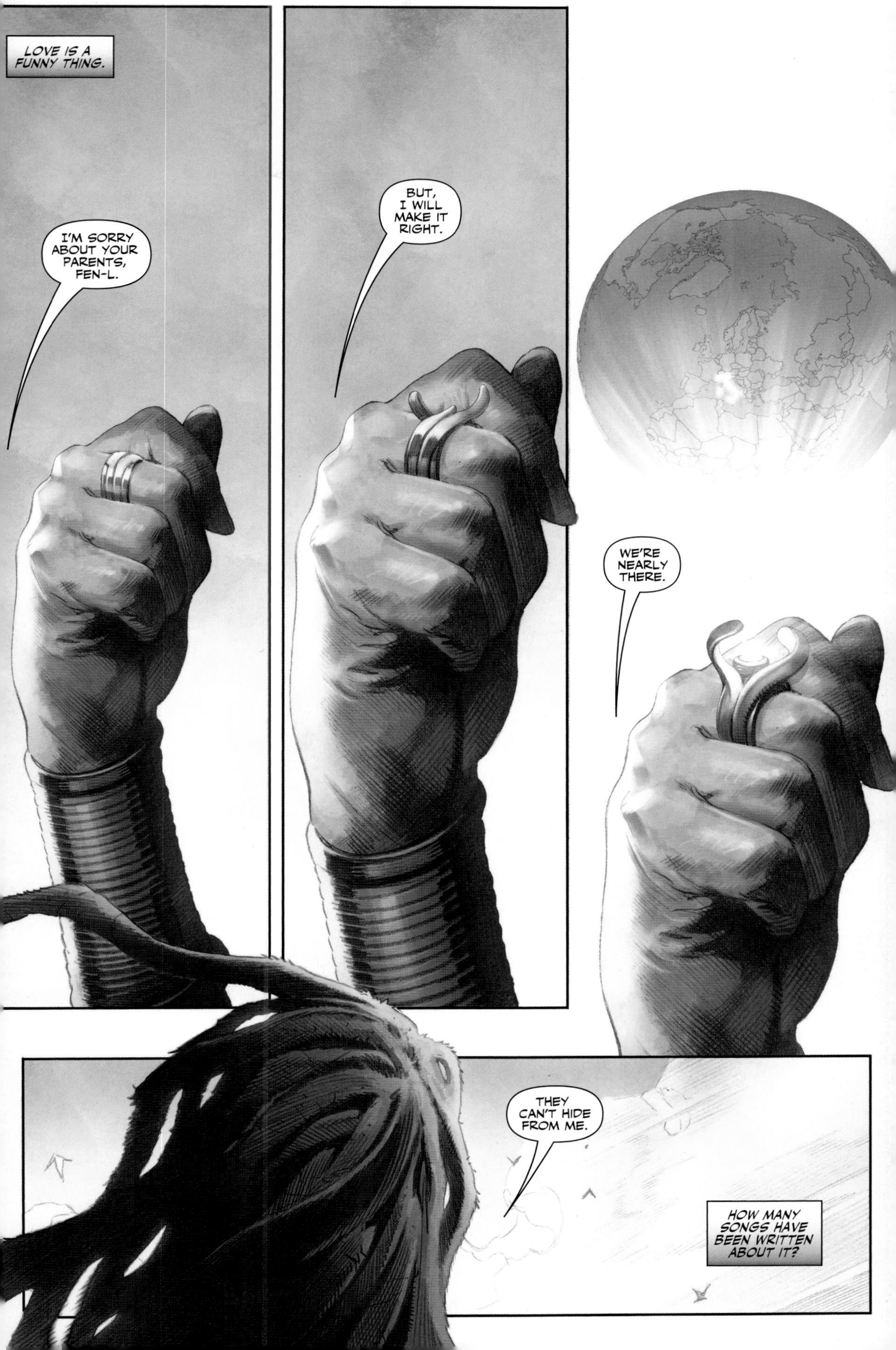
LOVE IS A FUNNY THING.
I'M SORRY ABOUT YOUR PARENTS, FEN-L.
BUT, I WILL MAKE IT RIGHT.
WE'RE NEARLY THERE.
THEY CAN'T HIDE FROM ME.
HOW MANY SONGS HAVE BEEN WRITTEN ABOUT IT?

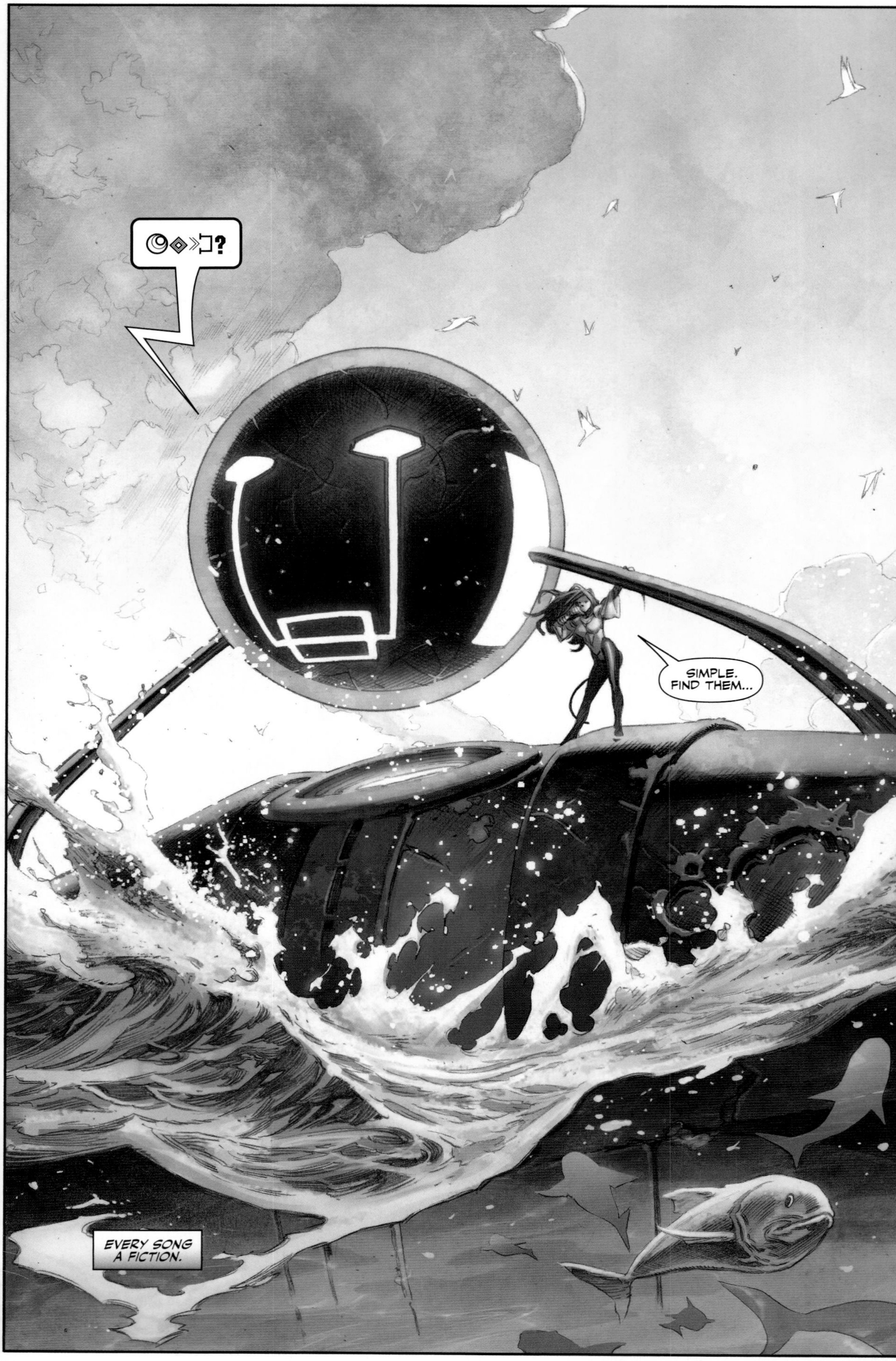
SIMPLE. FIND THEM...
EVERY SONG A FICTION.

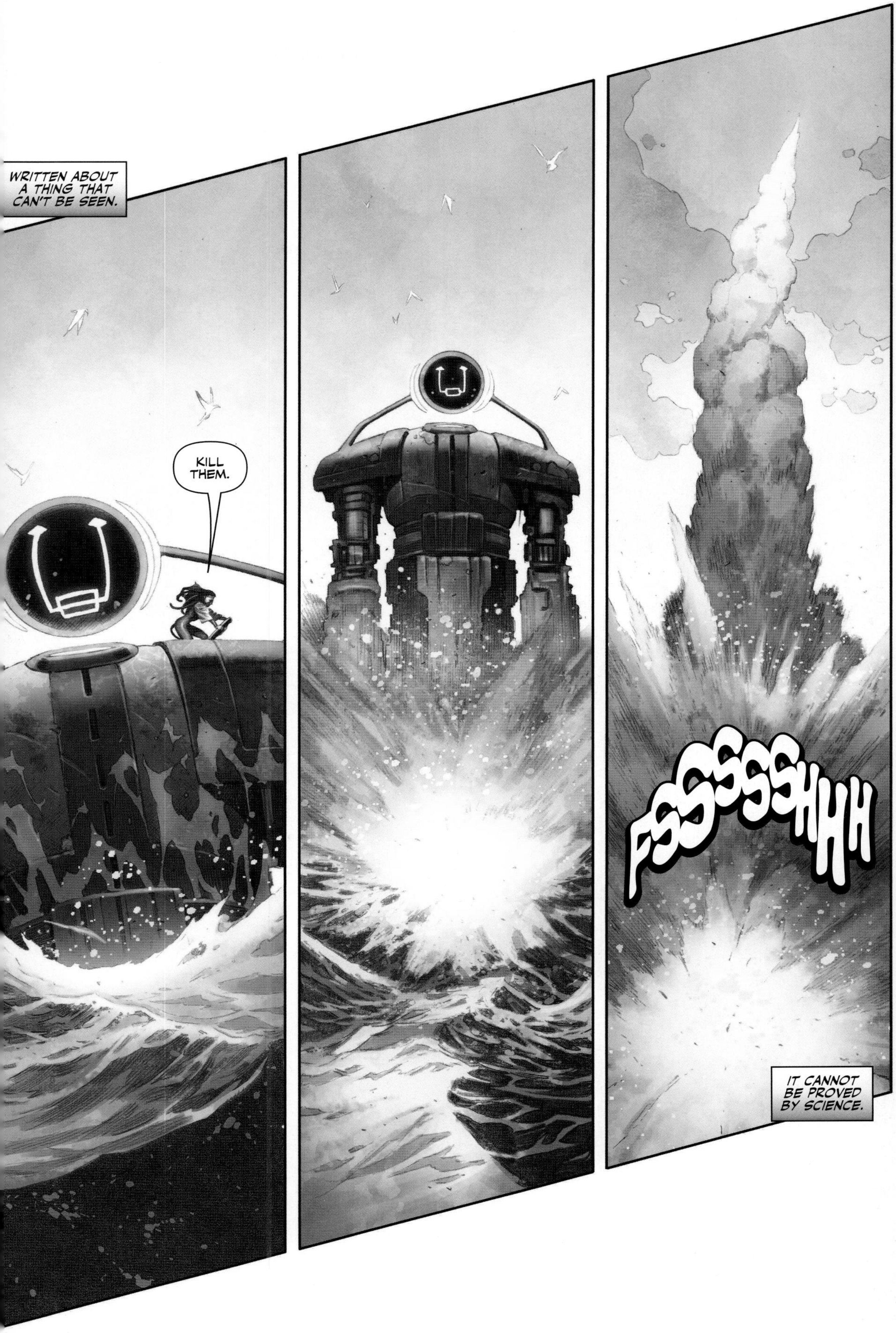
WRITTEN ABOUT A THING THAT CAN'T BE SEEN.
KILL THEM.
FSSSSSHHH
IT CANNOT BE PROVED BY SCIENCE.

YET, HERE
I AM.

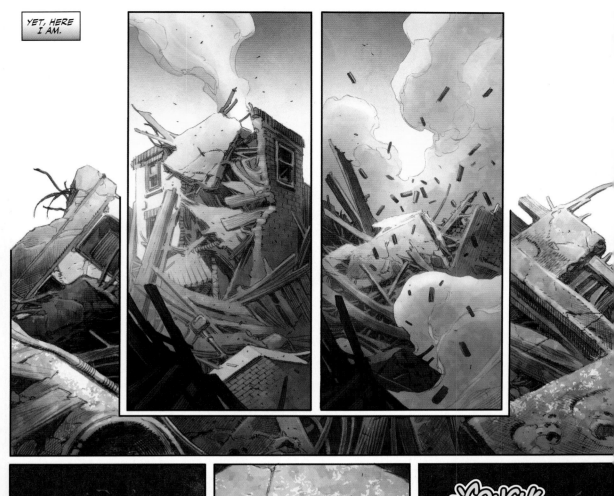

NGH...

=COUGH=
=COUGH=

IS THIS THE
PROOF?

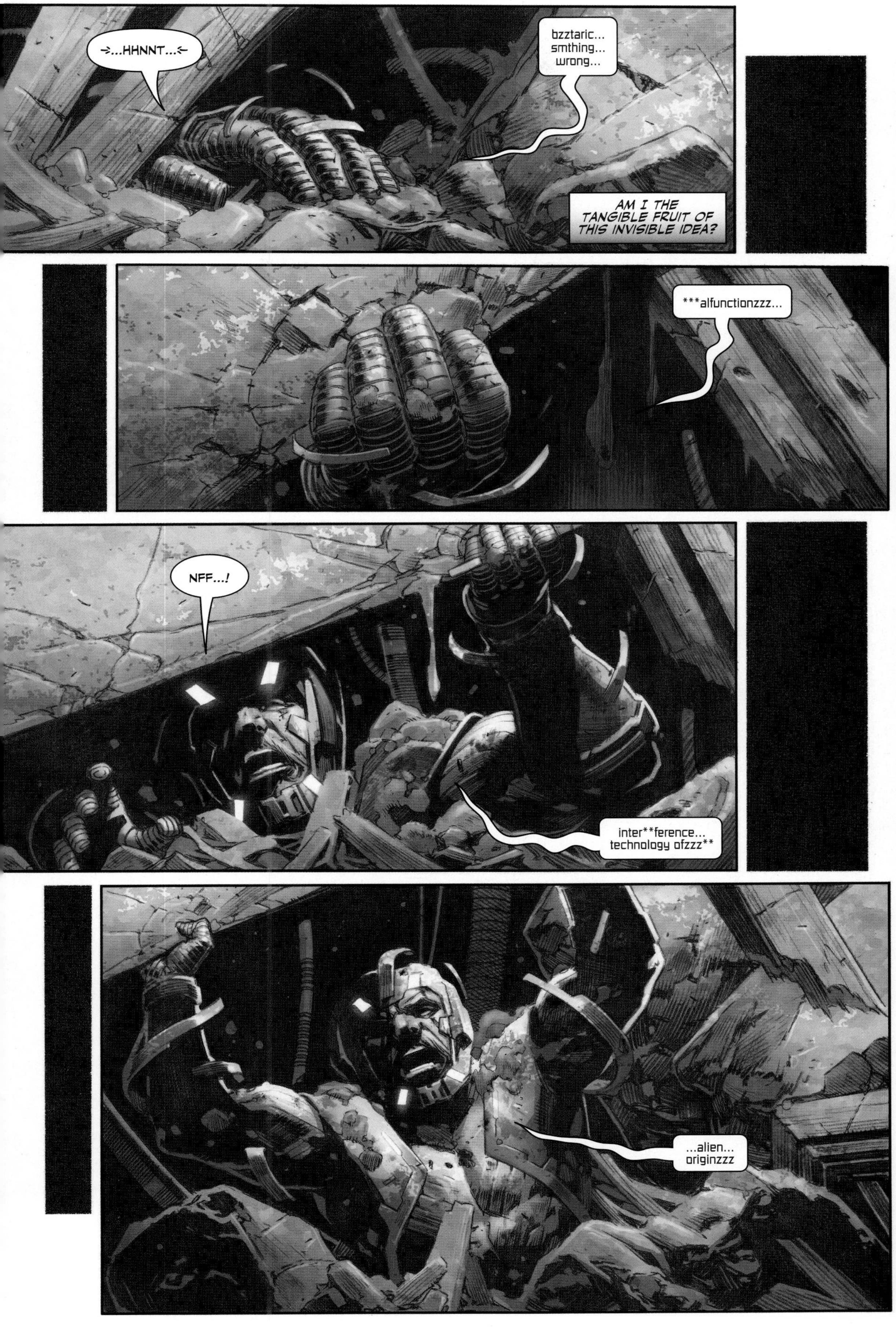

–>...HHNNT...<–
bzztaric... smthing... wrong...
AM I THE TANGIBLE FRUIT OF THIS INVISIBLE IDEA?
***alfunctionzzz...
NFF...!
inter**ference... technology ofzzz**
...alien... originzzz

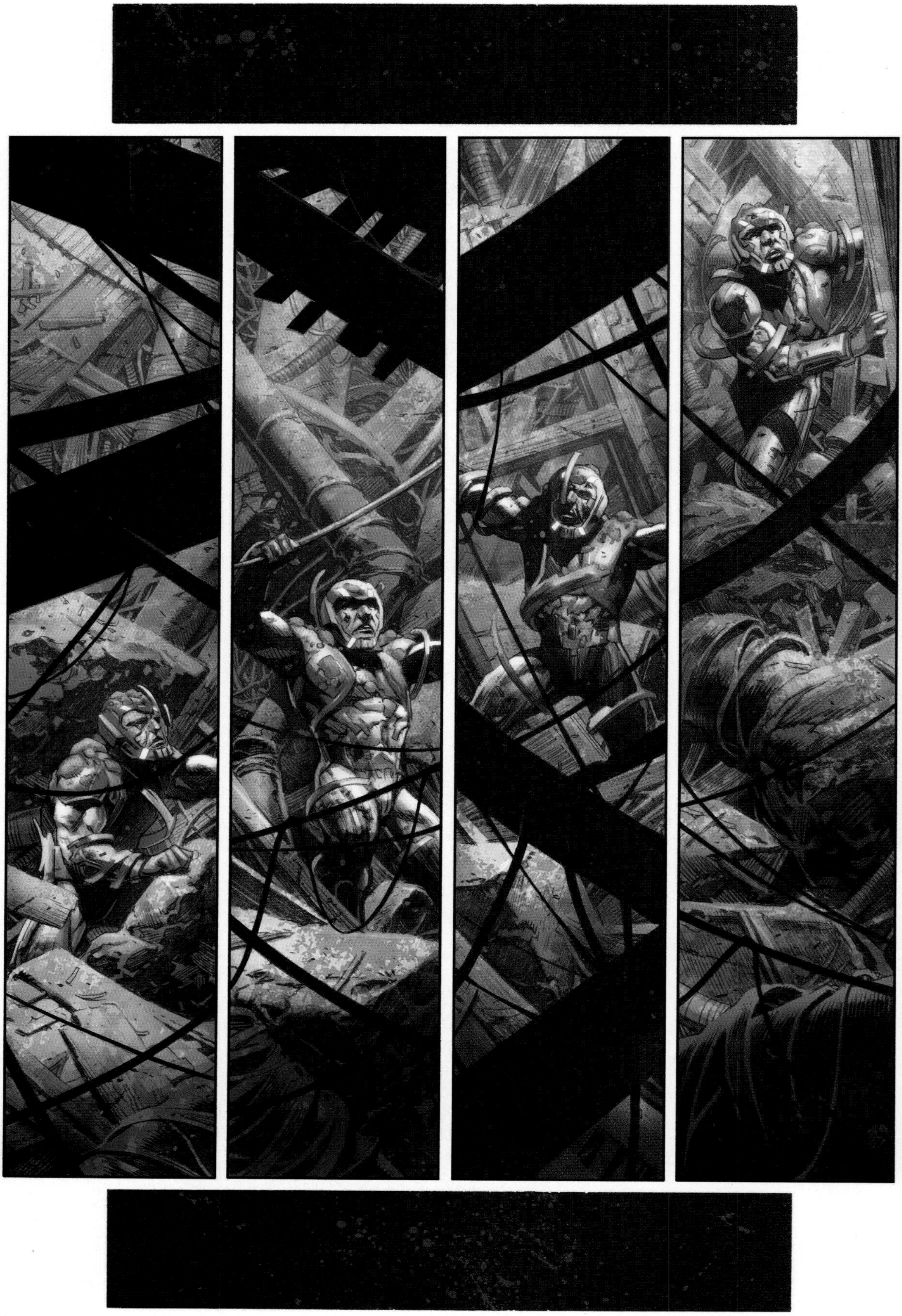

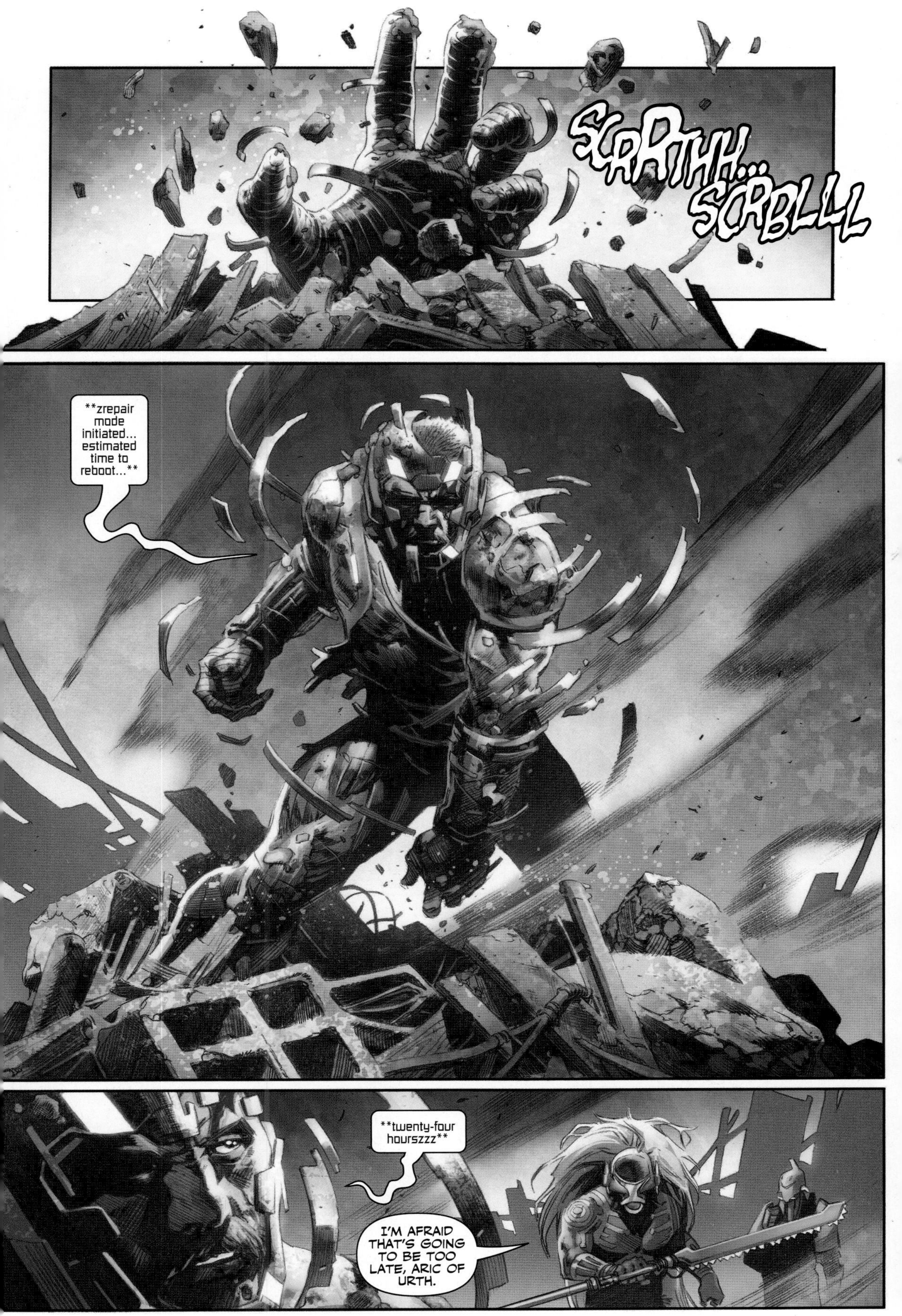
SCRRTHH... SCRBLLL
zrepair mode initiated... estimated time to reboot...
twenty-four hourszzz
I'M AFRAID THAT'S GOING TO BE TOO LATE, ARIC OF URTH.

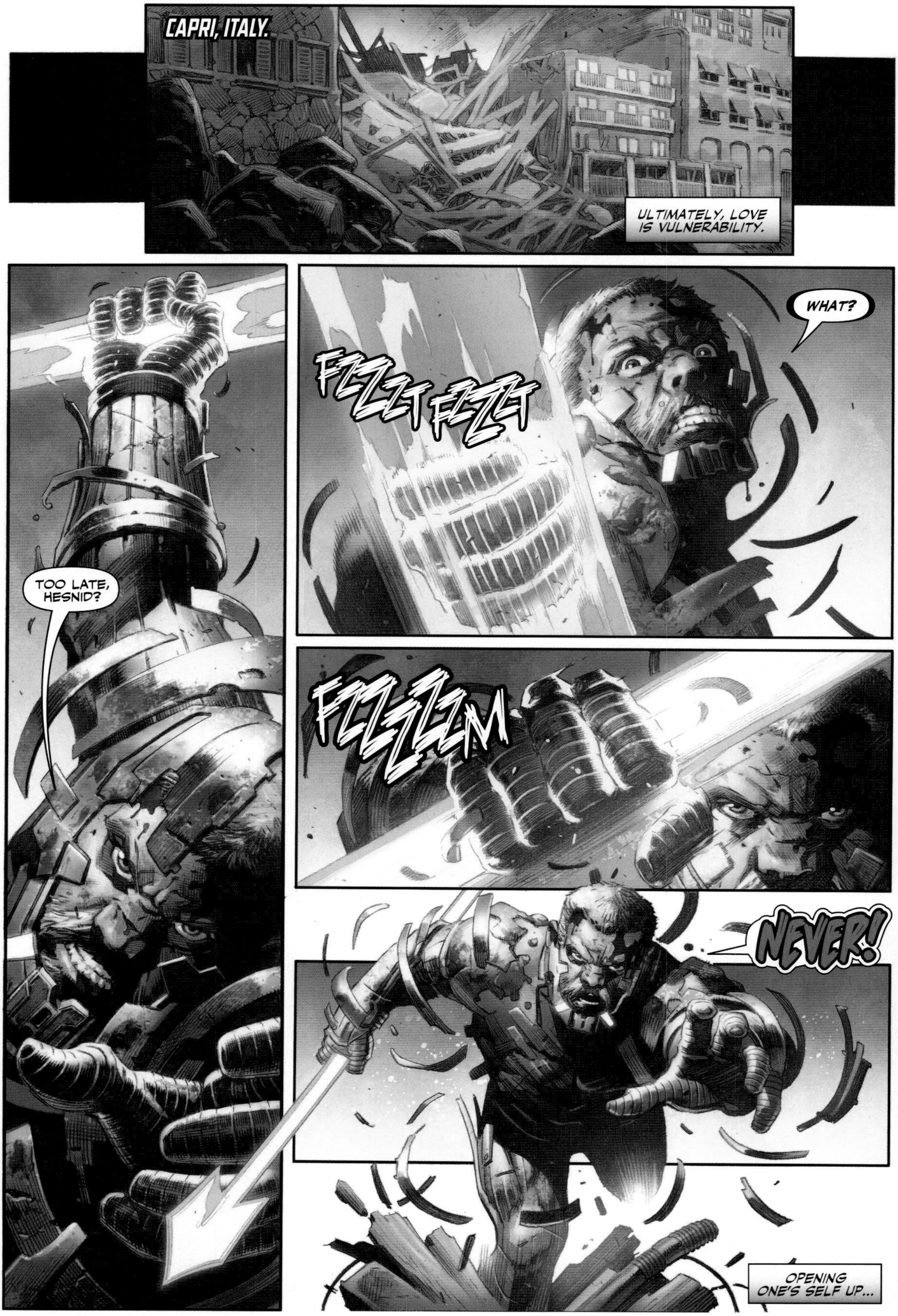
CAPRI, ITALY.
ULTIMATELY, LOVE IS VULNERABILITY.
TOO LATE, HESNID?
FZZZT FZZZT
WHAT?
FZZZZZM
NEVER!
OPENING ONE'S SELF UP...

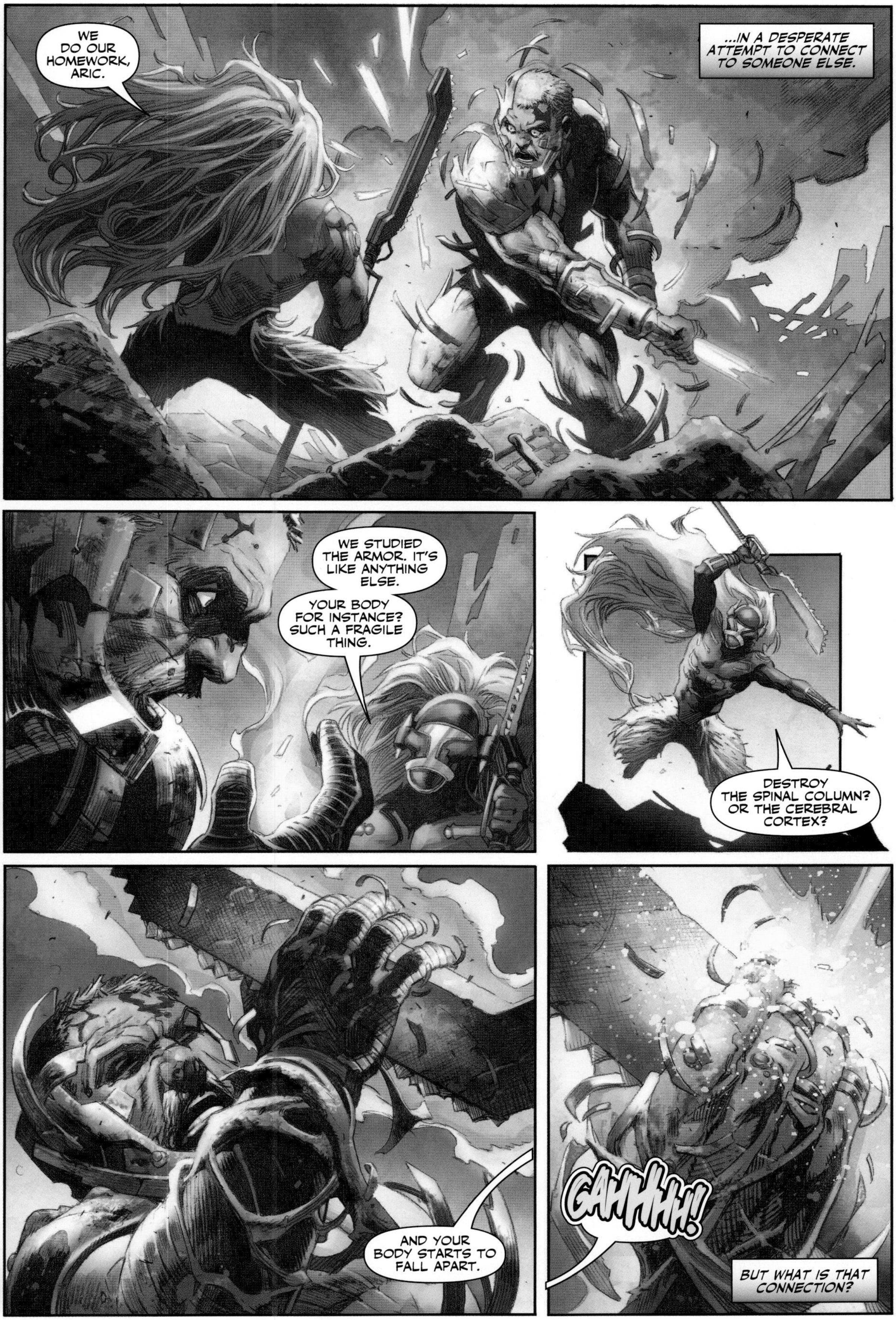
WE DO OUR HOMEWORK, ARIC.
...IN A DESPERATE ATTEMPT TO CONNECT TO SOMEONE ELSE.
WE STUDIED THE ARMOR. IT'S LIKE ANYTHING ELSE.
YOUR BODY FOR INSTANCE? SUCH A FRAGILE THING.
DESTROY THE SPINAL COLUMN? OR THE CEREBRAL CORTEX?
AND YOUR BODY STARTS TO FALL APART.
GAHHHH!
BUT WHAT IS THAT CONNECTION?

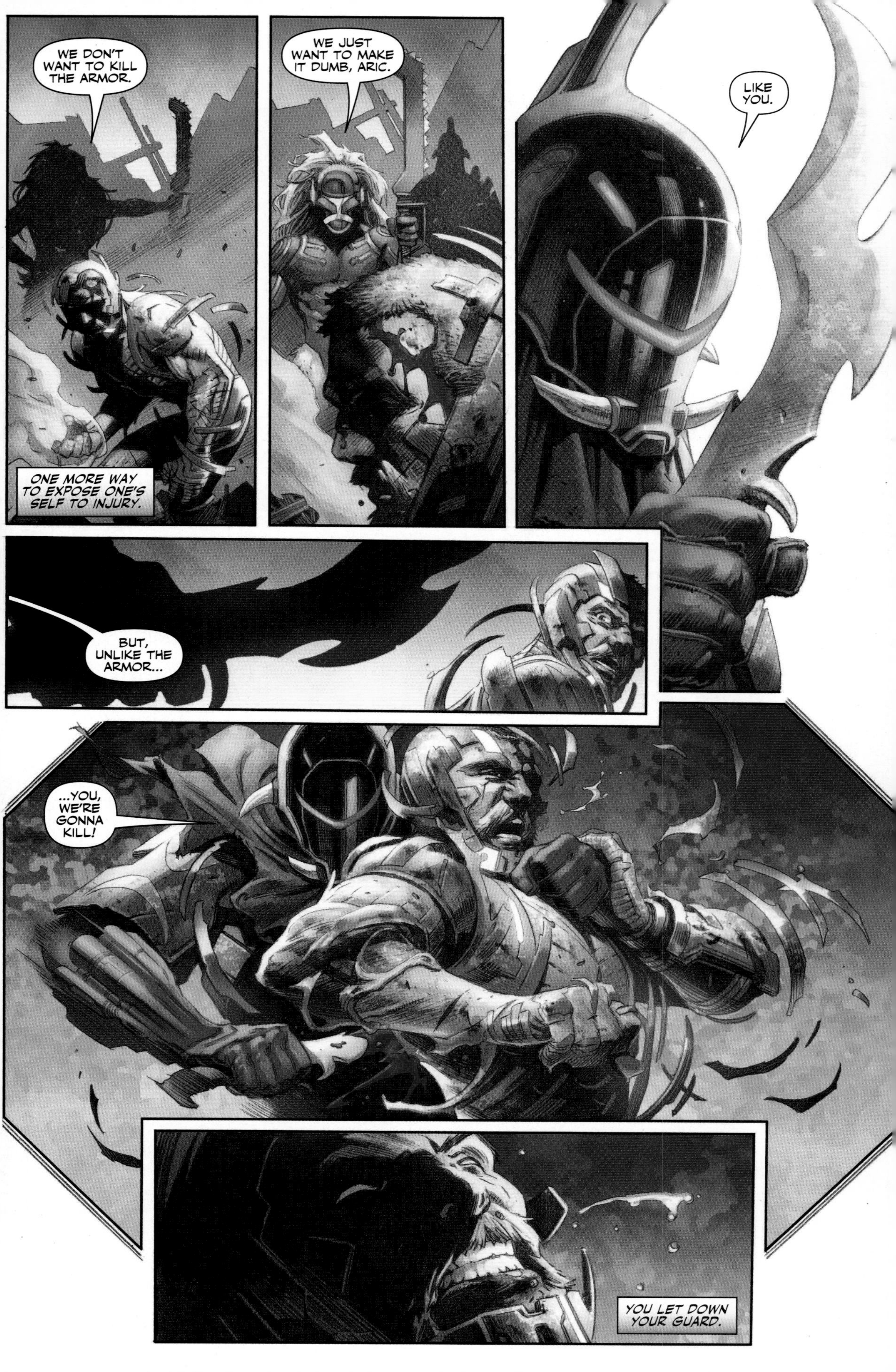
WE DON'T WANT TO KILL THE ARMOR.
ONE MORE WAY TO EXPOSE ONE'S SELF TO INJURY.
WE JUST WANT TO MAKE IT DUMB, ARIC.
LIKE YOU.
BUT, UNLIKE THE ARMOR...
...YOU, WE'RE GONNA KILL!
YOU LET DOWN YOUR GUARD.

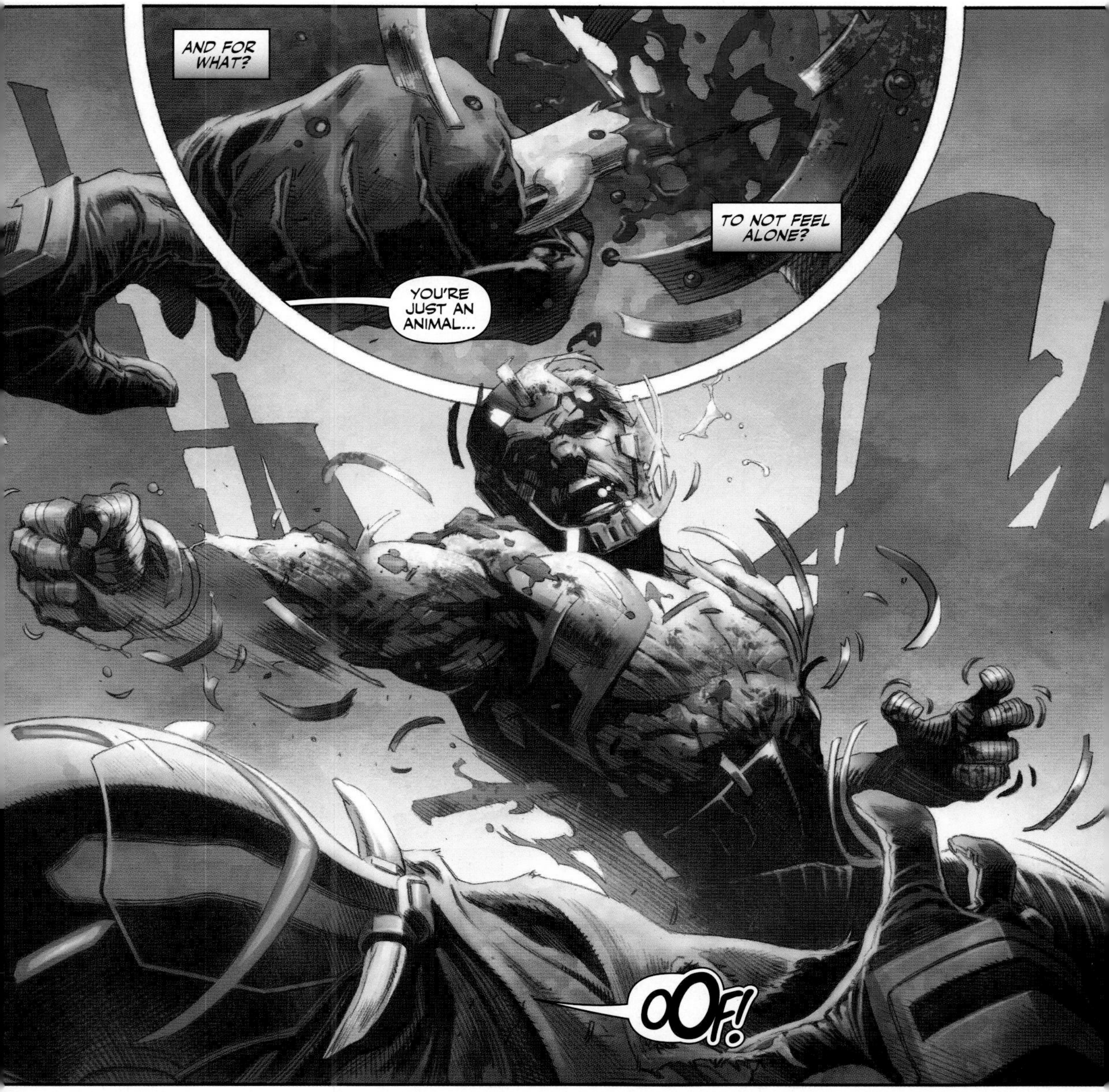
AND FOR WHAT?
TO NOT FEEL ALONE?
YOU'RE JUST AN ANIMAL...
OOF!

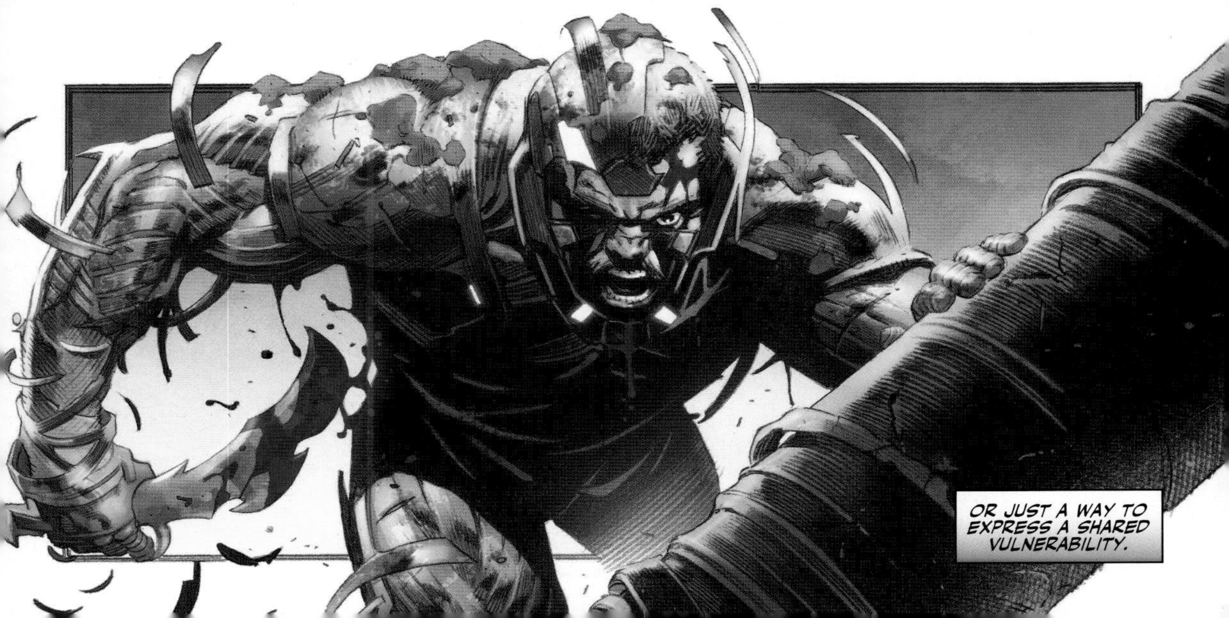
OR JUST A WAY TO EXPRESS A SHARED VULNERABILITY.

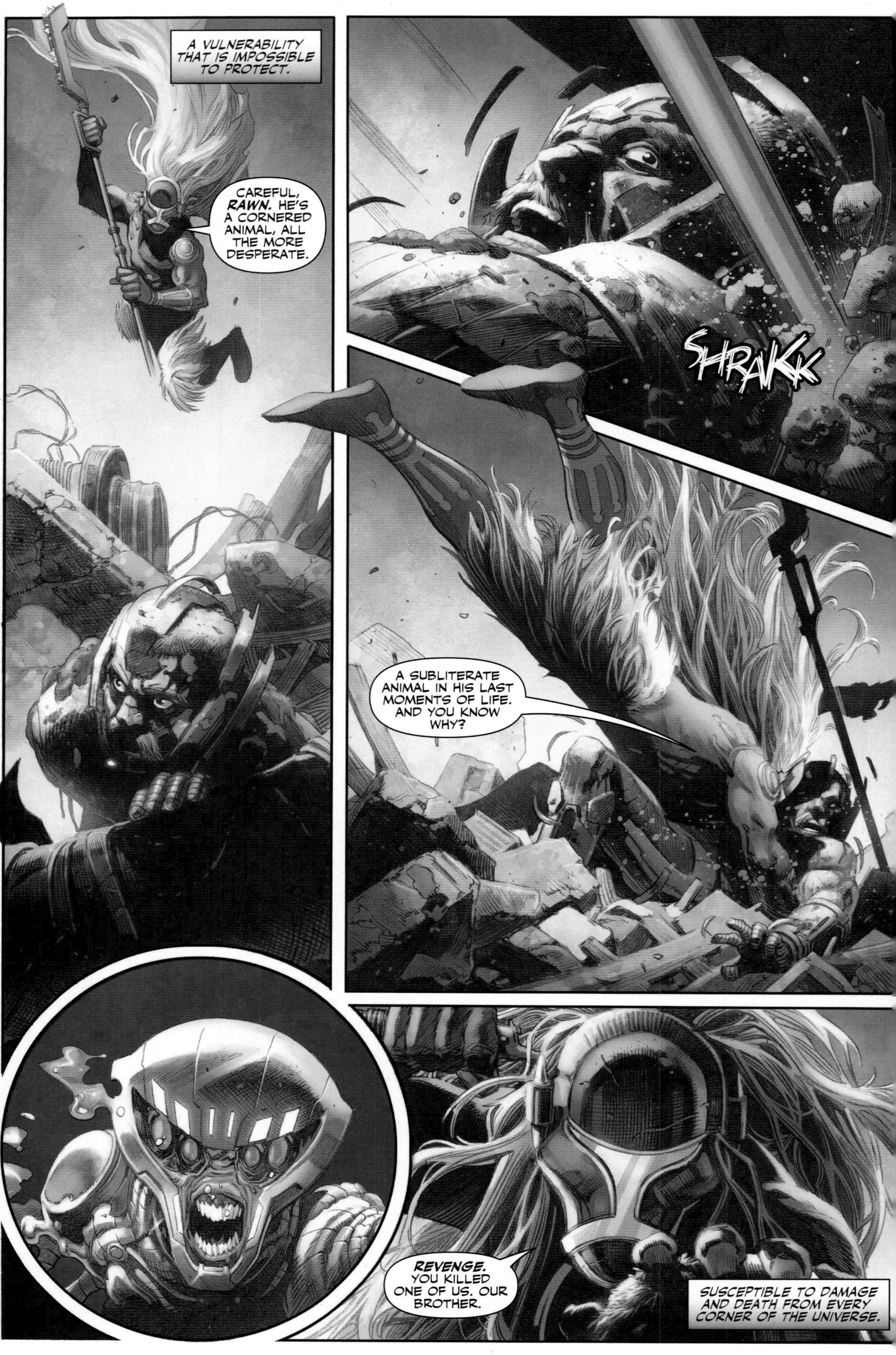
A VULNERABILITY THAT IS IMPOSSIBLE TO PROTECT.
CAREFUL, RAWN. HE'S A CORNERED ANIMAL, ALL THE MORE DESPERATE.
SHRAKK
A SUBLITERATE ANIMAL IN HIS LAST MOMENTS OF LIFE. AND YOU KNOW WHY?
REVENGE. YOU KILLED ONE OF US. OUR BROTHER.
SUSCEPTIBLE TO DAMAGE AND DEATH FROM EVERY CORNER OF THE UNIVERSE.

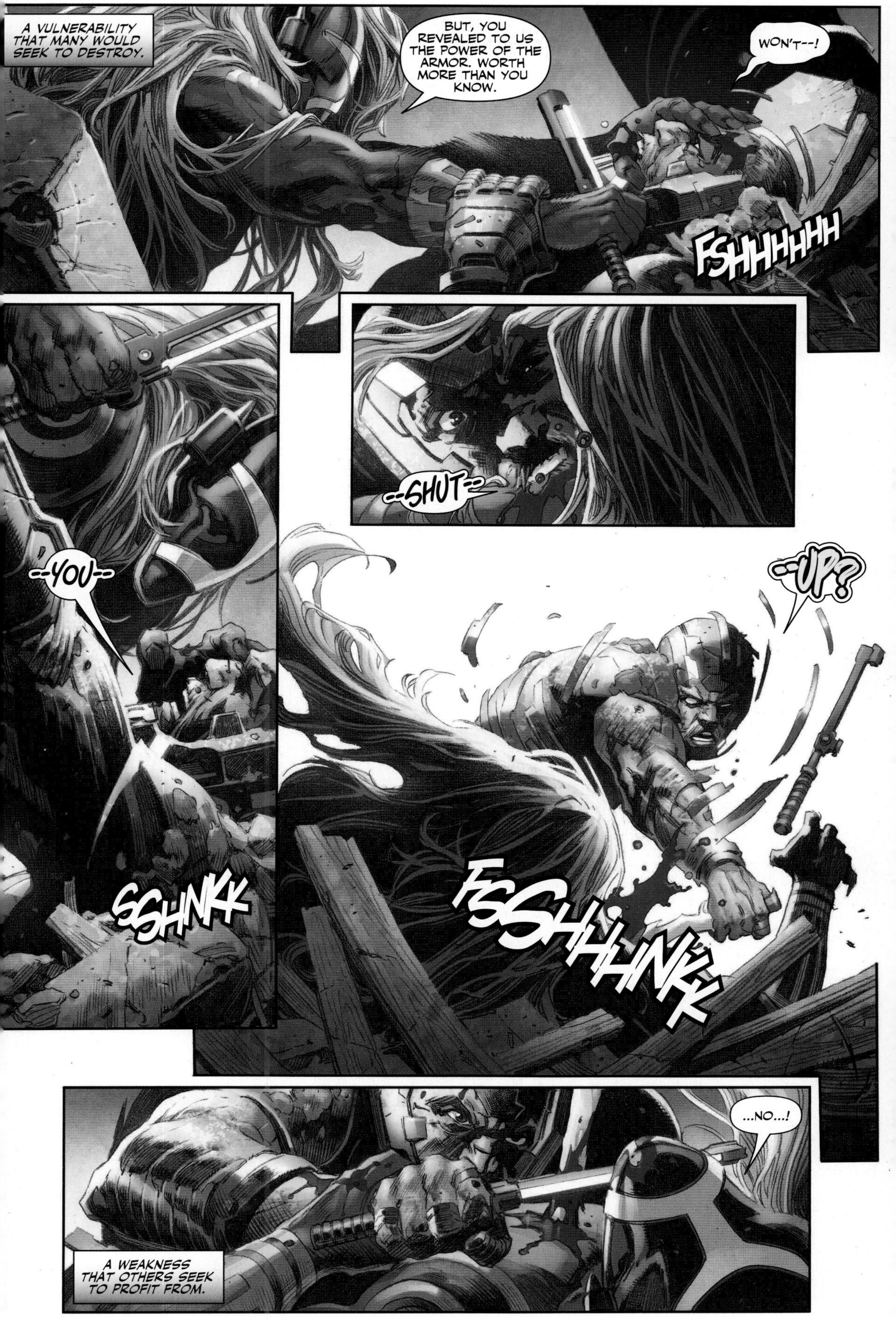
A VULNERABILITY THAT MANY WOULD SEEK TO DESTROY.
BUT, YOU REVEALED TO US THE POWER OF THE ARMOR. WORTH MORE THAN YOU KNOW.
WON'T--!
FSHHHHHH
--YOU--
--SHUT--
--UP?
SSHNKK
FSSHHUNKK
...NO...!
A WEAKNESS THAT OTHERS SEEK TO PROFIT FROM.

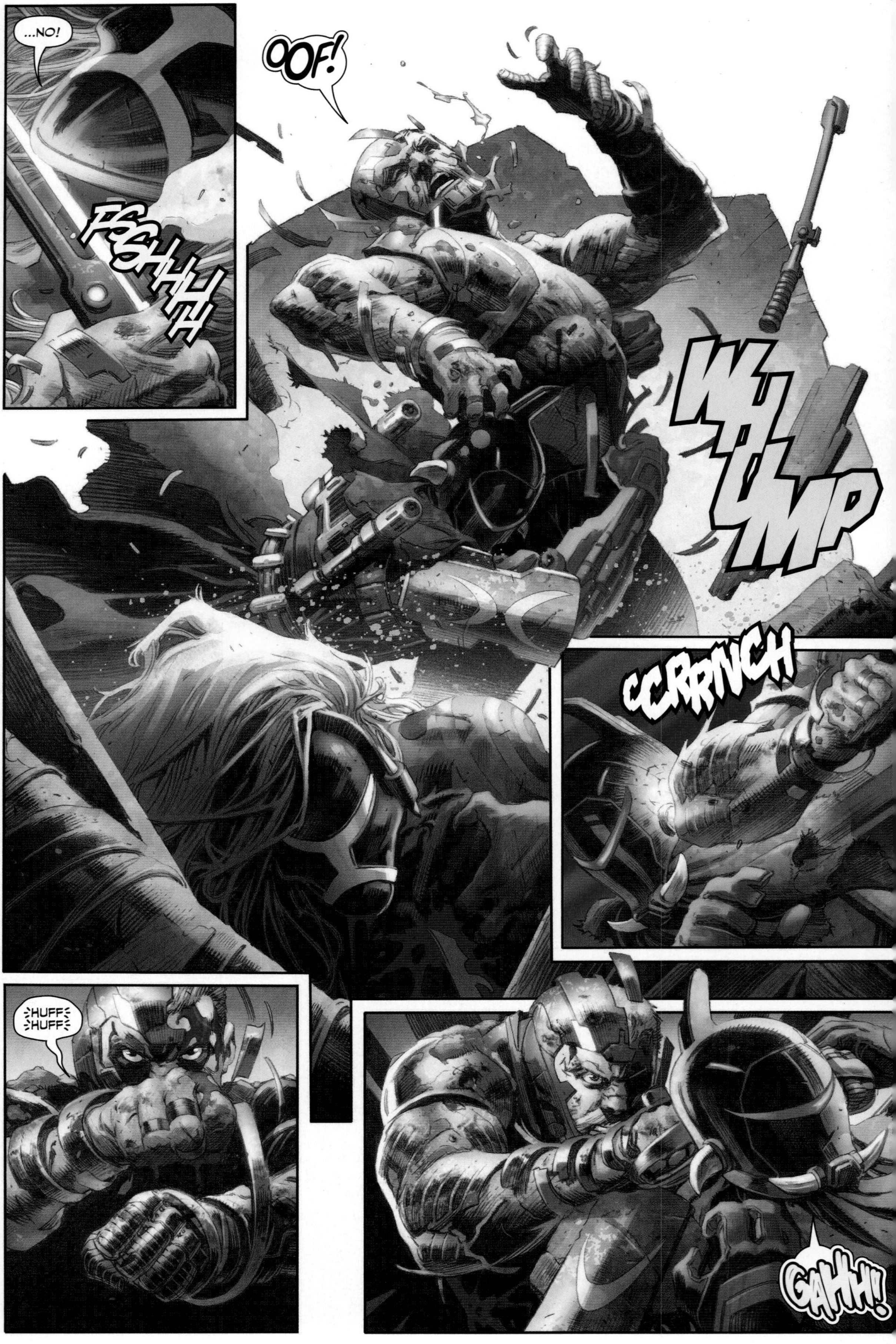
...NO!
FSCHHHH
OOF!
WHUMP
CCRRNCH
HUFF HUFF
GAHHH!

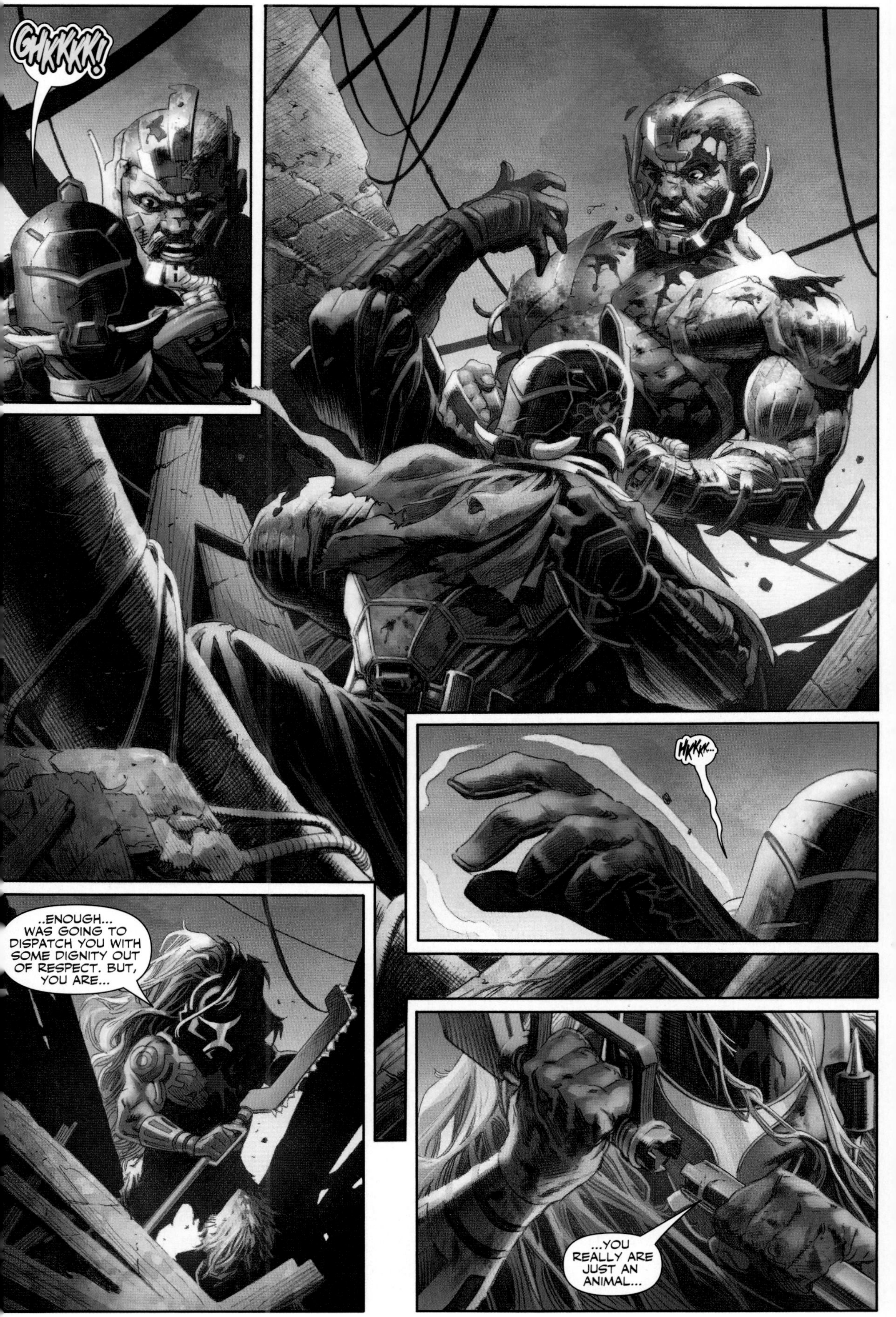
GHKKKK!
HKKKK...
..ENOUGH... WAS GOING TO DISPATCH YOU WITH SOME DIGNITY OUT OF RESPECT. BUT, YOU ARE...
...YOU REALLY ARE JUST AN ANIMAL...

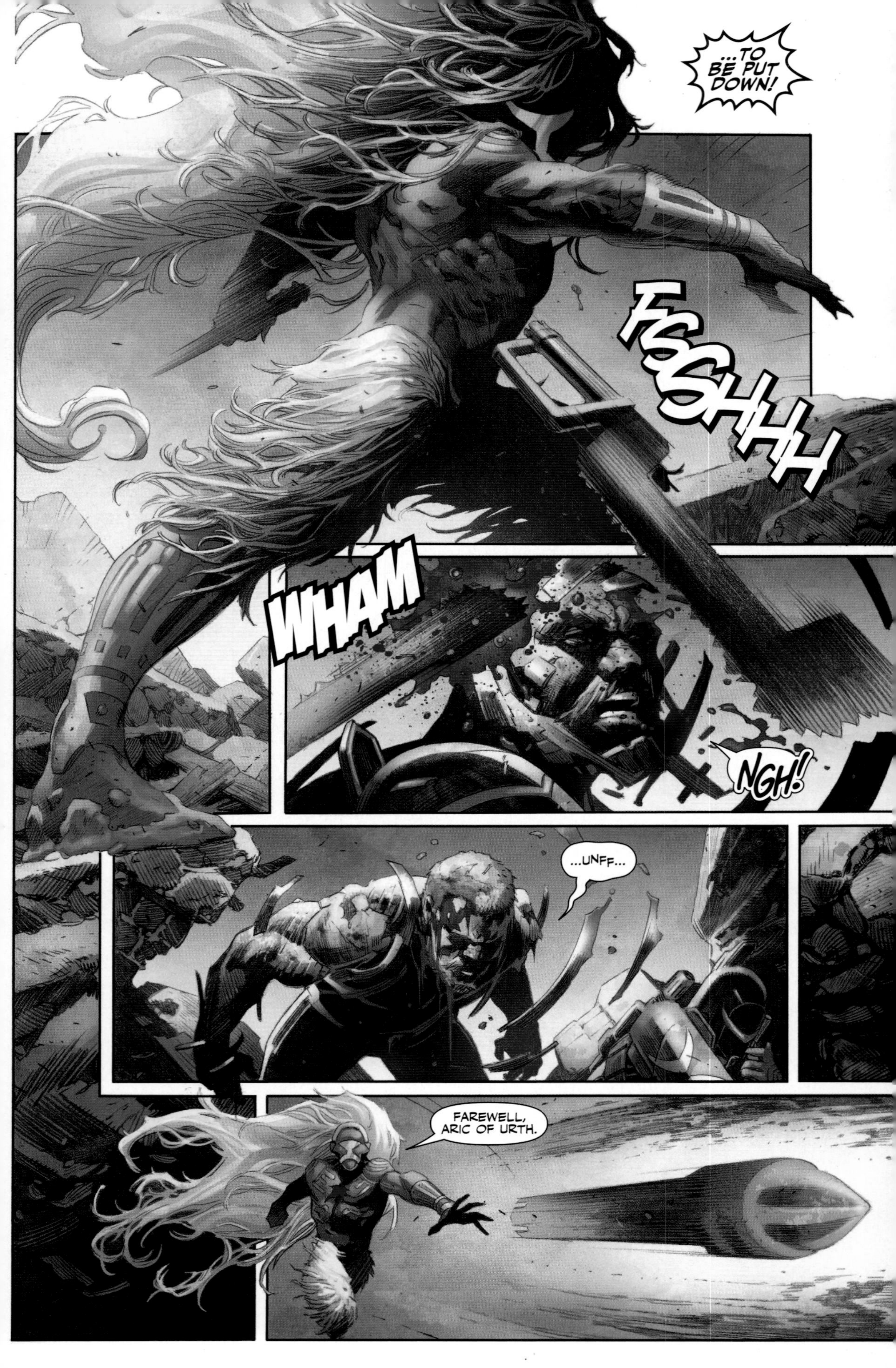
...TO BE PUT DOWN!
FSSHHHH
WHAM
NGH!
...UNFF...
FAREWELL, ARIC OF URTH.

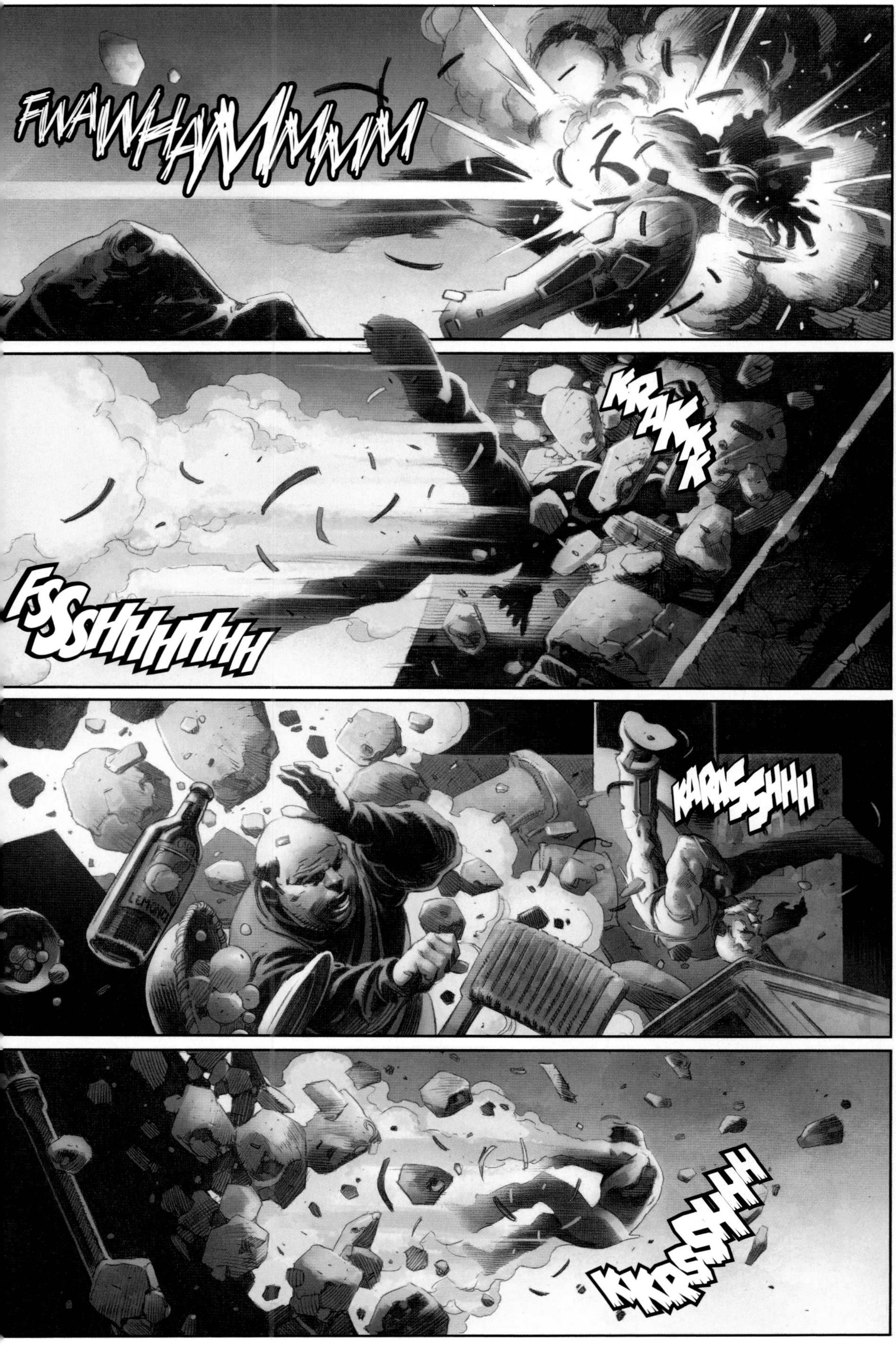
FWAWHAWMMMM
KRAKKK
FSSSHHHHHHH
KARASSHHH
KKRSSHHH

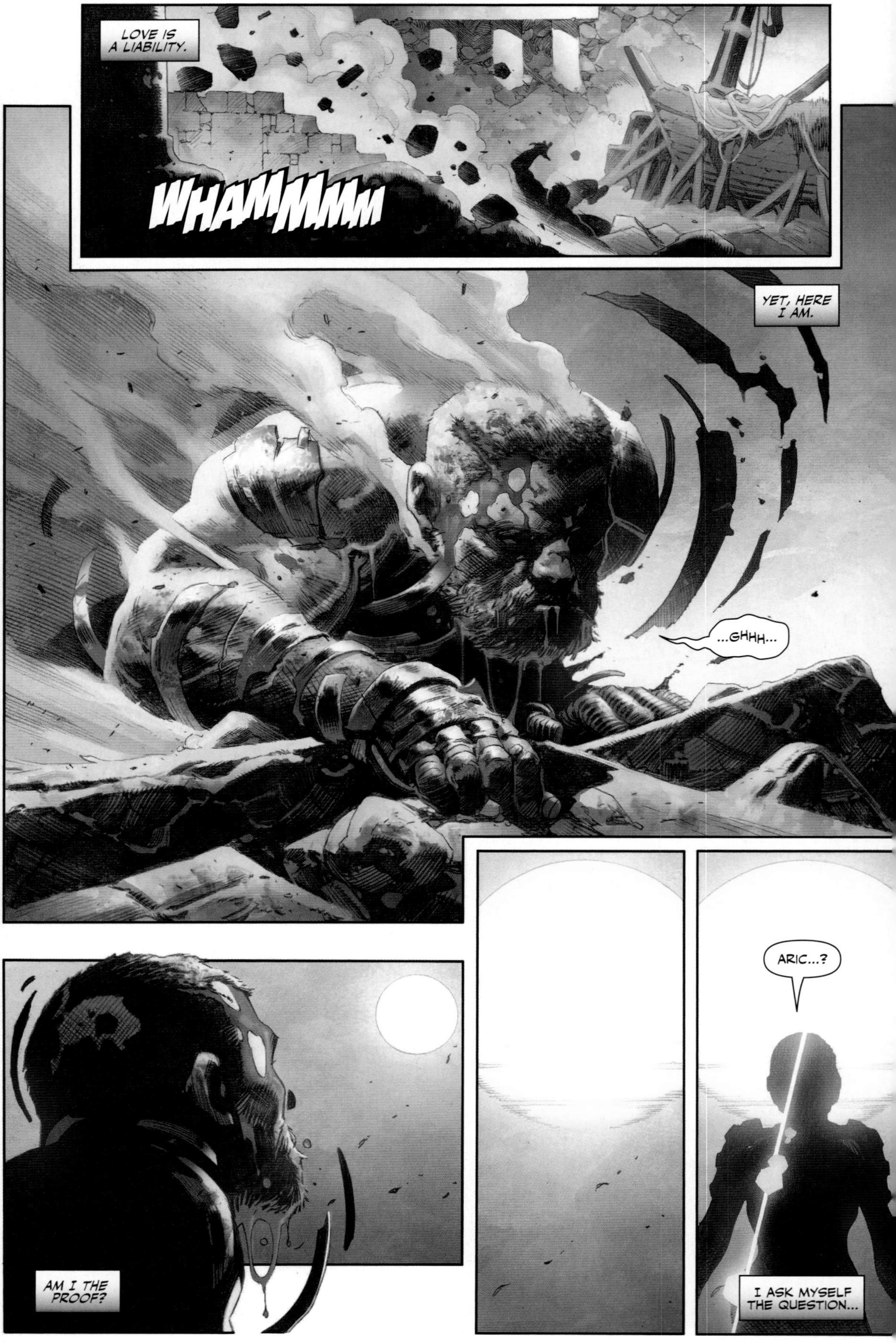
LOVE IS A LIABILITY.
WHAMMMM
YET, HERE I AM.
...GHHH...
AM I THE PROOF?
ARIC...?
I ASK MYSELF THE QUESTION...

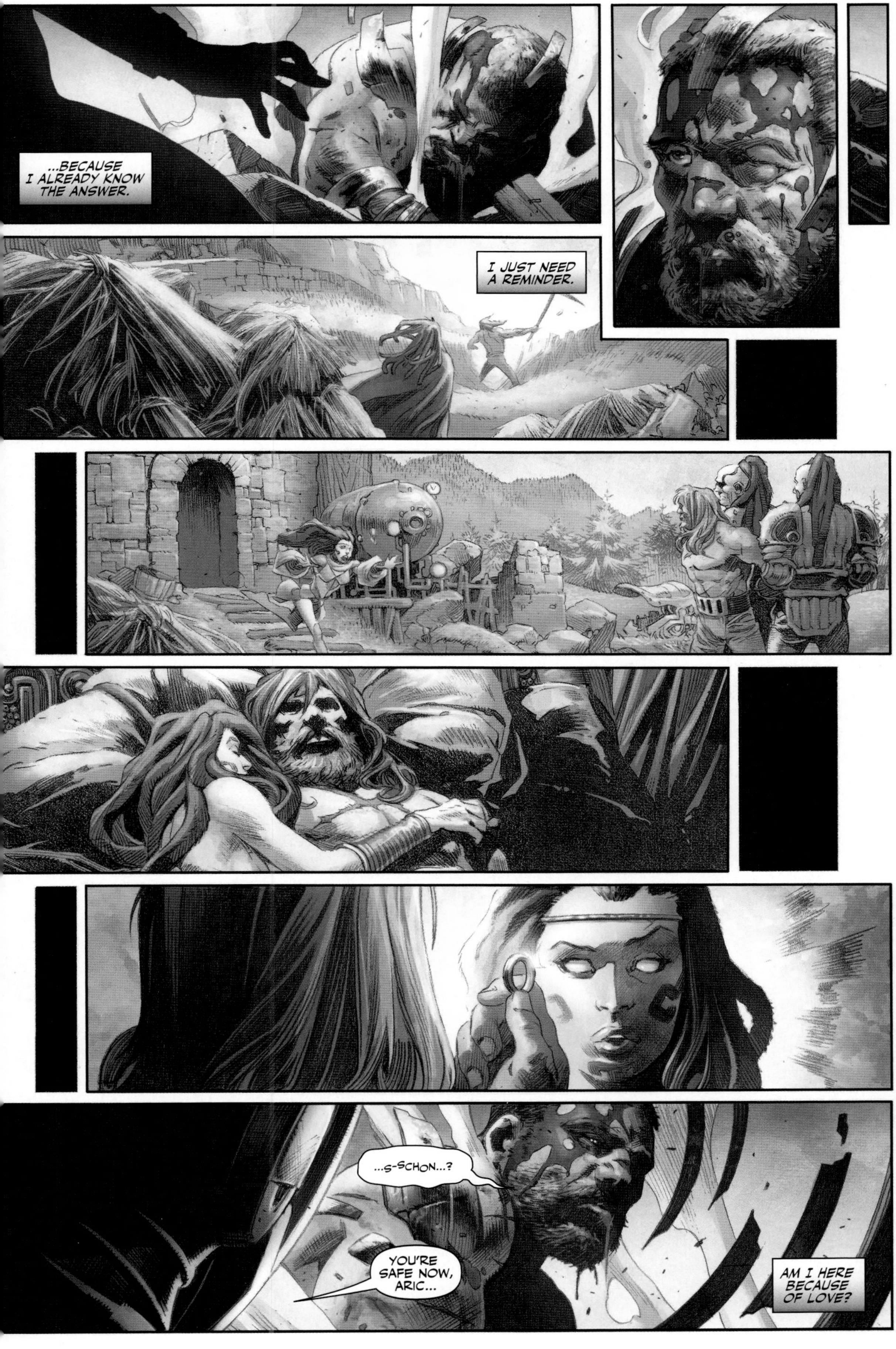

...BECAUSE I ALREADY KNOW THE ANSWER.
I JUST NEED A REMINDER.
...S-SCHON...?
YOU'RE SAFE NOW, ARIC...
AM I HERE BECAUSE OF LOVE?

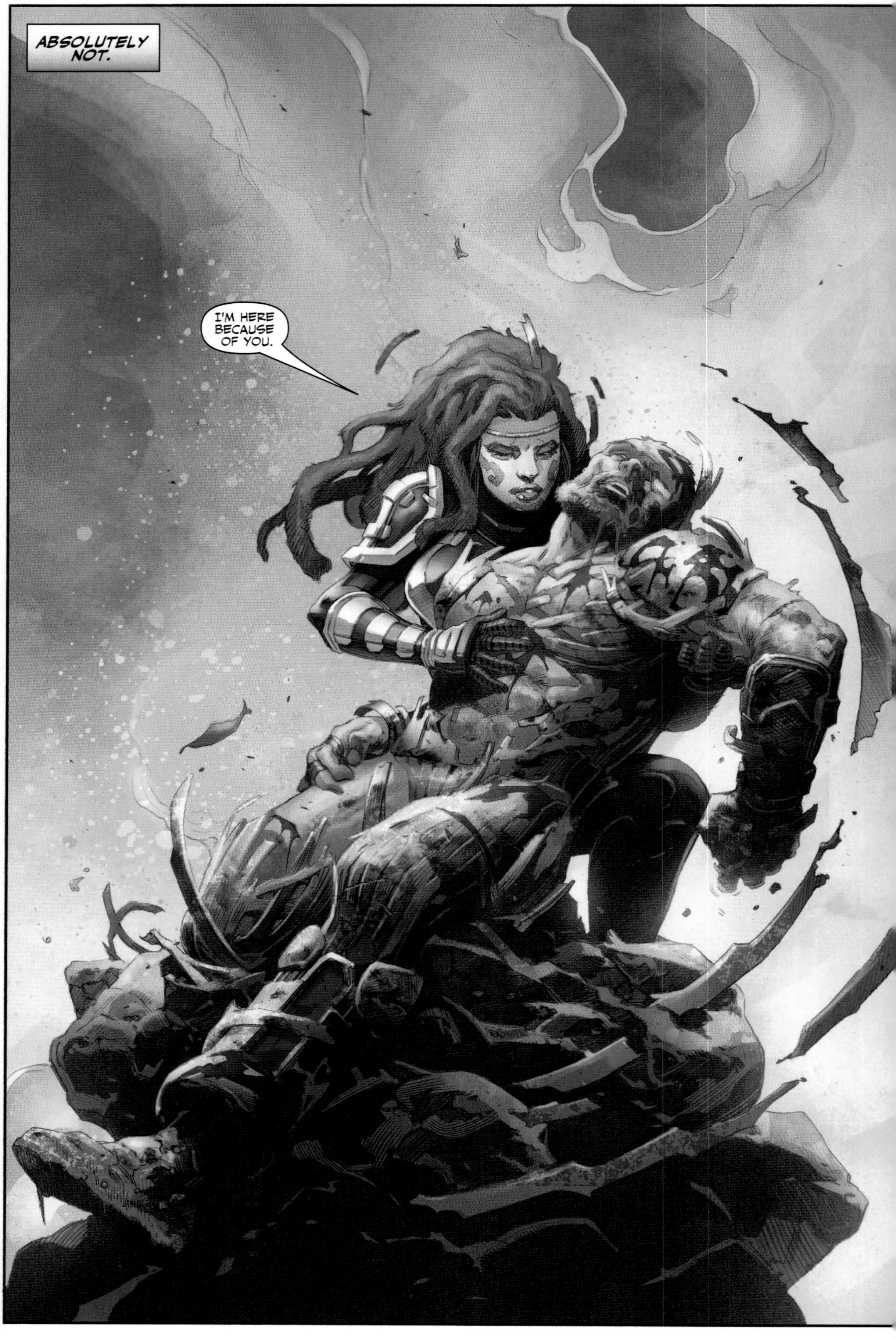
ABSOLUTELY NOT.
I'M HERE BECAUSE OF YOU.

X-O MANOWAR®

ERO

ISSUE 25

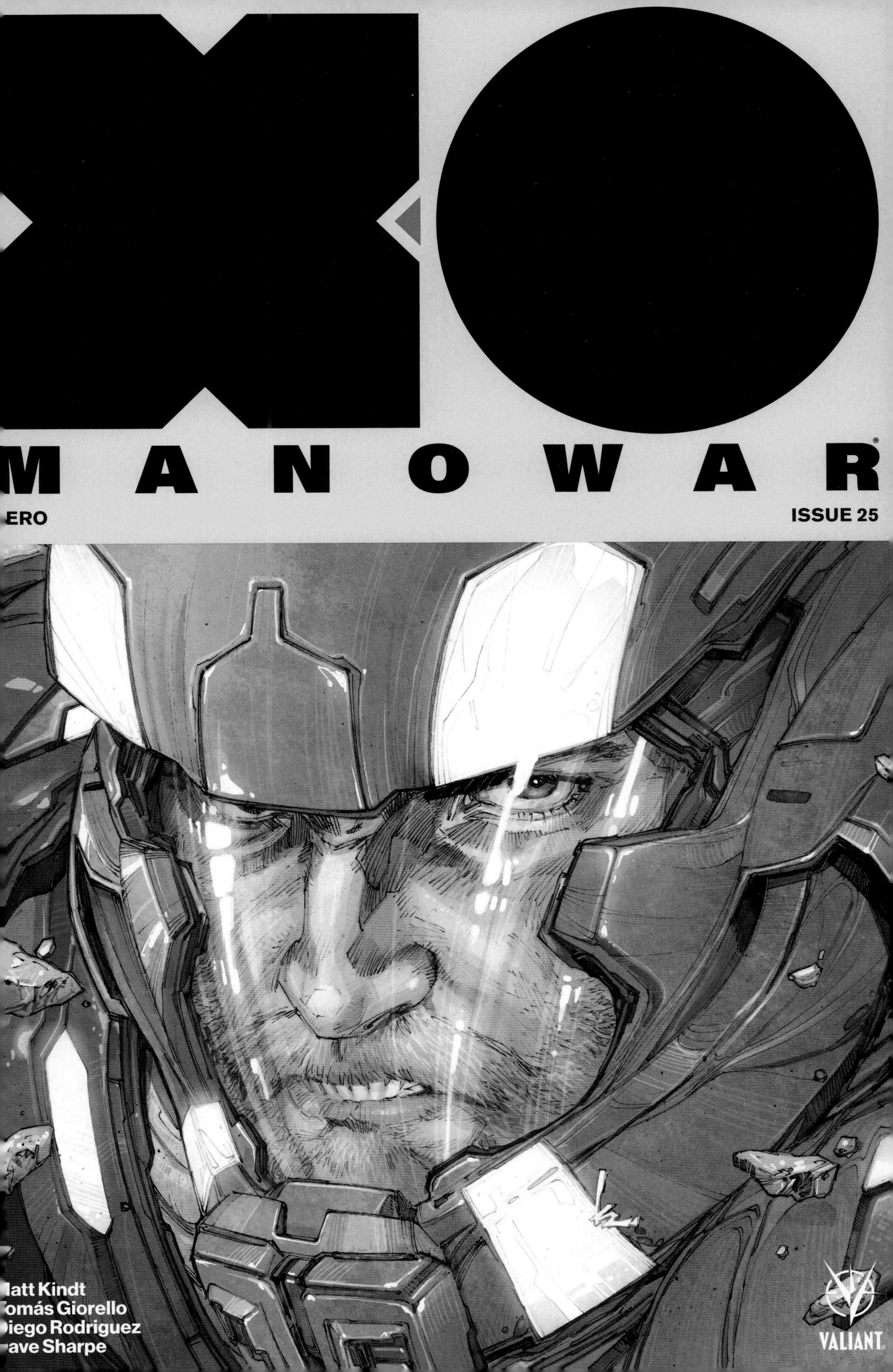

latt Kindt
omás Giorello
iego Rodriguez
ave Sharpe

VALIANT

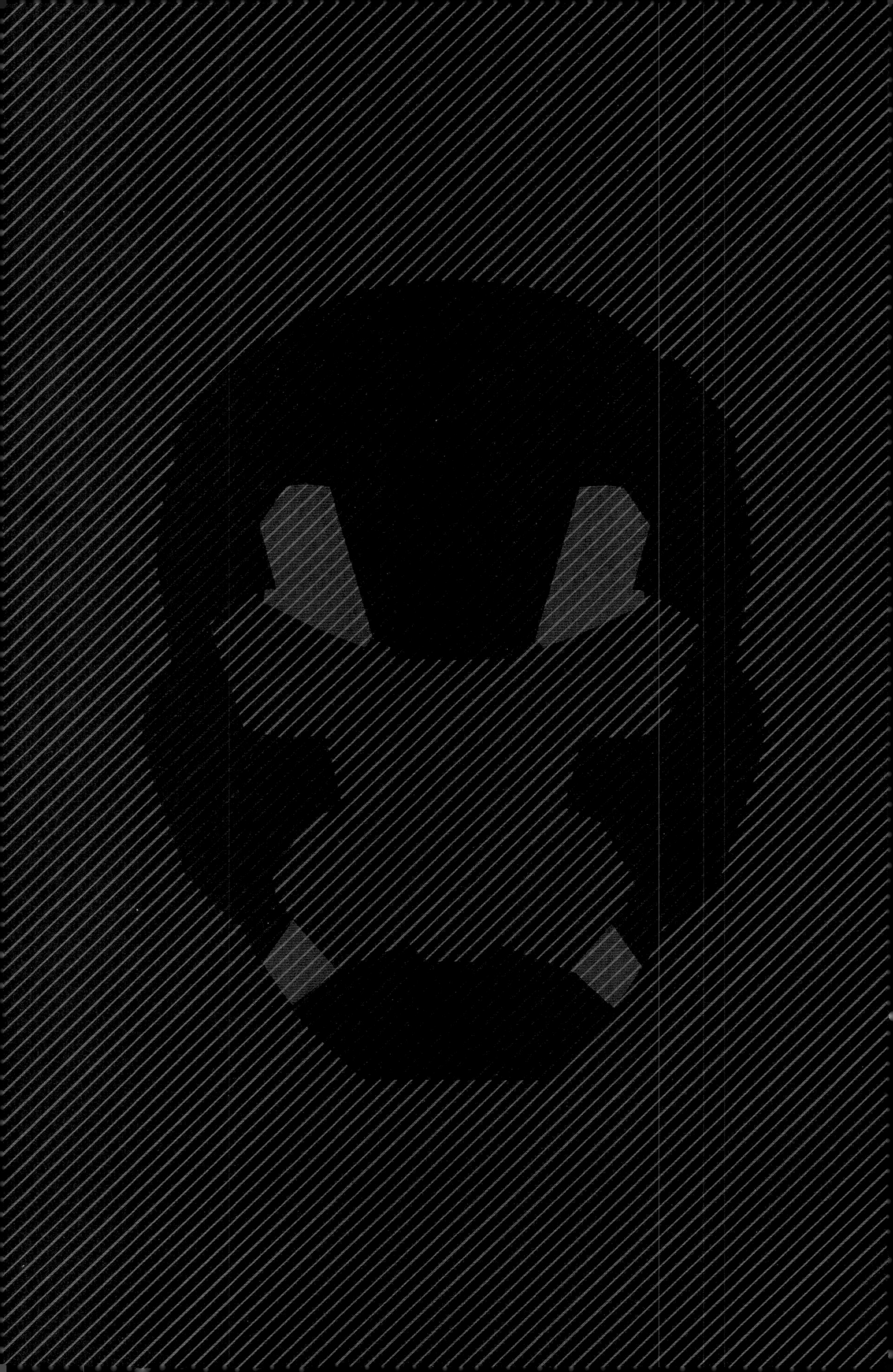

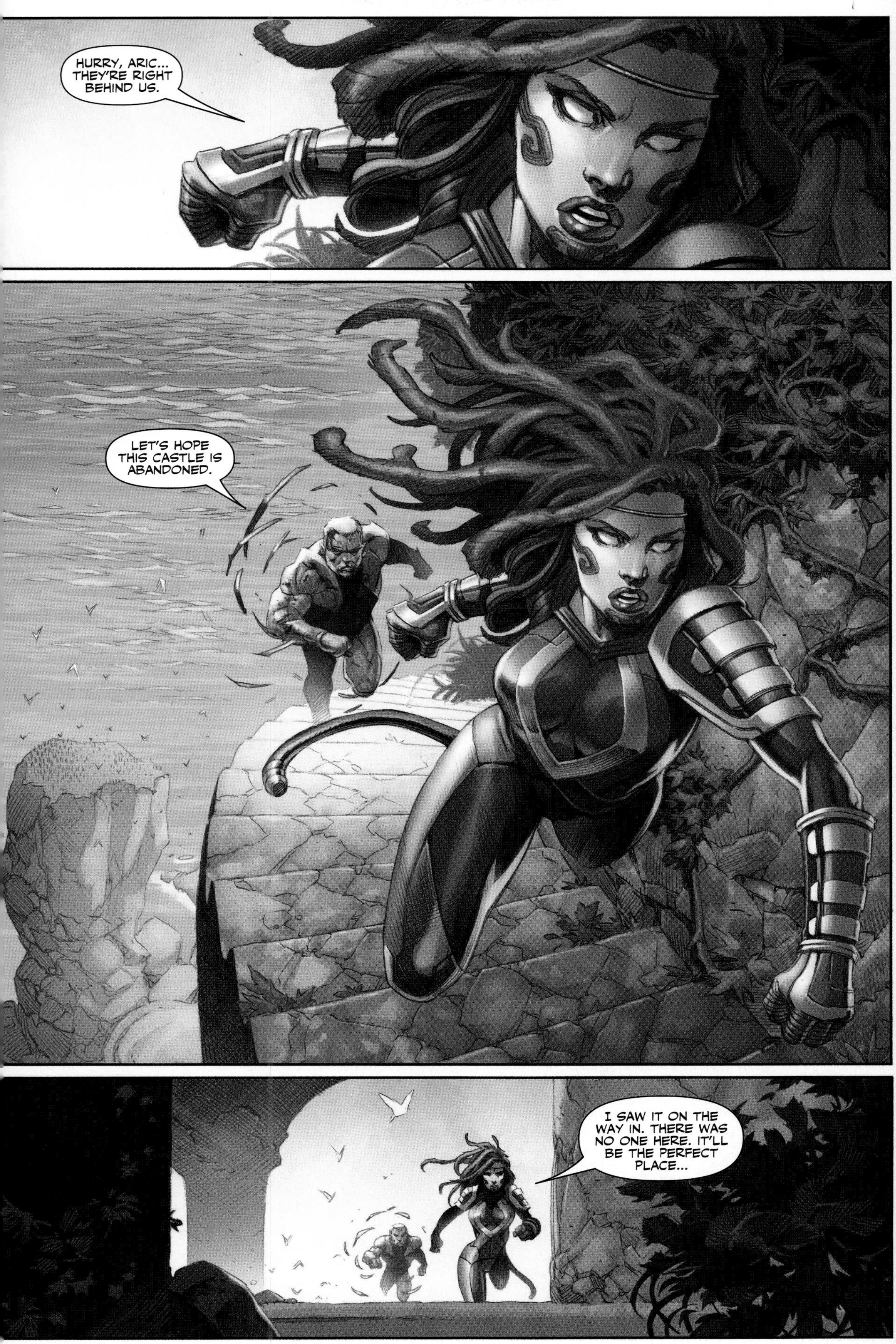
HURRY, ARIC... THEY'RE RIGHT BEHIND US.
LET'S HOPE THIS CASTLE IS ABANDONED.
I SAW IT ON THE WAY IN. THERE WAS NO ONE HERE. IT'LL BE THE PERFECT PLACE...

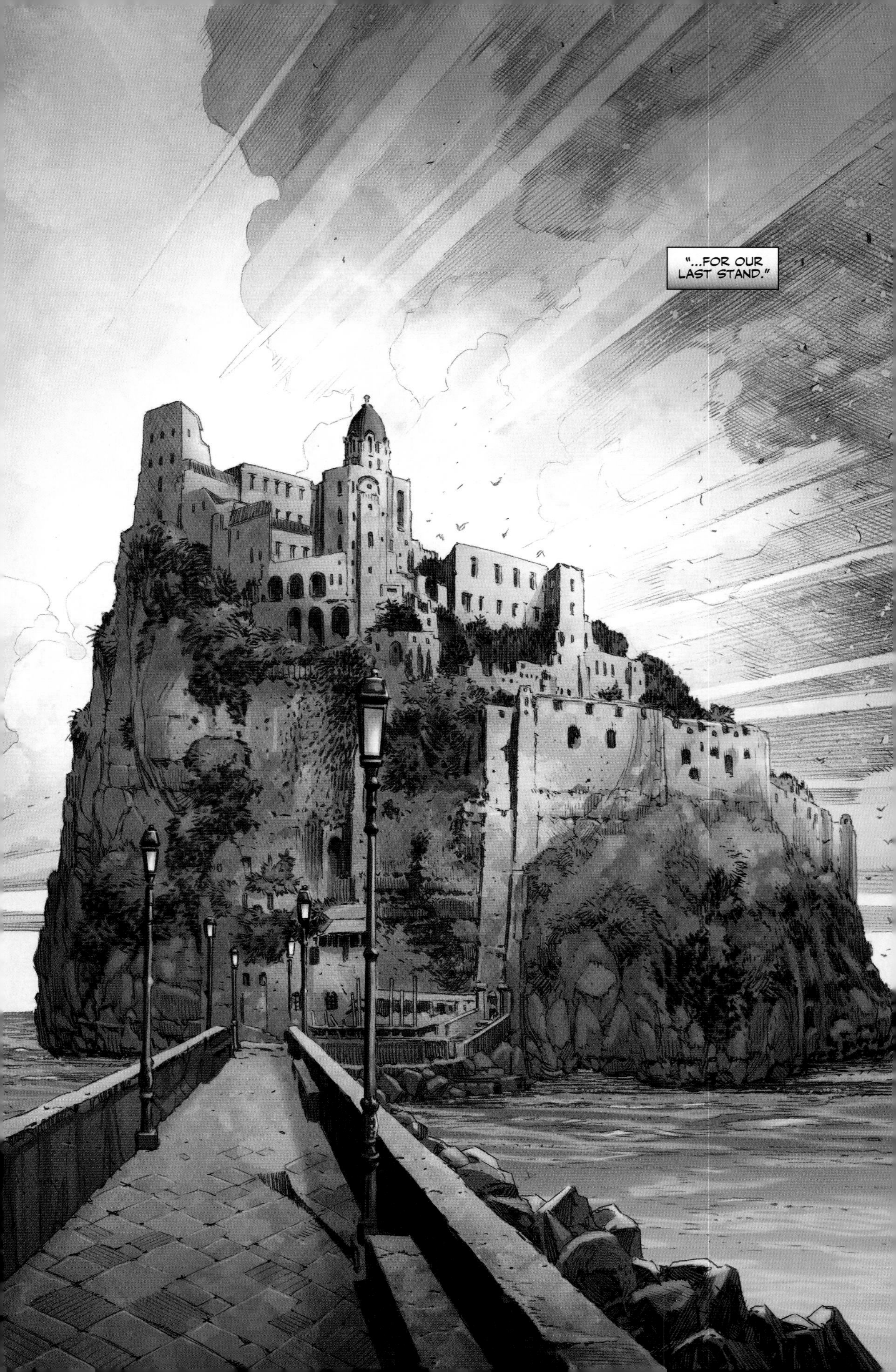
"...FOR OUR LAST STAND."

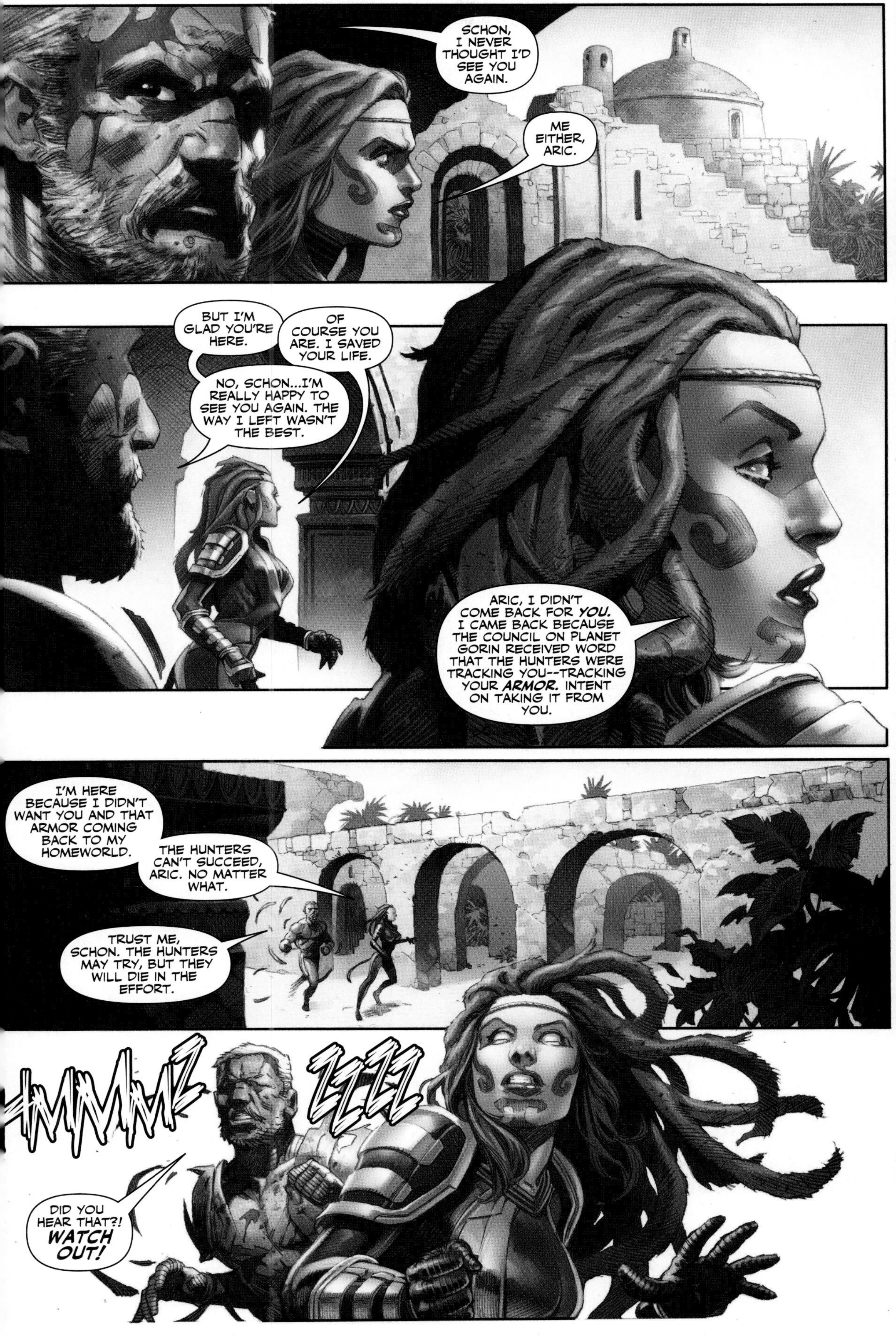
SCHON, I NEVER THOUGHT I'D SEE YOU AGAIN.
ME EITHER, ARIC.
BUT I'M GLAD YOU'RE HERE.
OF COURSE YOU ARE. I SAVED YOUR LIFE.
NO, SCHON...I'M REALLY HAPPY TO SEE YOU AGAIN. THE WAY I LEFT WASN'T THE BEST.
ARIC, I DIDN'T COME BACK FOR *YOU.* I CAME BACK BECAUSE THE COUNCIL ON PLANET GORIN RECEIVED WORD THAT THE HUNTERS WERE TRACKING YOU--TRACKING YOUR ***ARMOR.*** INTENT ON TAKING IT FROM YOU.
I'M HERE BECAUSE I DIDN'T WANT YOU AND THAT ARMOR COMING BACK TO MY HOMEWORLD.
THE HUNTERS CAN'T SUCCEED, ARIC. NO MATTER WHAT.
TRUST ME, SCHON. THE HUNTERS MAY TRY, BUT THEY WILL DIE IN THE EFFORT.
HMMMZ
ZZZZ
DID YOU HEAR THAT?! ***WATCH OUT!***

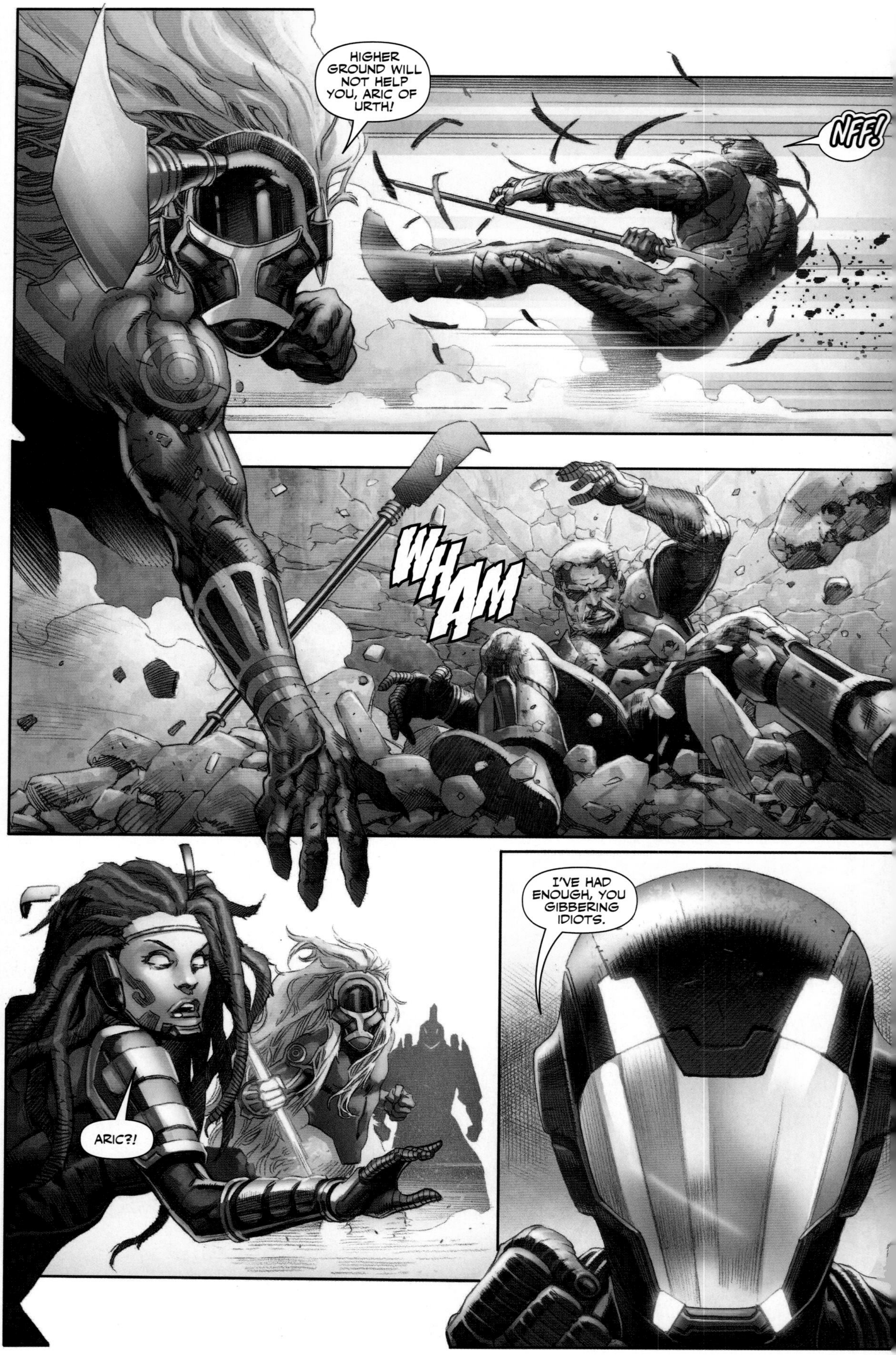
HIGHER GROUND WILL NOT HELP YOU, ARIC OF URTH!
NFF!
WHAM
ARIC?!
I'VE HAD ENOUGH, YOU GIBBERING IDIOTS.

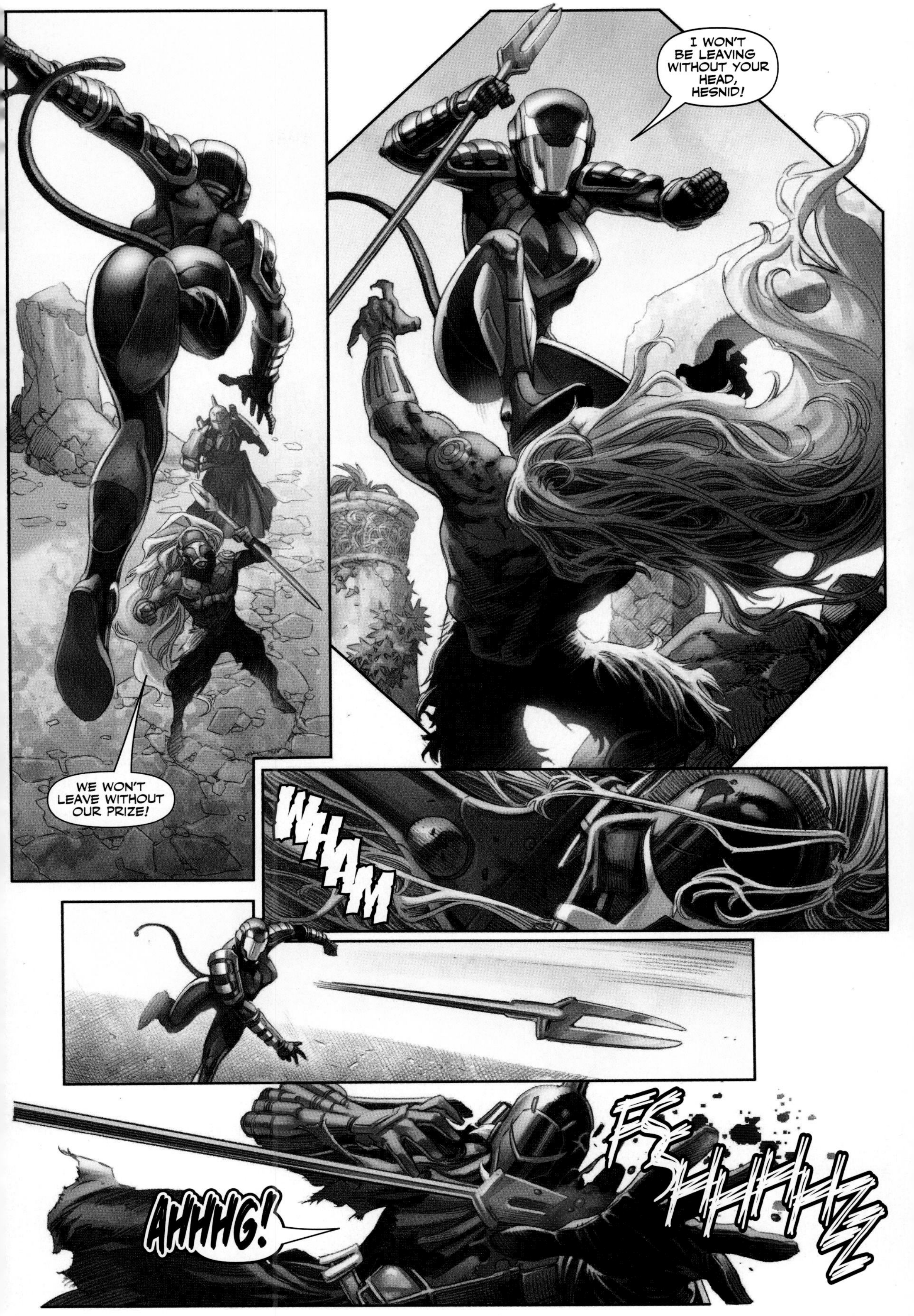

I WON'T BE LEAVING WITHOUT YOUR HEAD, HESNID!
WE WON'T LEAVE WITHOUT OUR PRIZE!
WHAM
AHHHG!
FSSHHHHHZ

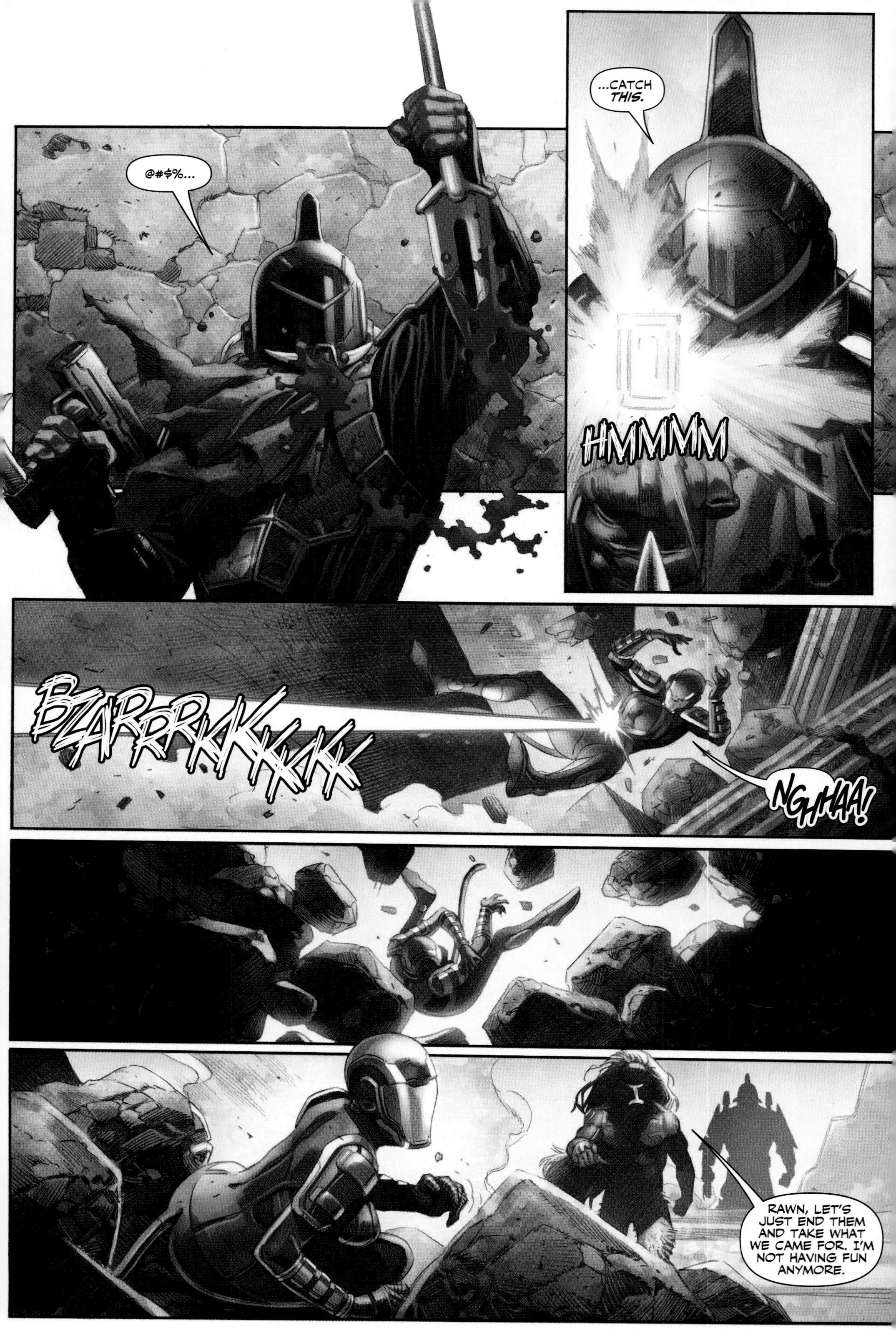

@#$%...
...CATCH THIS.
HMMMM
BZARRRKKKKKK
NGHHAA!
RAWN, LET'S JUST END THEM AND TAKE WHAT WE CAME FOR. I'M NOT HAVING FUN ANYMORE.

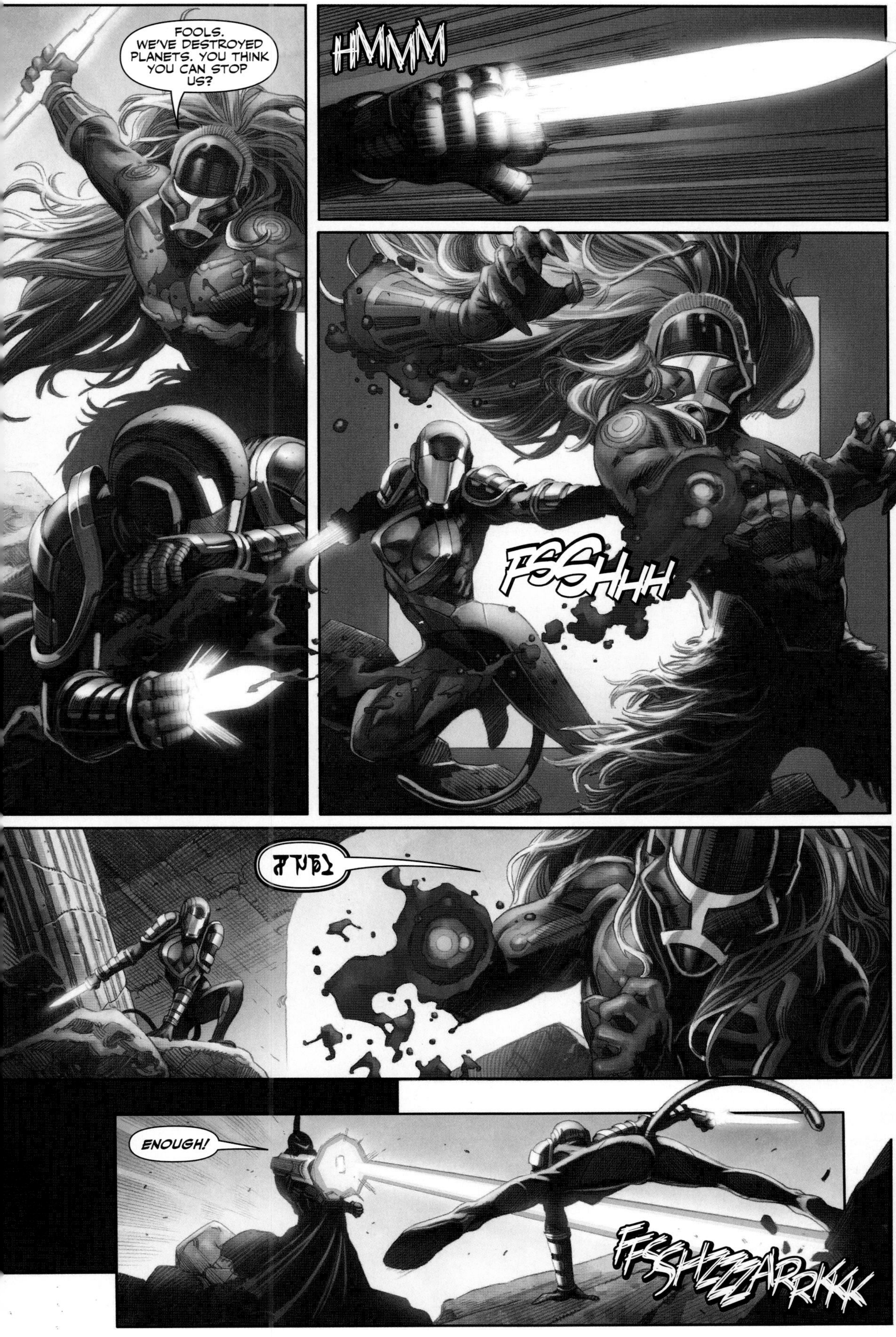
FOOLS. WE'VE DESTROYED PLANETS. YOU THINK YOU CAN STOP US?
HMMM
FSSHHH
ENOUGH!
FFSSHZZZARRKKK

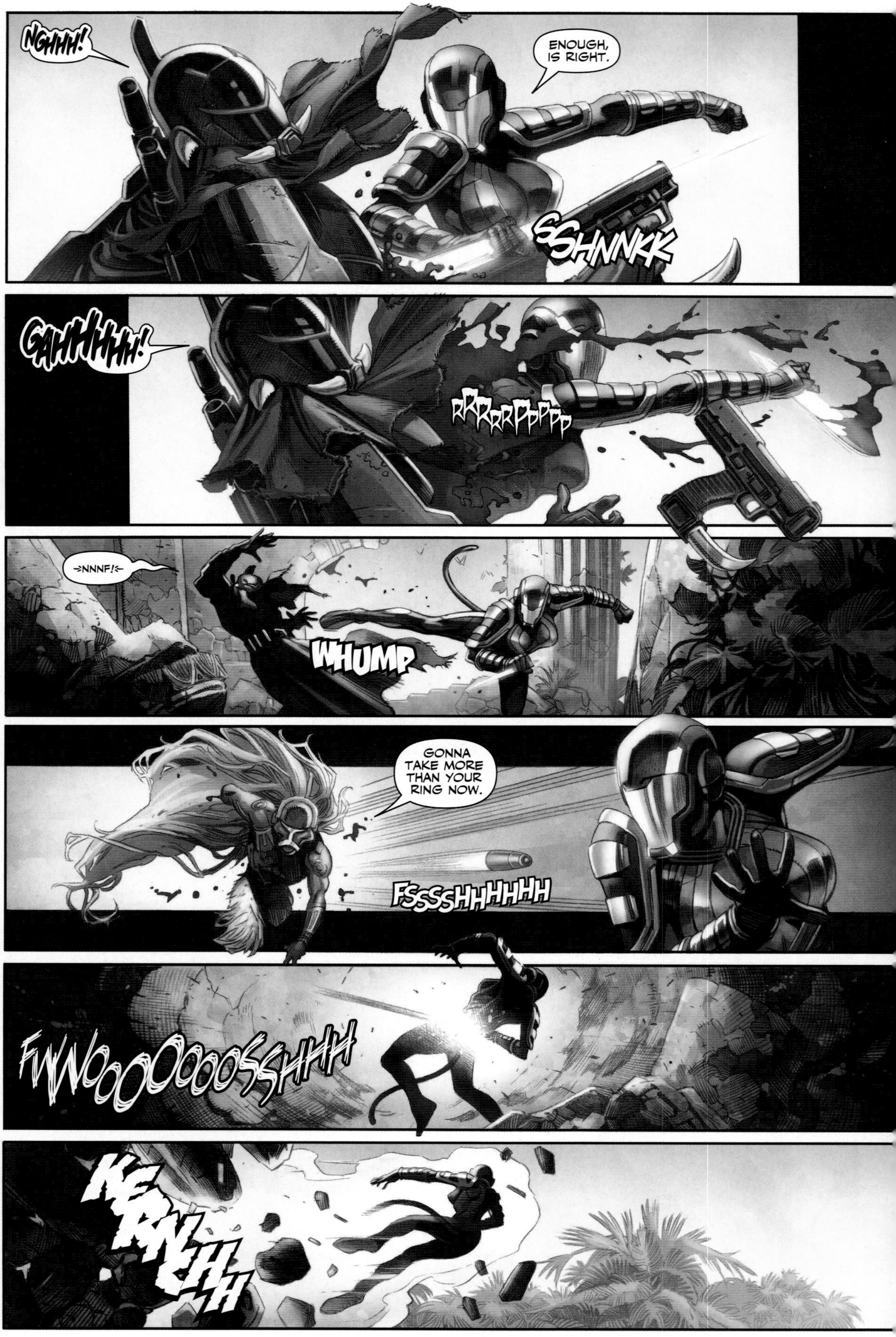
NGHHH!
ENOUGH, IS RIGHT.
SSHNNKK
GAHHHHHH!
RRRRRRPPPPP
NNNF!
WHUMP
GONNA TAKE MORE THAN YOUR RING NOW.
FSSSSHHHHHH
FWWOOOOOOOSSHHH
KERRNCHH

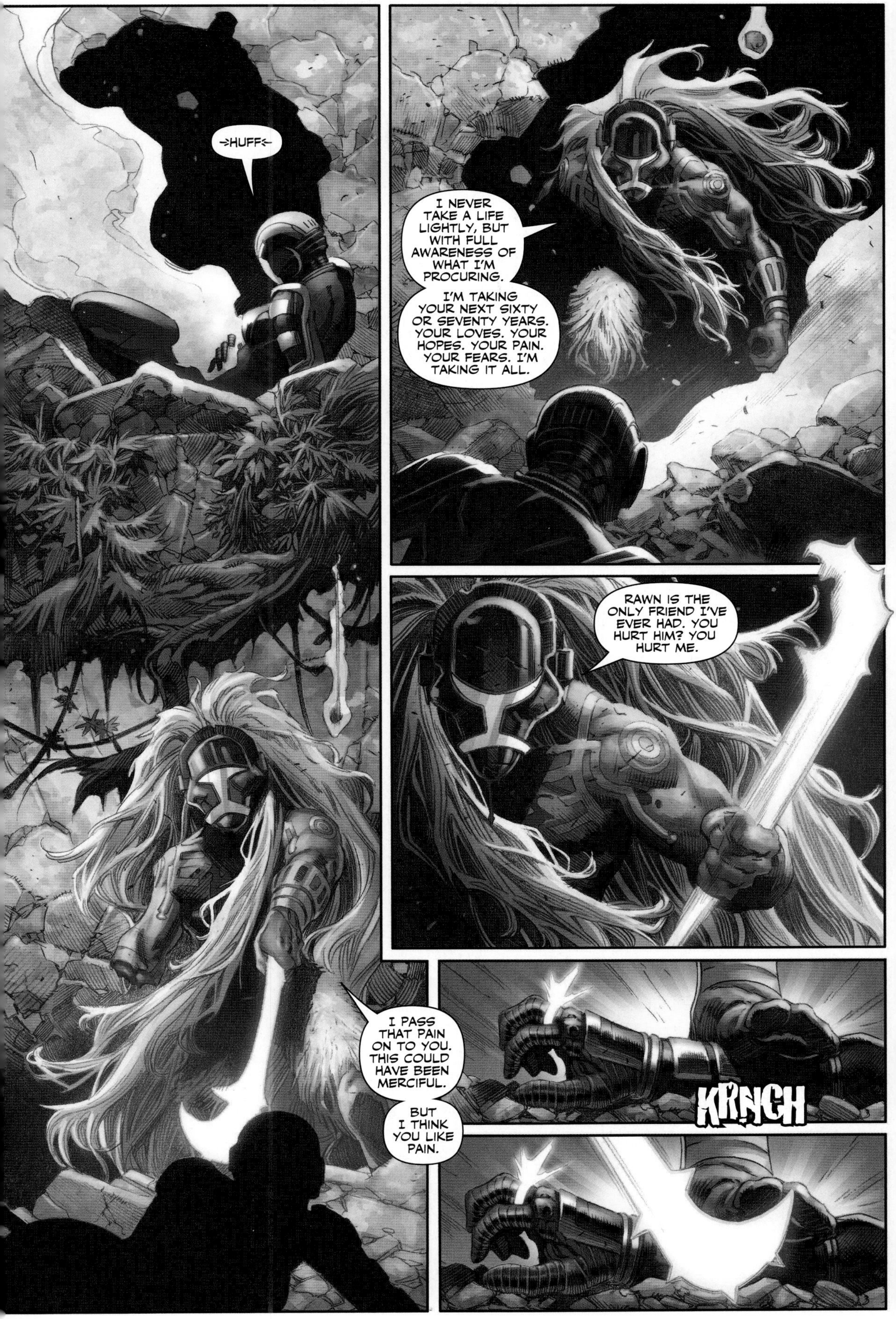

—HUFF—
I NEVER TAKE A LIFE LIGHTLY, BUT WITH FULL AWARENESS OF WHAT I'M PROCURING.
I'M TAKING YOUR NEXT SIXTY OR SEVENTY YEARS. YOUR LOVES. YOUR HOPES. YOUR PAIN. YOUR FEARS. I'M TAKING IT ALL.
RAWN IS THE ONLY FRIEND I'VE EVER HAD. YOU HURT HIM? YOU HURT ME.
I PASS THAT PAIN ON TO YOU. THIS COULD HAVE BEEN MERCIFUL.
BUT I THINK YOU LIKE PAIN.
KRNCH

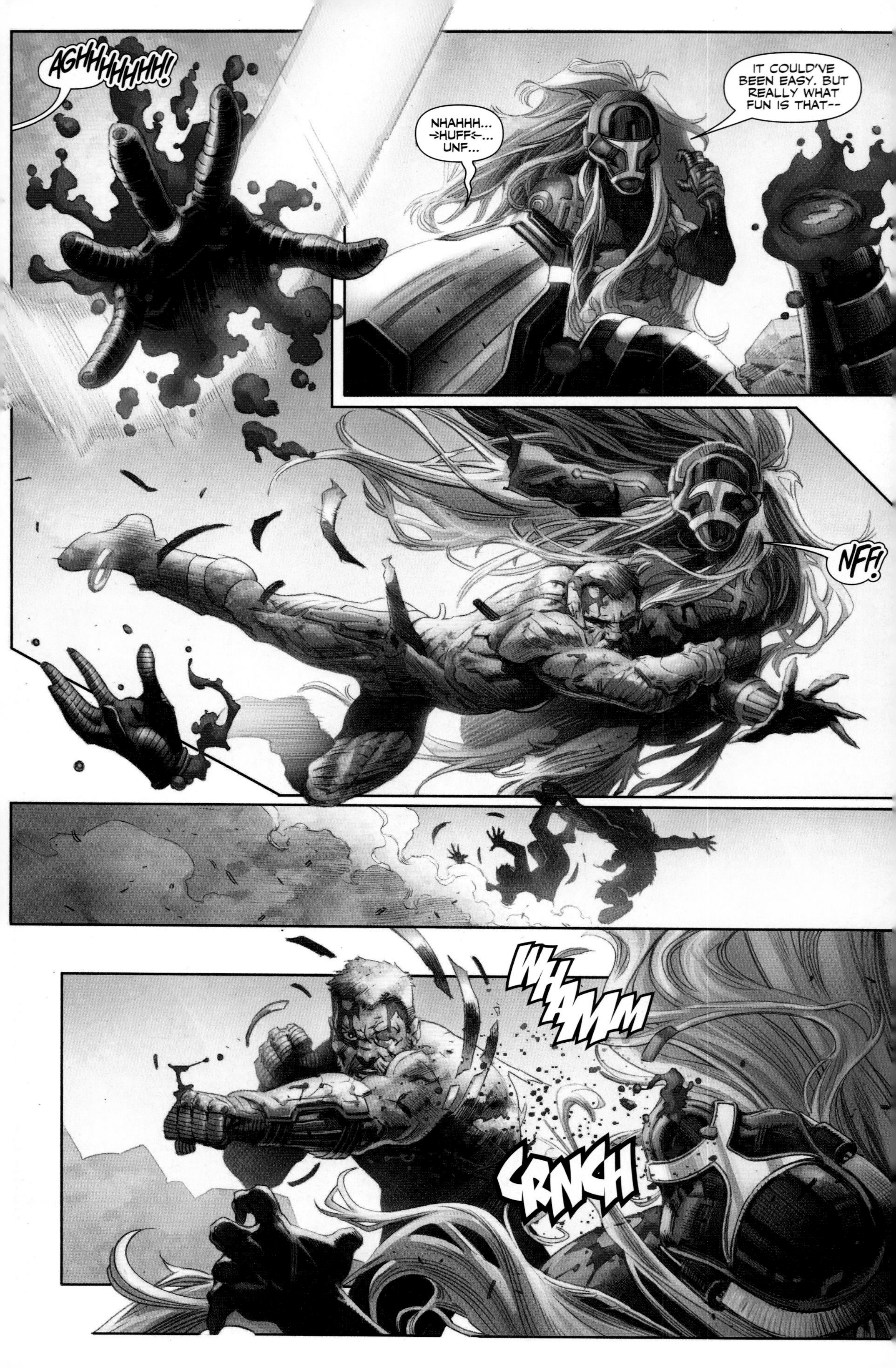
AGHHHHHHH!
NHAHHH... >HUFF<... UNF...
IT COULD'VE BEEN EASY. BUT REALLY WHAT FUN IS THAT--
NFF!
WHAMM
CRNCH

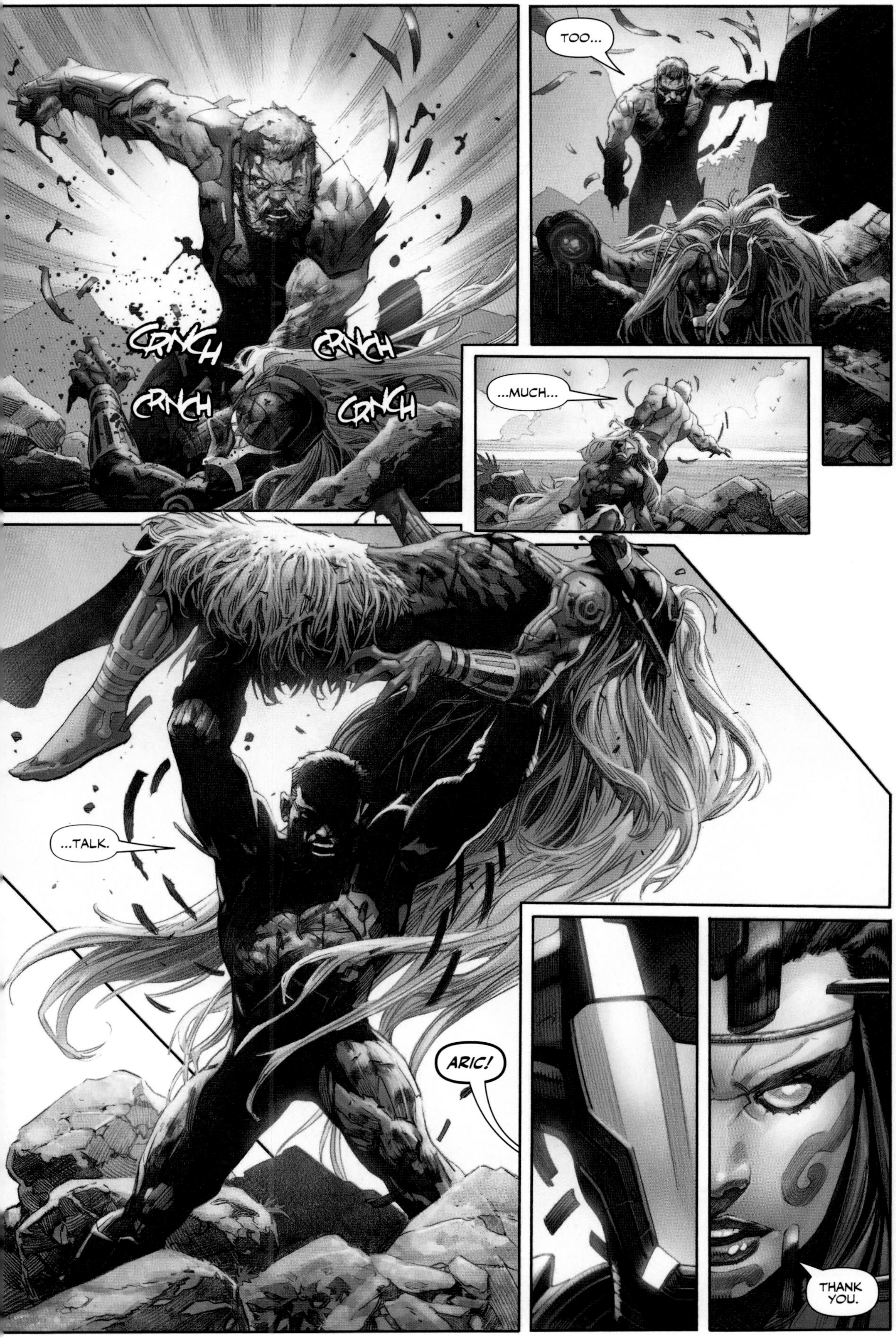
CRNCH
CRNCH
CRNCH
CRNCH
TOO...
...MUCH...
...TALK.
ARIC!
THANK YOU.

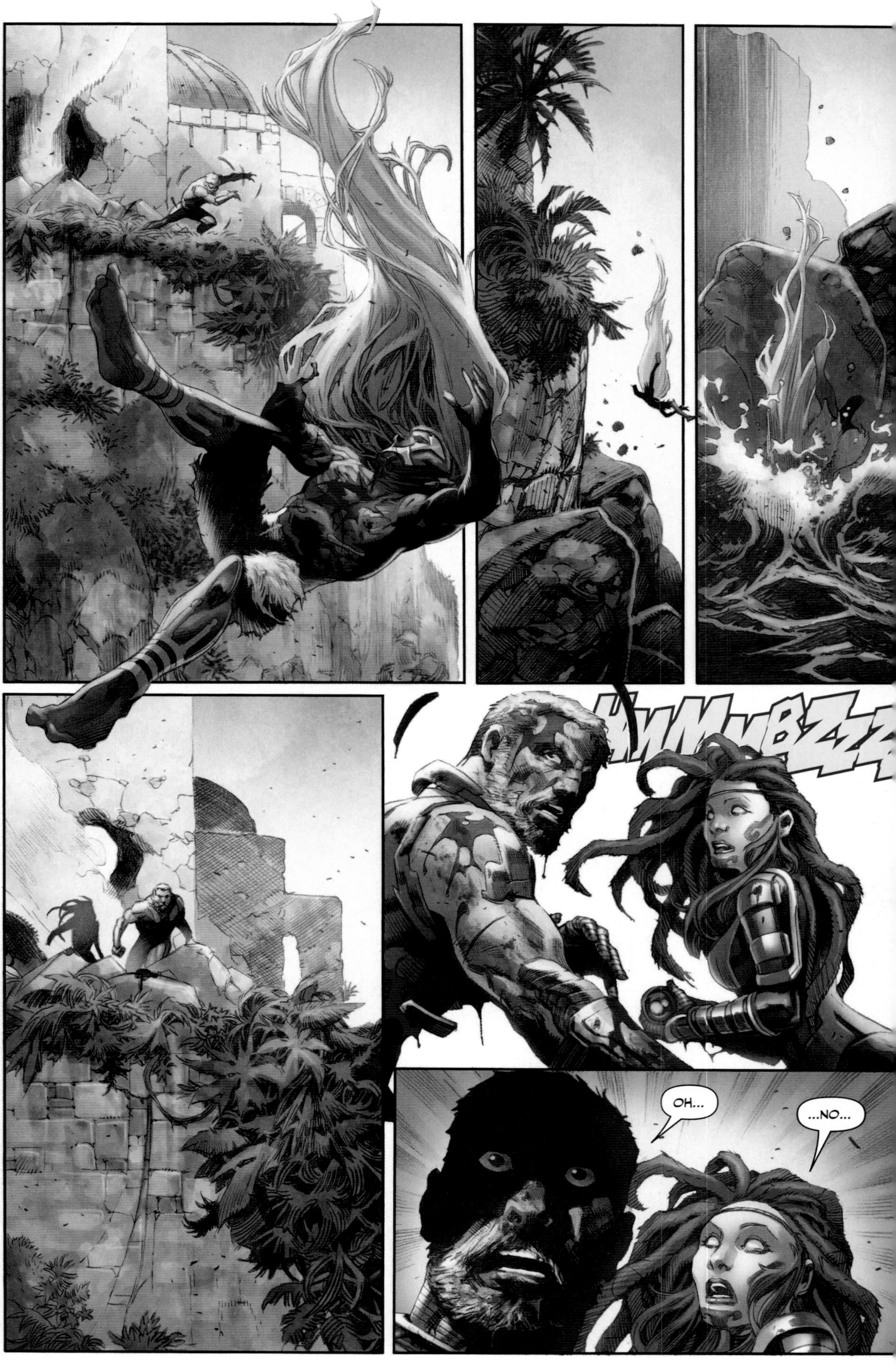
HUMMBZZZ
OH...
...NO...

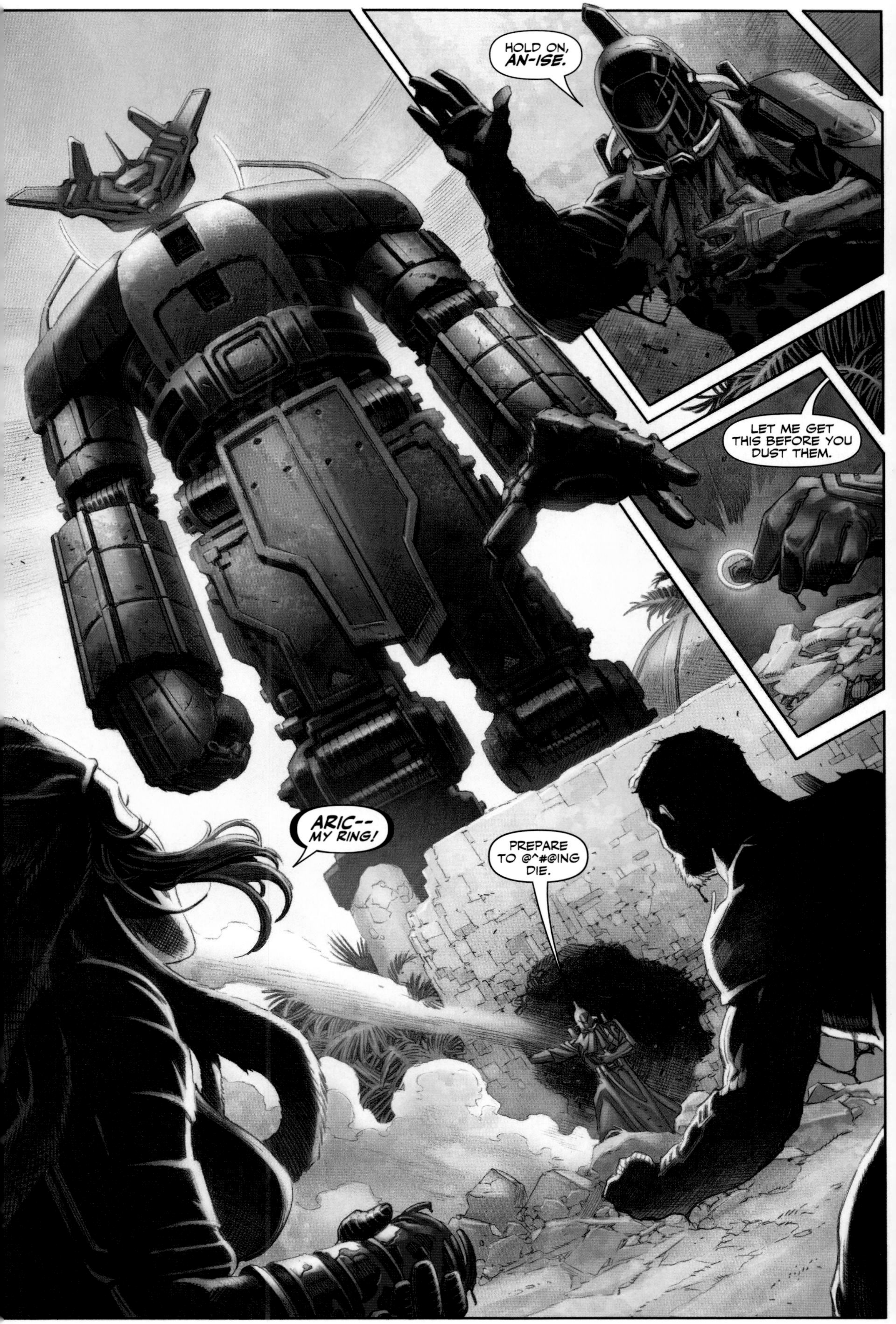
HOLD ON, AN-ISE.
LET ME GET THIS BEFORE YOU DUST THEM.
ARIC-- MY RING!
PREPARE TO @^#@ING DIE.

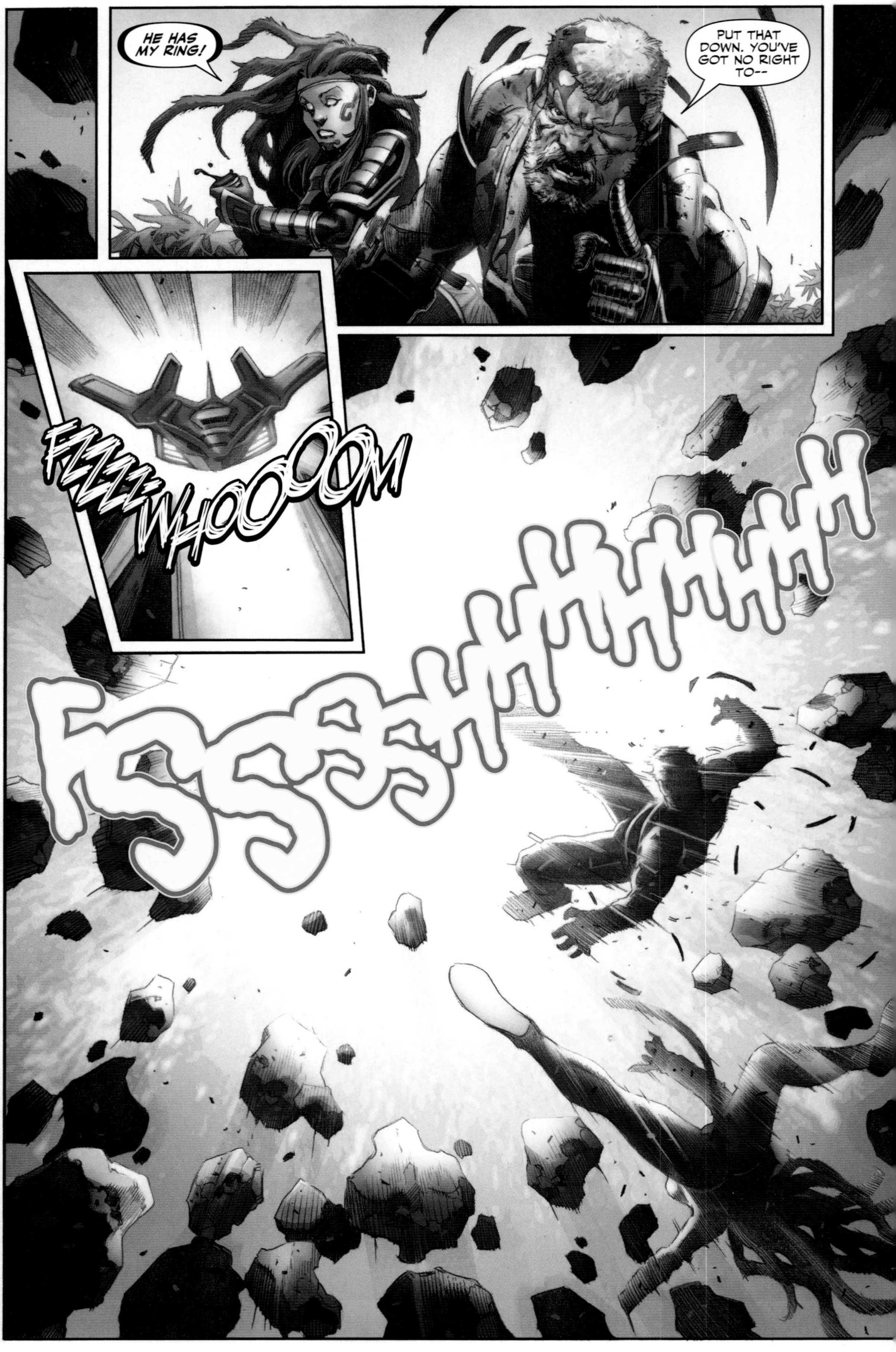
HE HAS MY RING!
PUT THAT DOWN. YOU'VE GOT NO RIGHT TO--
FZZZZ WHOOOOOM
FSSSSHHHHHHHHH

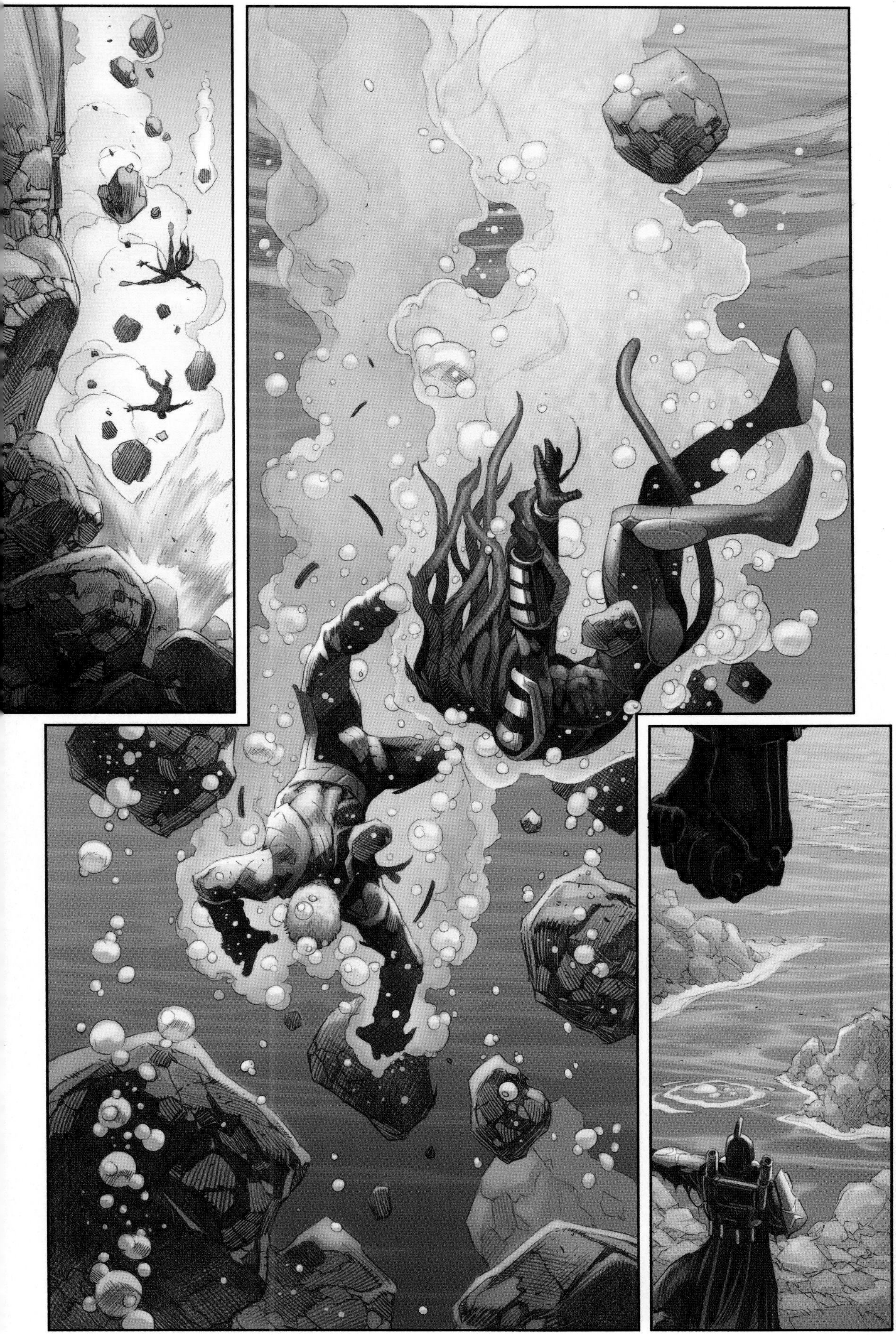

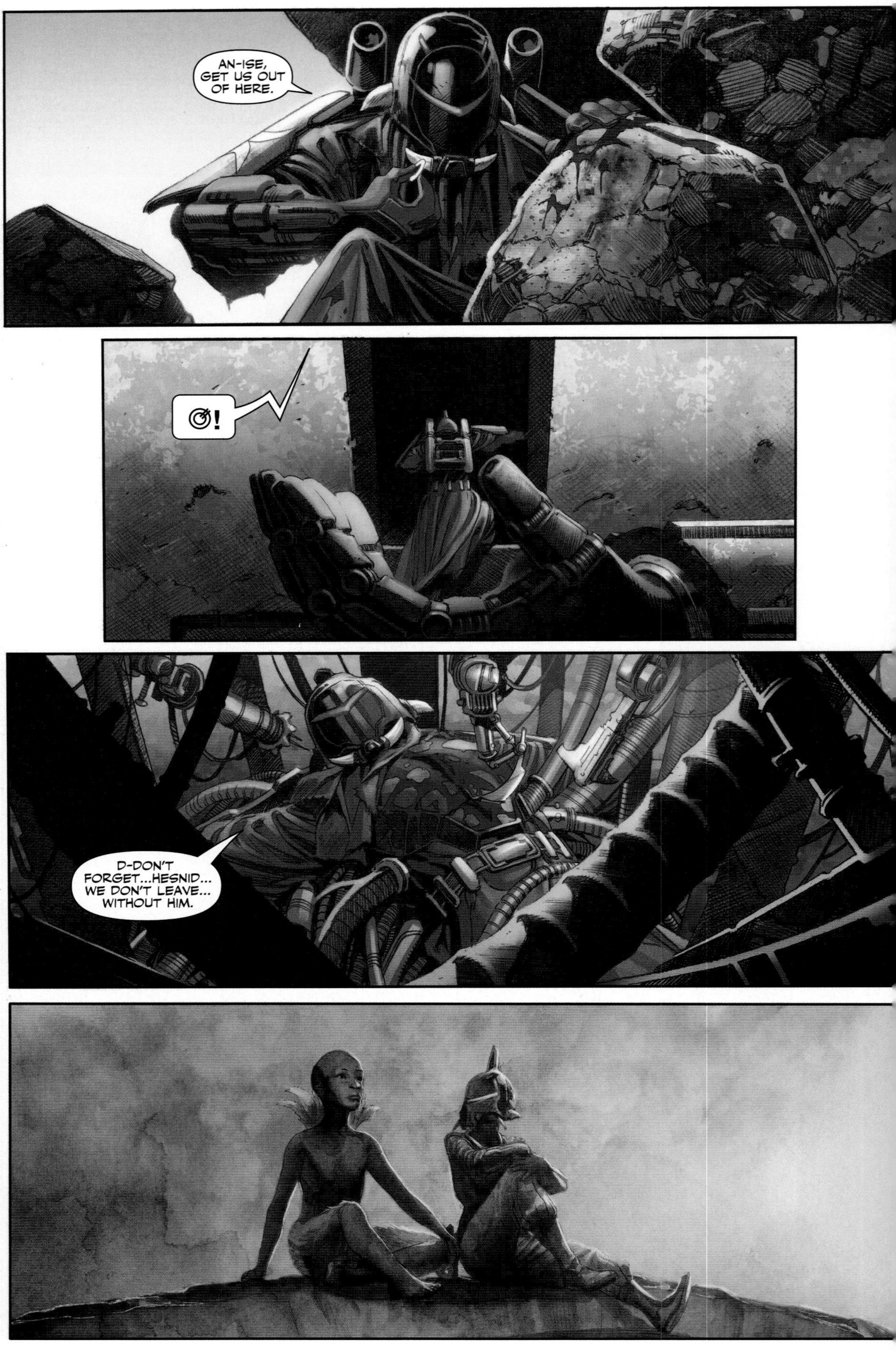
AN-ISE, GET US OUT OF HERE.
!
D-DON'T FORGET...HESNID... WE DON'T LEAVE... WITHOUT HIM.

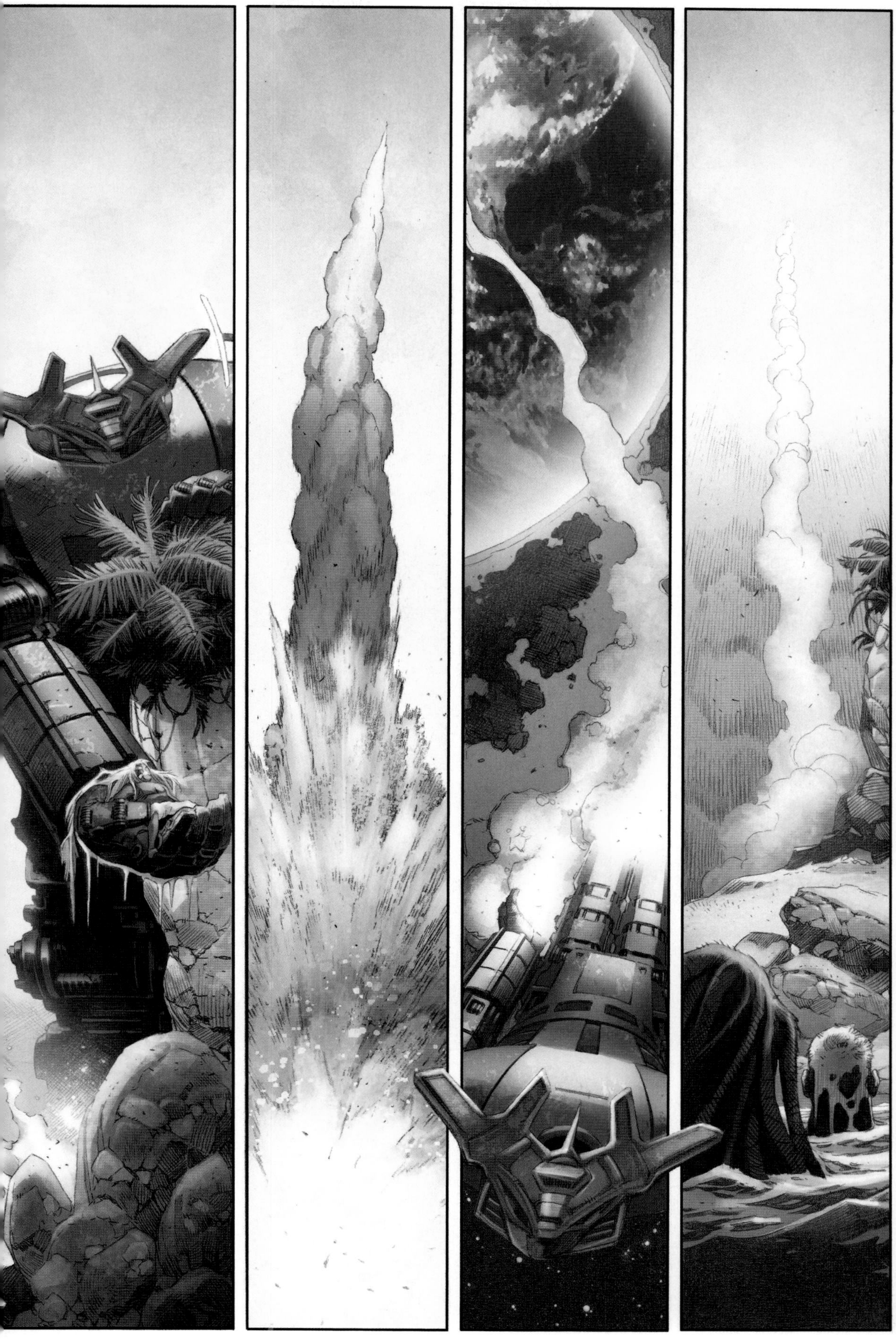

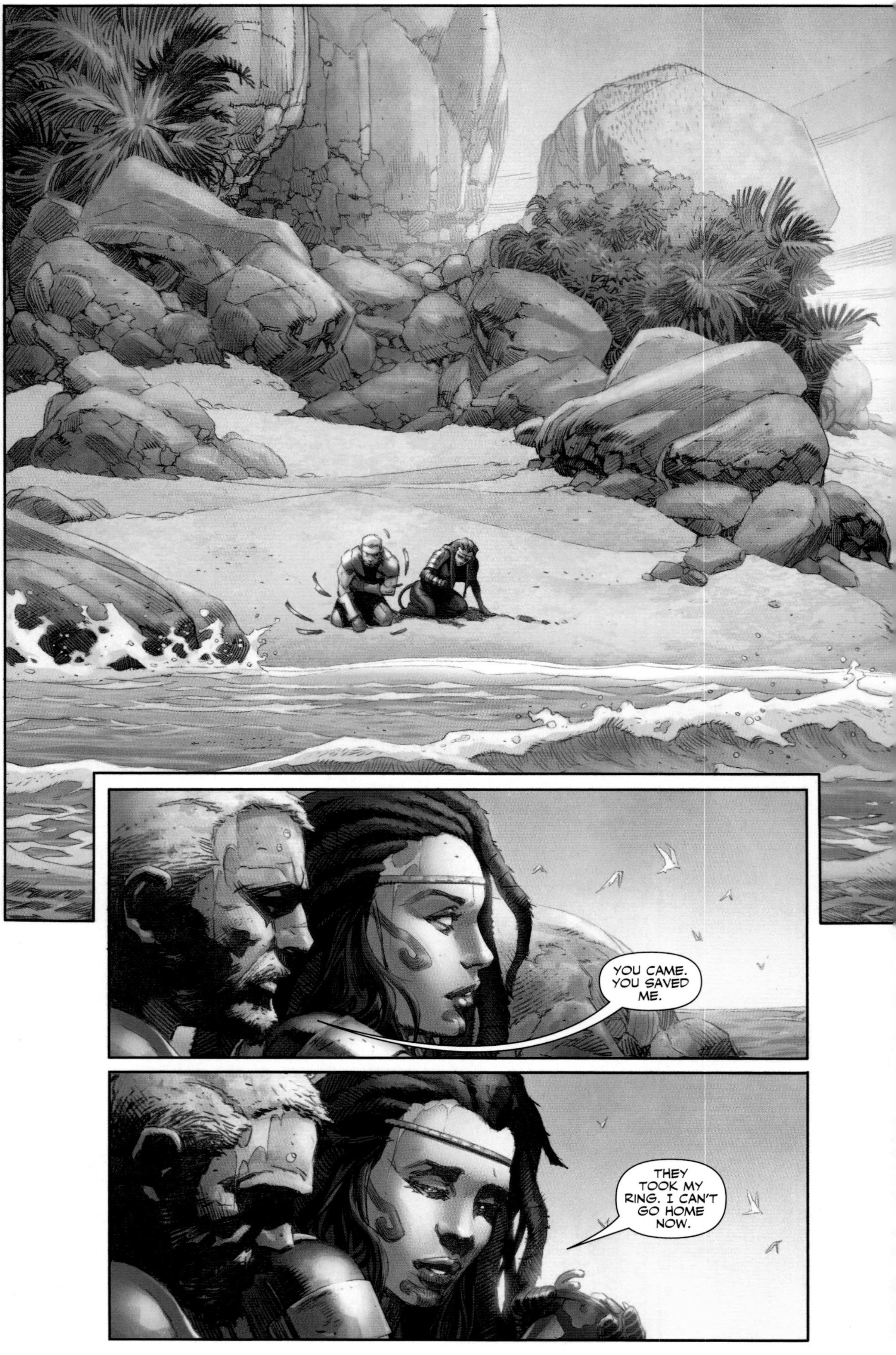
YOU CAME. YOU SAVED ME.
THEY TOOK MY RING. I CAN'T GO HOME NOW.

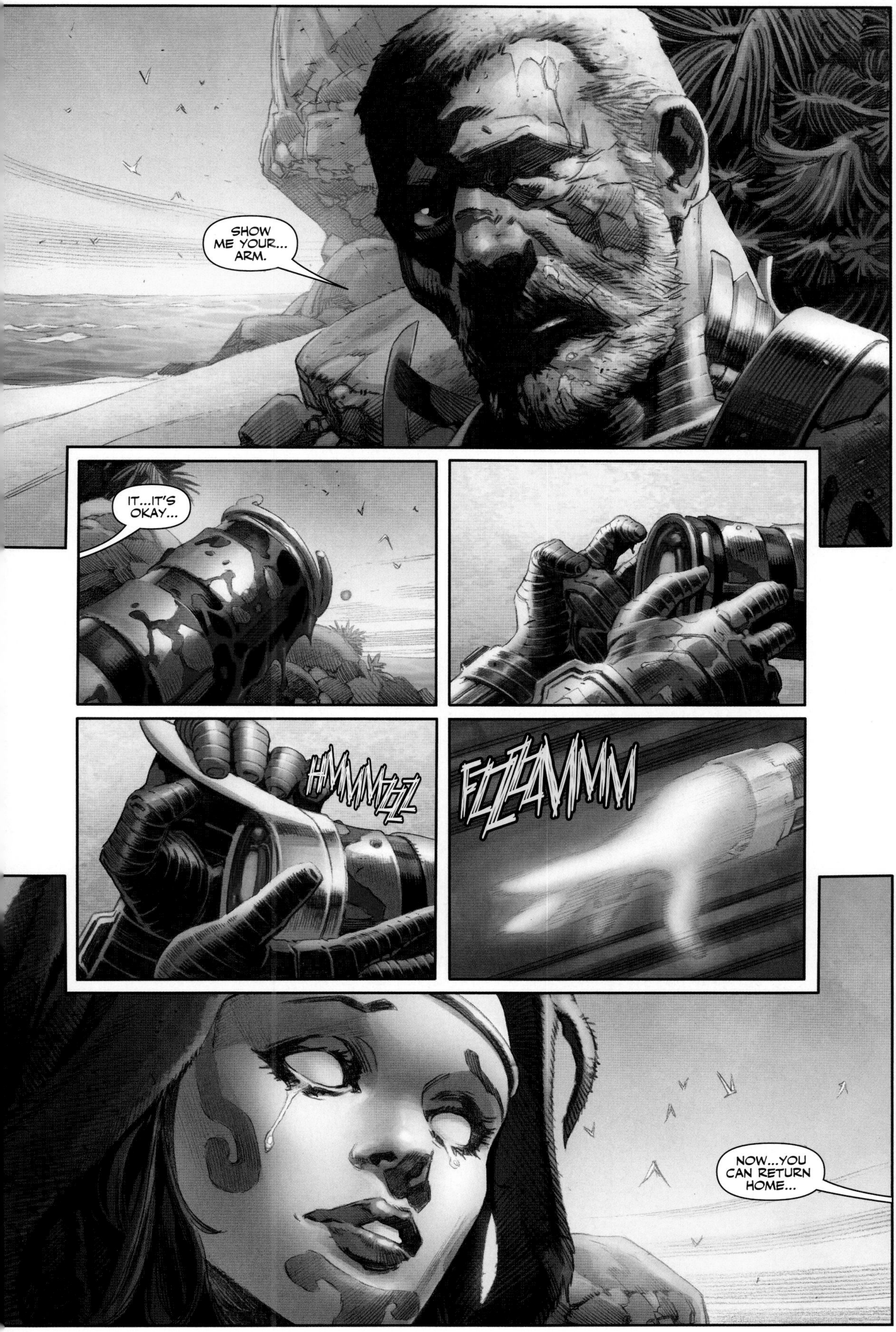
SHOW ME YOUR... ARM.
IT...IT'S OKAY...
HMMMZZZ
FZZZMMM
NOW...YOU CAN RETURN HOME...

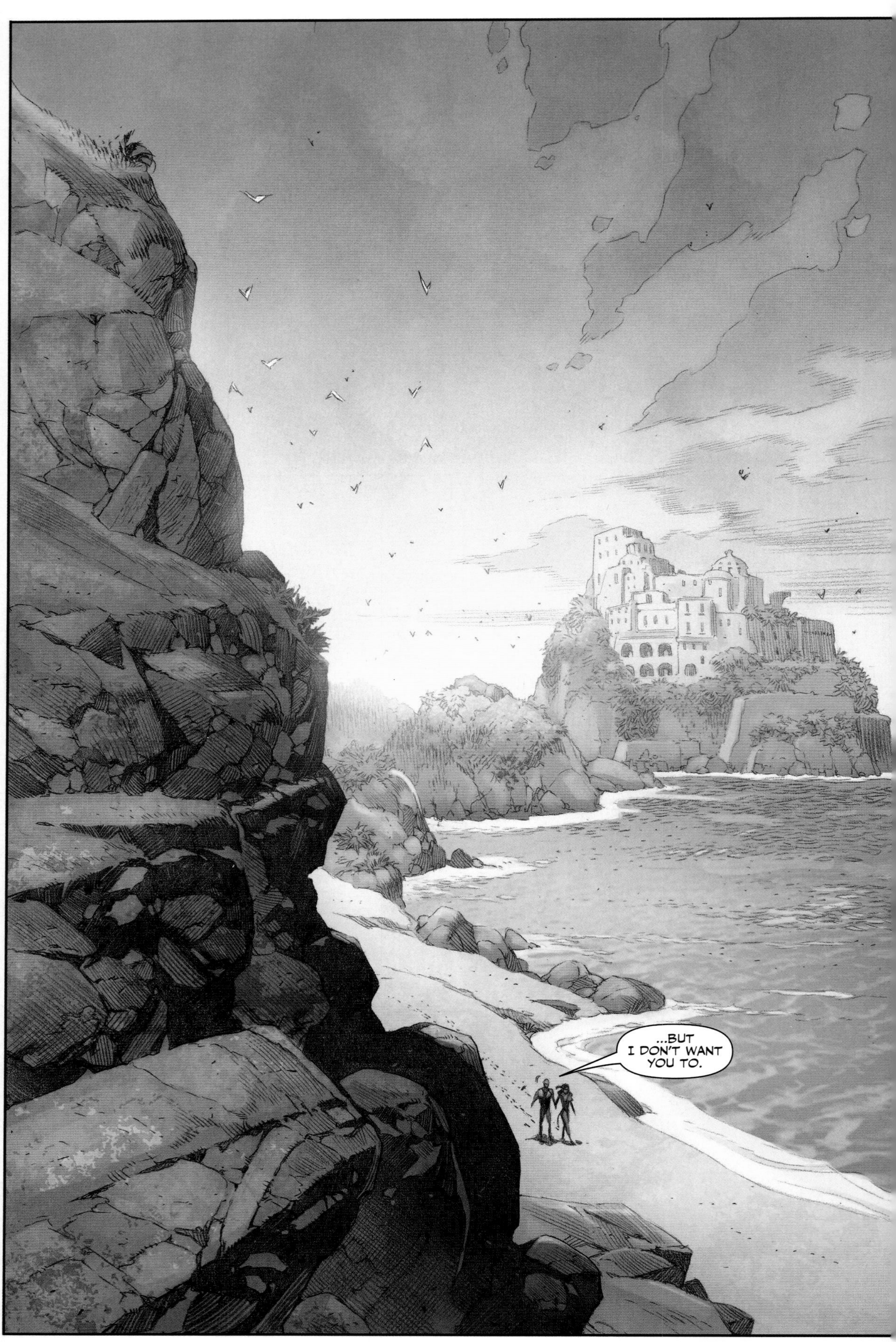
...BUT I DON'T WANT YOU TO.

X-O MANOWAR®

ERO

ISSUE 26

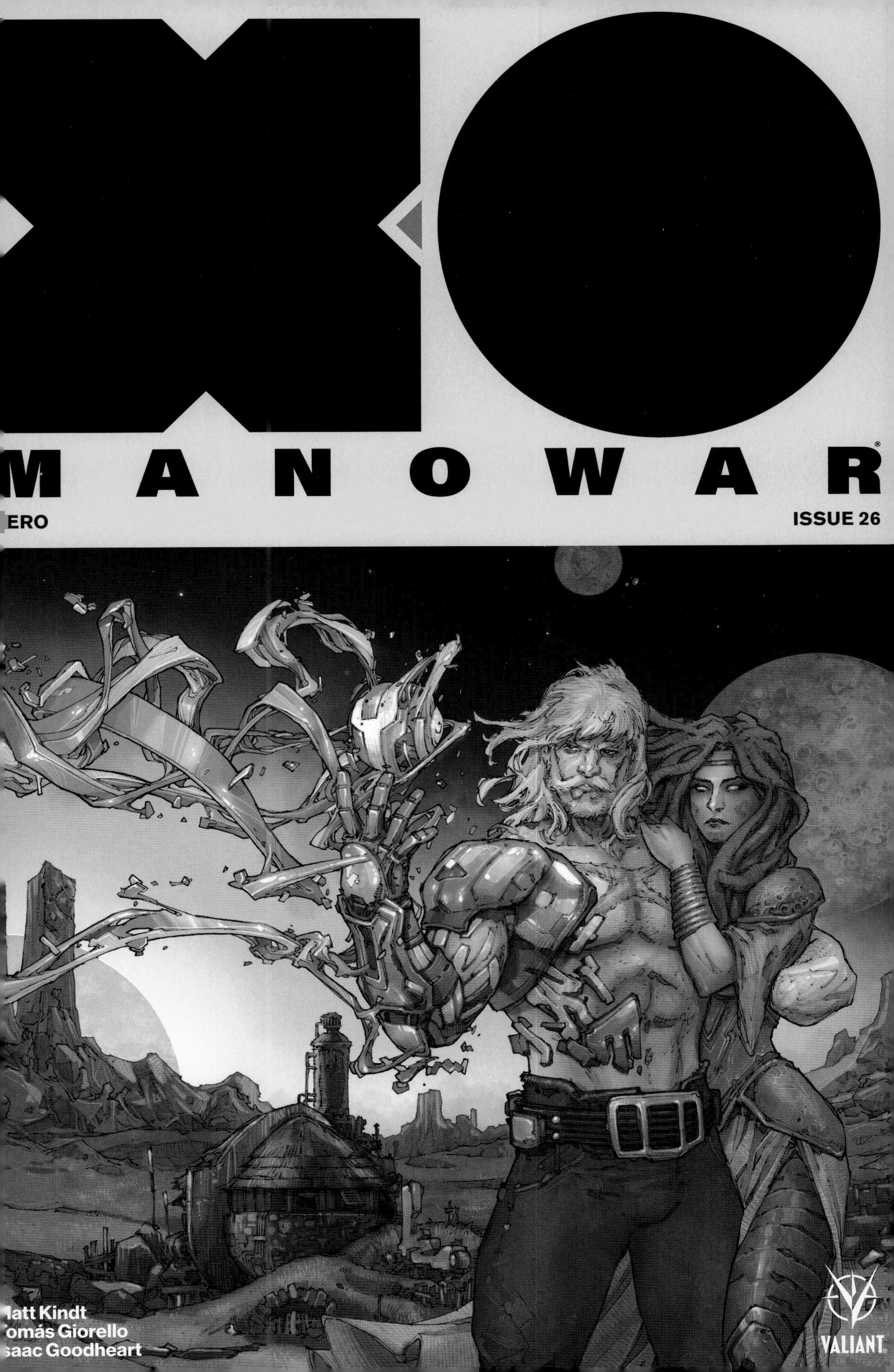

latt Kindt
omás Giorello
saac Goodheart
VALIANT

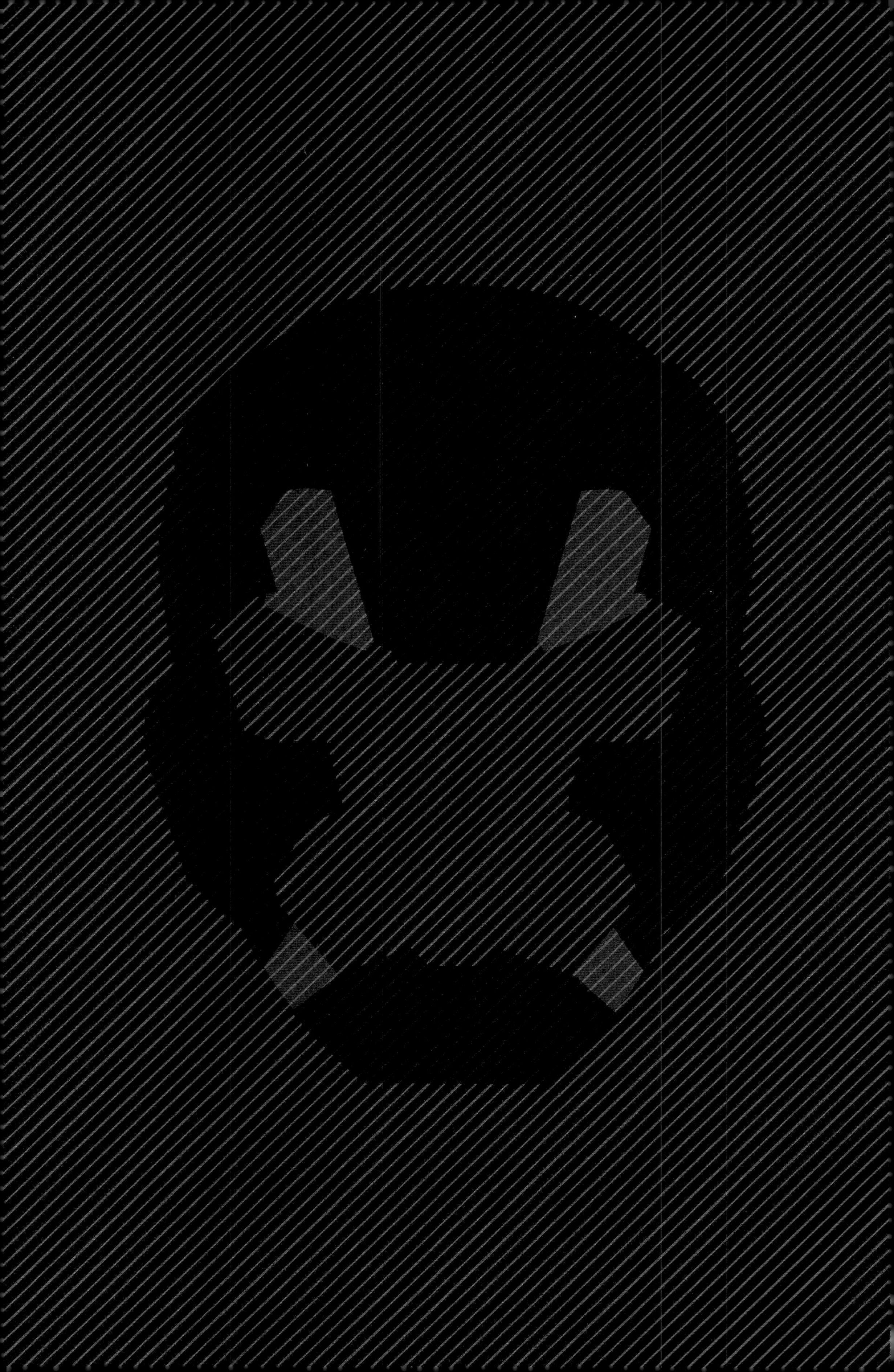

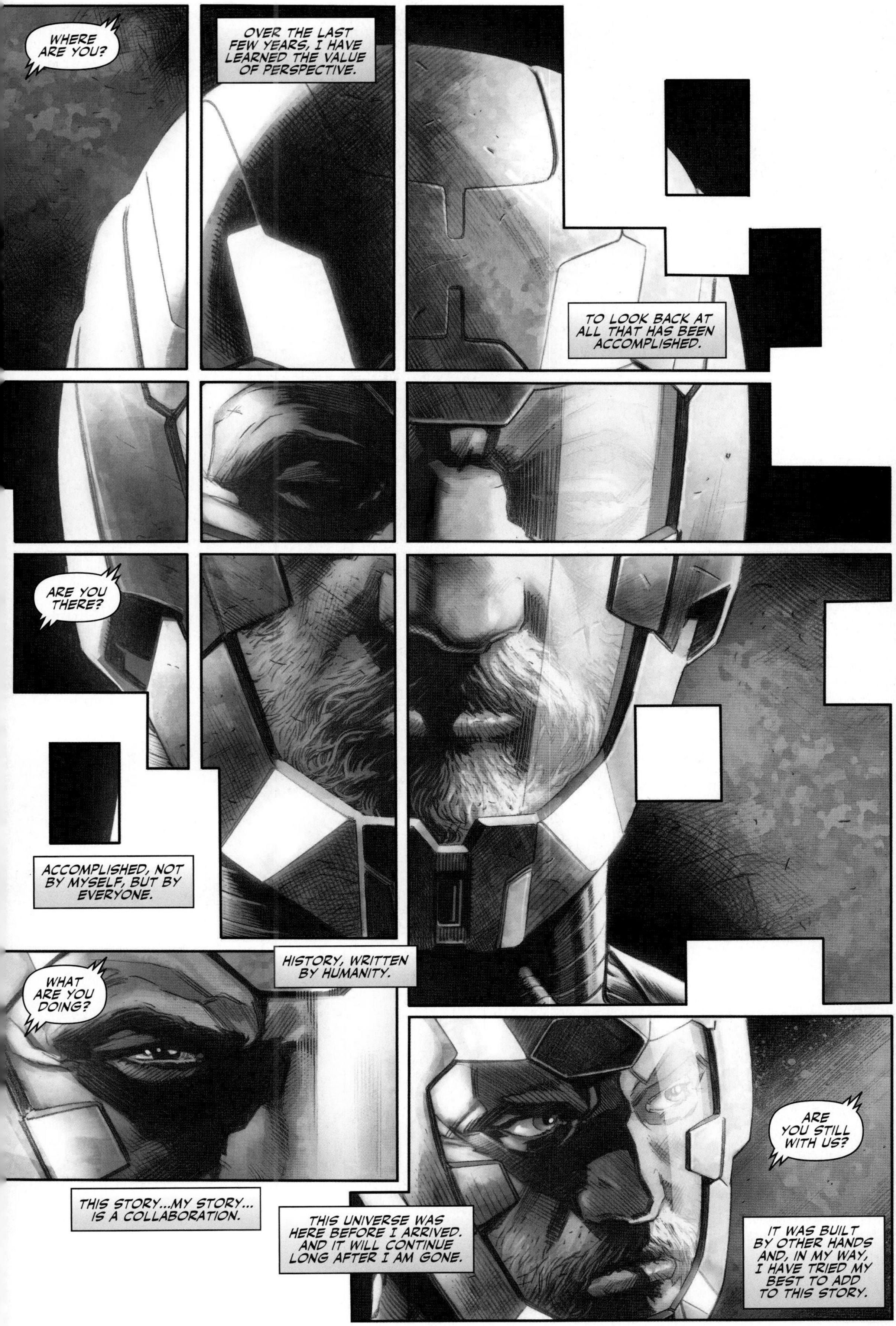
WHERE ARE YOU?
OVER THE LAST FEW YEARS, I HAVE LEARNED THE VALUE OF PERSPECTIVE.
TO LOOK BACK AT ALL THAT HAS BEEN ACCOMPLISHED.
ARE YOU THERE?
ACCOMPLISHED, NOT BY MYSELF, BUT BY EVERYONE.
HISTORY, WRITTEN BY HUMANITY.
WHAT ARE YOU DOING?
ARE YOU STILL WITH US?
THIS STORY...MY STORY... IS A COLLABORATION.
THIS UNIVERSE WAS HERE BEFORE I ARRIVED. AND IT WILL CONTINUE LONG AFTER I AM GONE.
IT WAS BUILT BY OTHER HANDS AND, IN MY WAY, I HAVE TRIED MY BEST TO ADD TO THIS STORY.

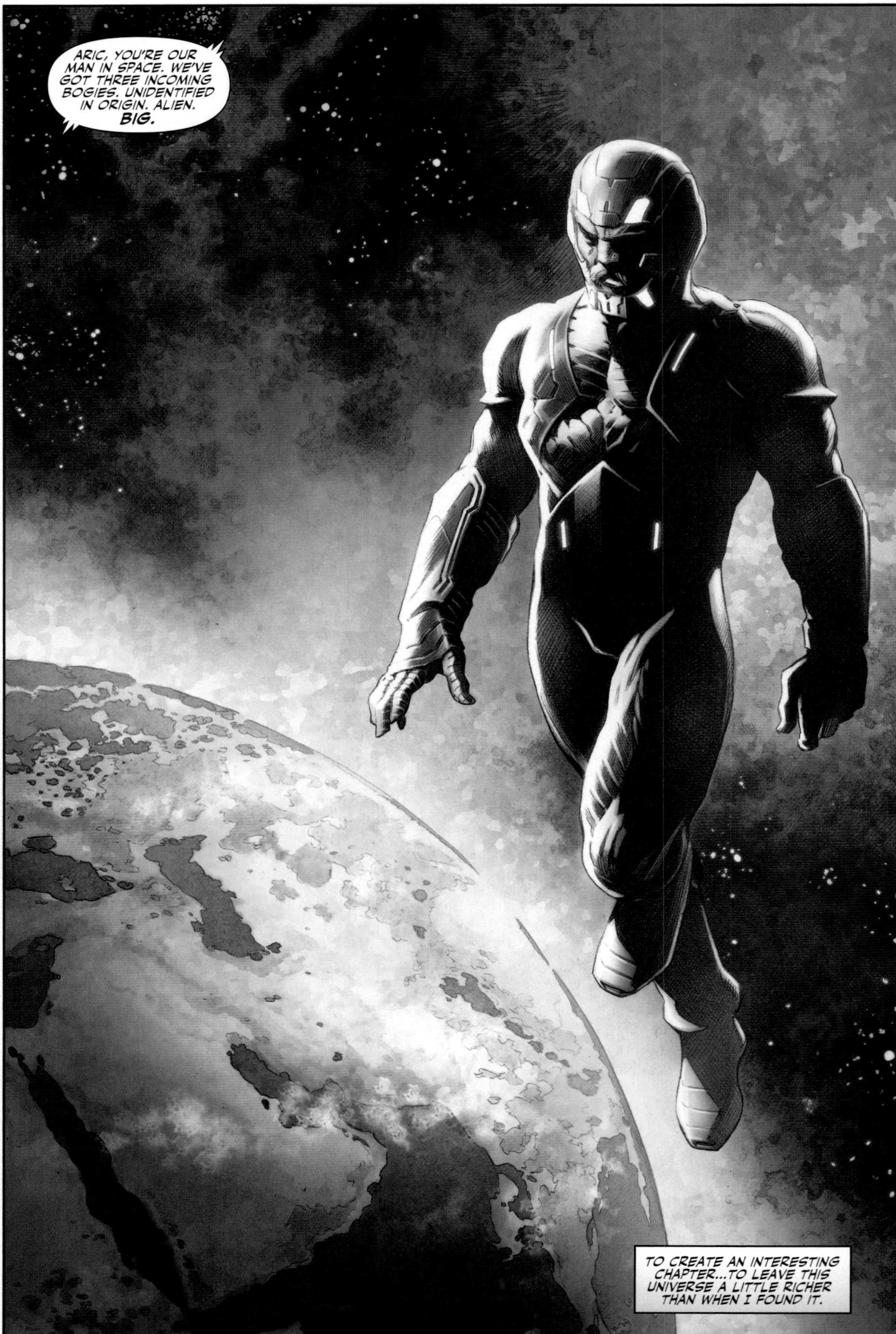
ARIC, YOU'RE OUR MAN IN SPACE. WE'VE GOT THREE INCOMING BOGIES. UNIDENTIFIED IN ORIGIN. ALIEN. BIG.
TO CREATE AN INTERESTING CHAPTER...TO LEAVE THIS UNIVERSE A LITTLE RICHER THAN WHEN I FOUND IT.

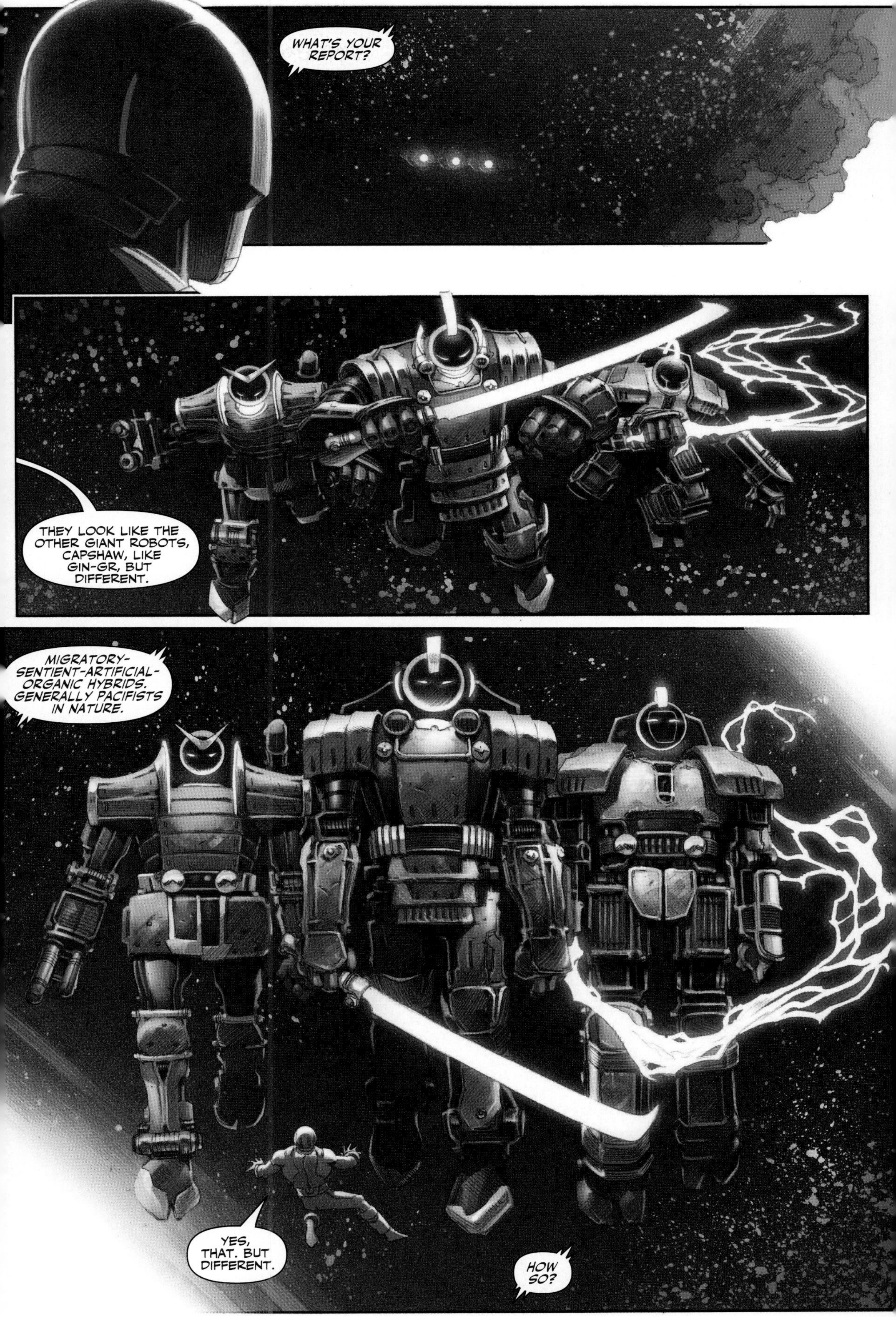
WHAT'S YOUR REPORT?
THEY LOOK LIKE THE OTHER GIANT ROBOTS, CAPSHAW, LIKE GIN-GR, BUT DIFFERENT.
MIGRATORY-SENTIENT-ARTIFICIAL-ORGANIC HYBRIDS. GENERALLY PACIFISTS IN NATURE.
YES, THAT. BUT DIFFERENT.
HOW SO?

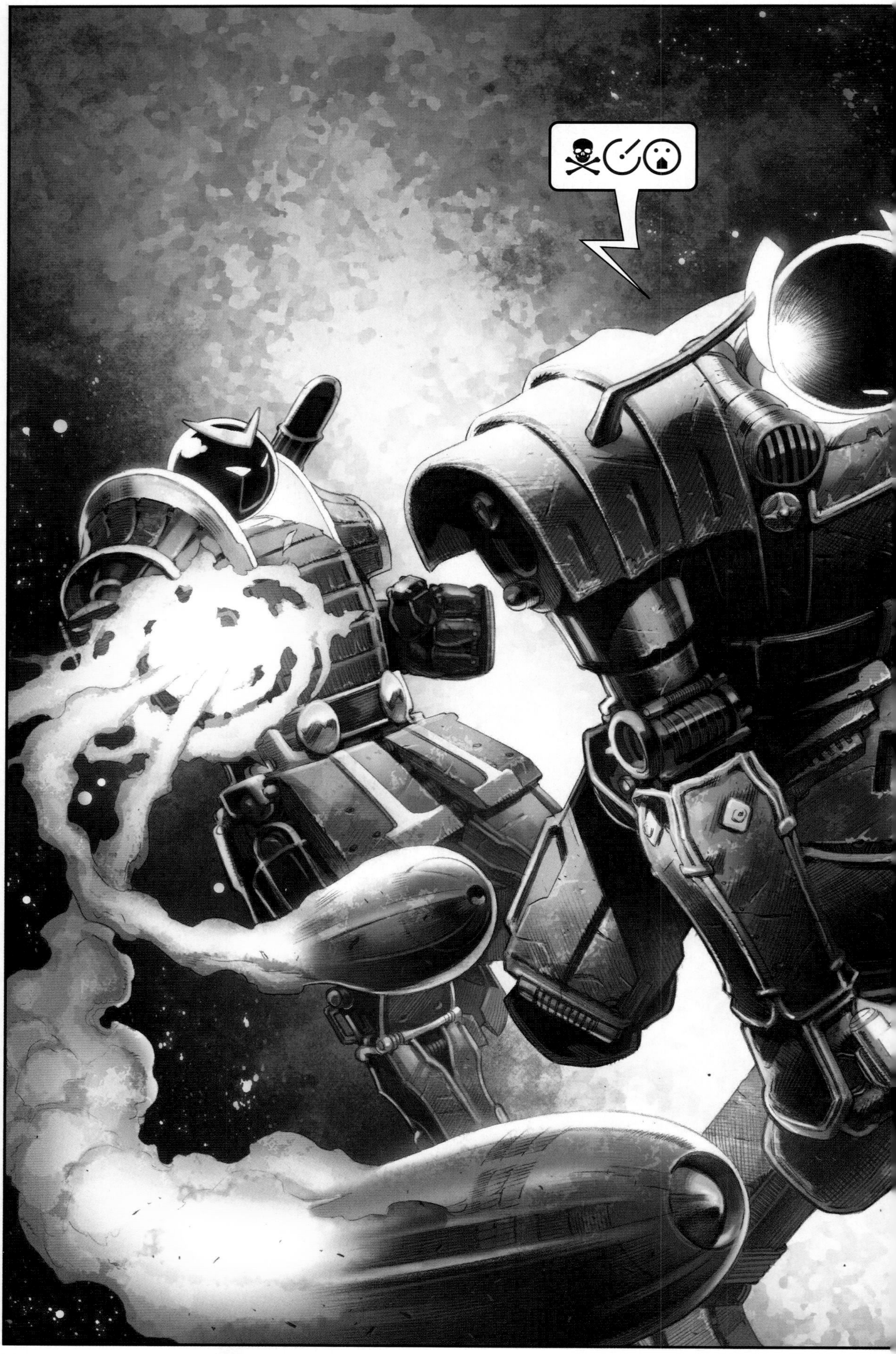

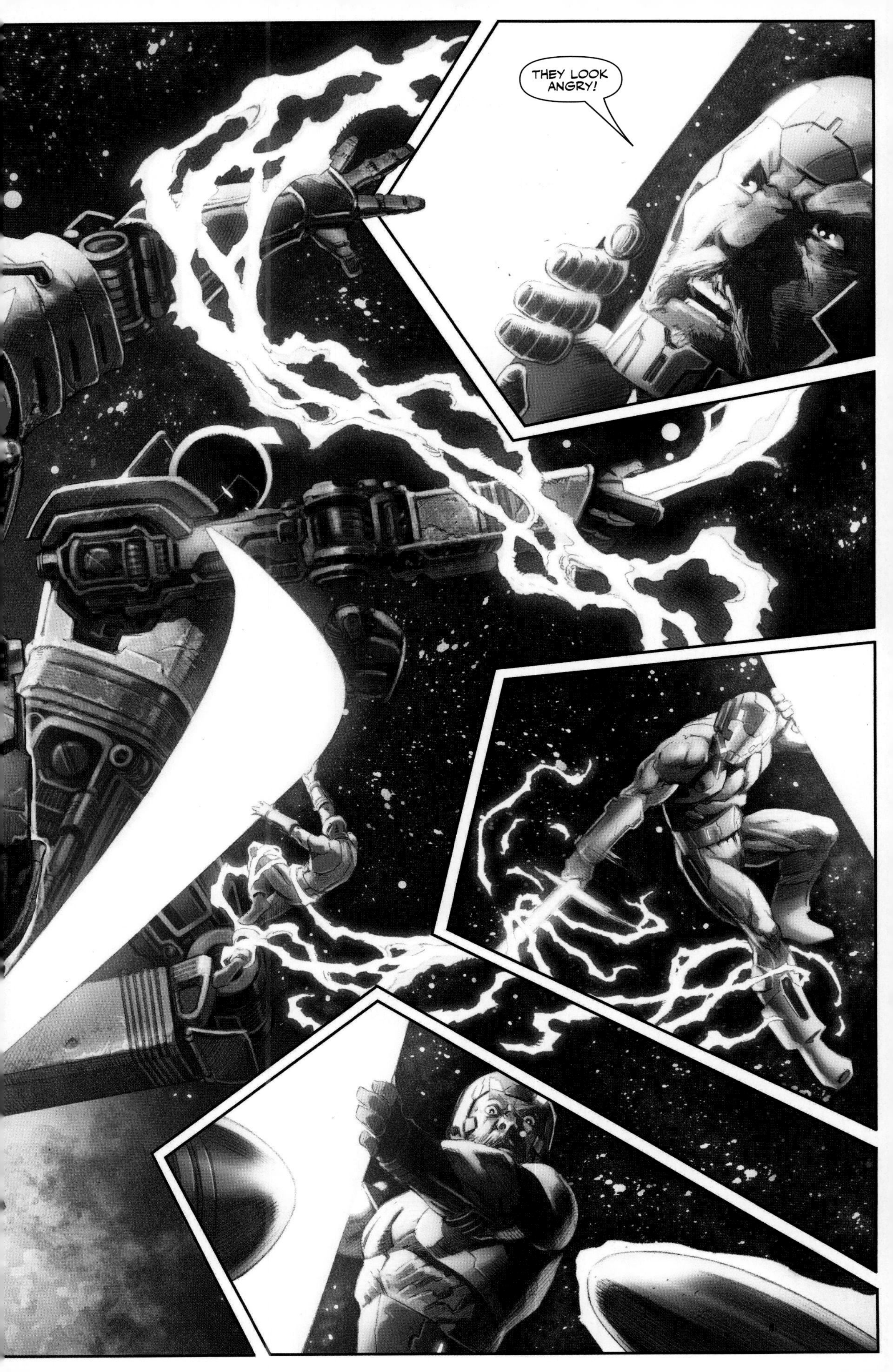
THEY LOOK ANGRY!

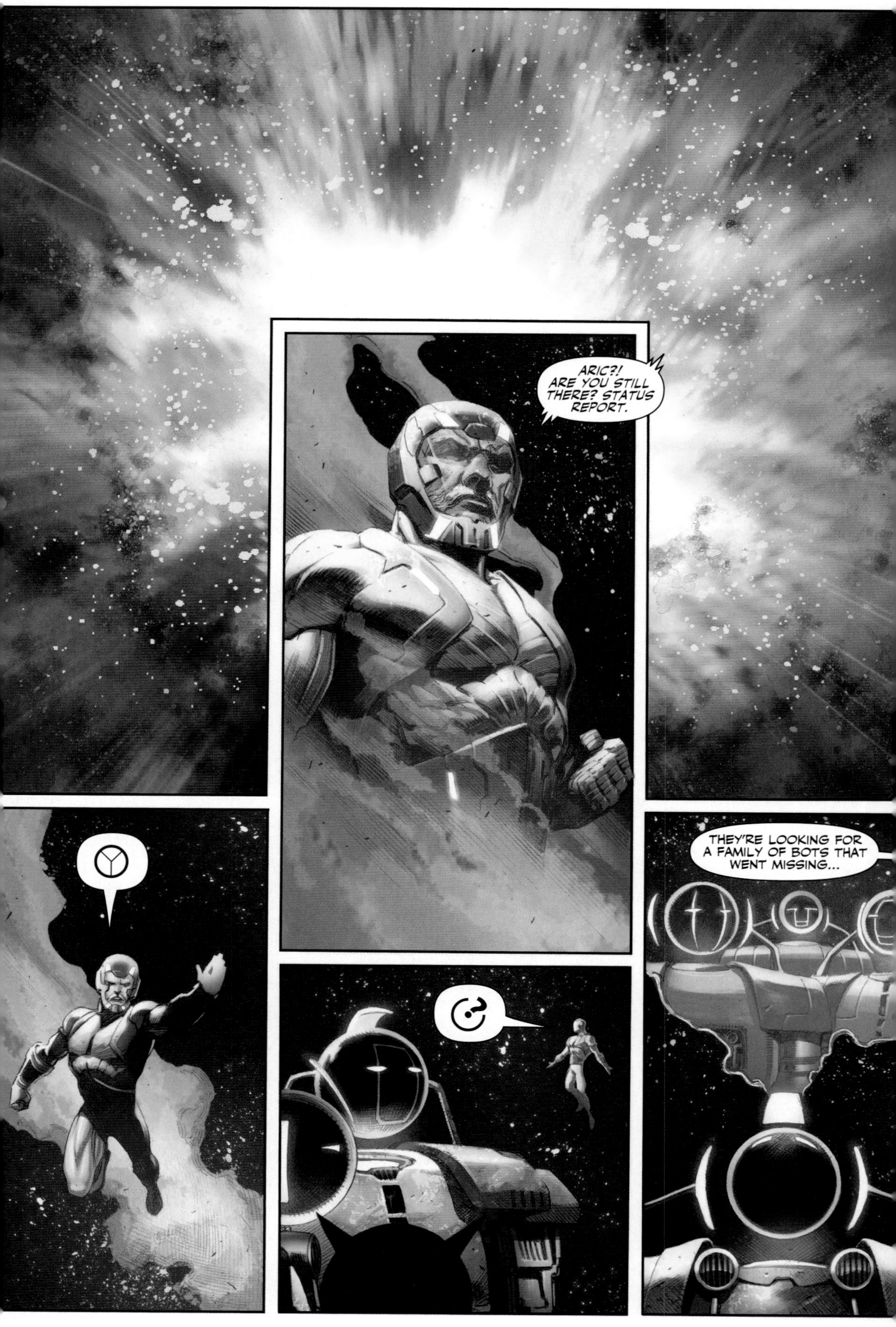
ARIC?! ARE YOU STILL THERE? STATUS REPORT.
THEY'RE LOOKING FOR A FAMILY OF BOTS THAT WENT MISSING...

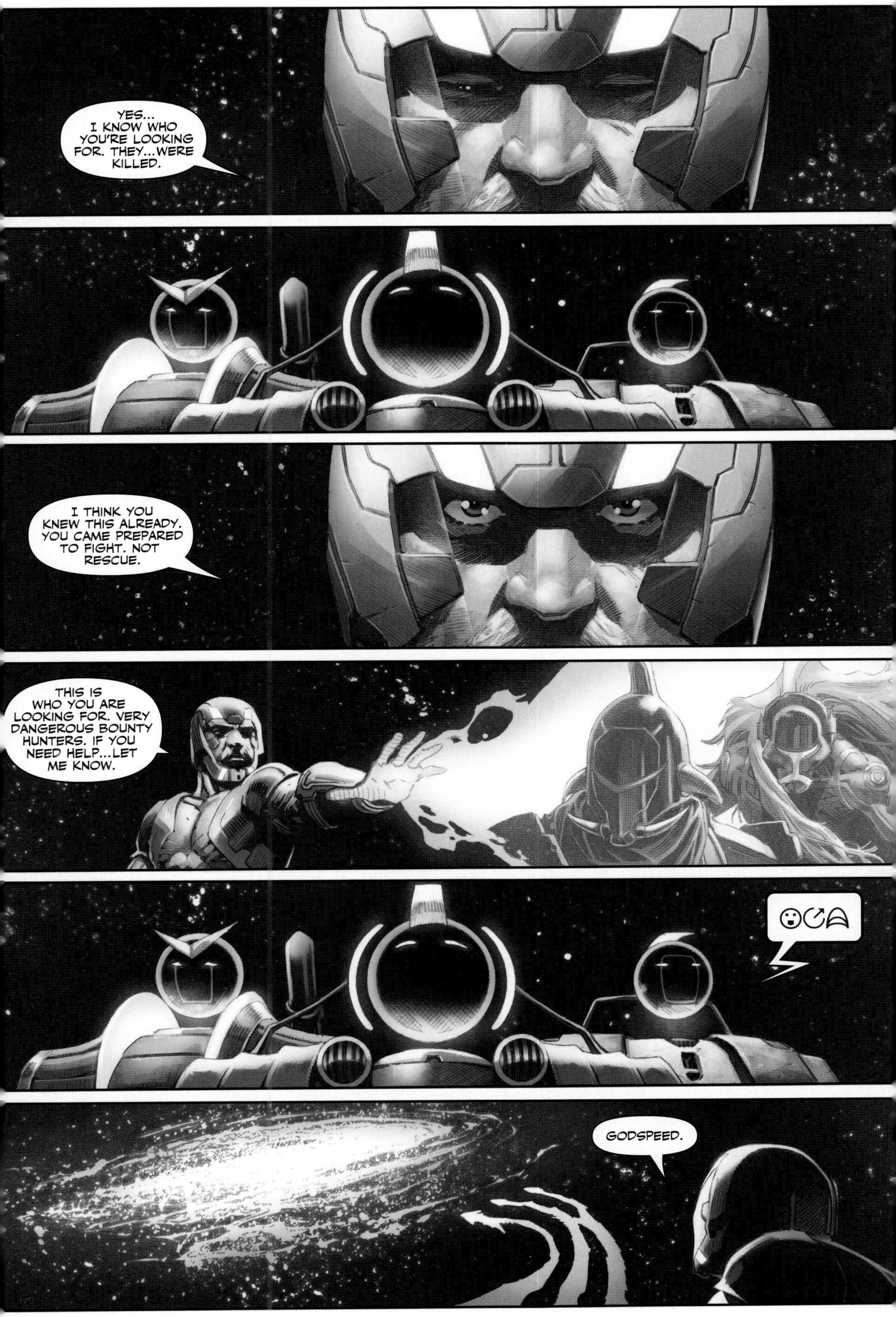
YES... I KNOW WHO YOU'RE LOOKING FOR. THEY...WERE KILLED.
I THINK YOU KNEW THIS ALREADY. YOU CAME PREPARED TO FIGHT. NOT RESCUE.
THIS IS WHO YOU ARE LOOKING FOR. VERY DANGEROUS BOUNTY HUNTERS. IF YOU NEED HELP...LET ME KNOW.
GODSPEED.

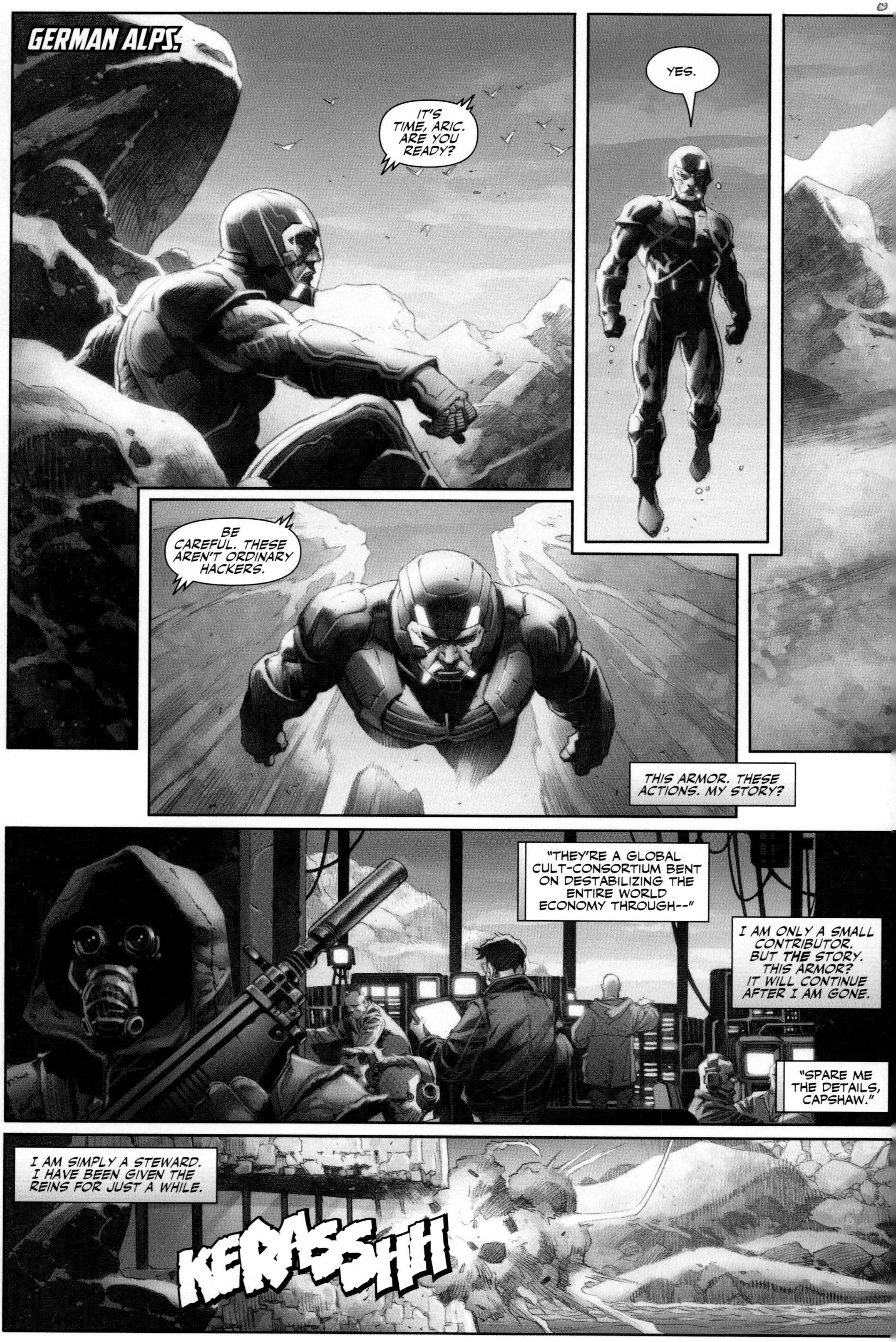
GERMAN ALPS.
IT'S TIME, ARIC. ARE YOU READY?
YES.
BE CAREFUL. THESE AREN'T ORDINARY HACKERS.
THIS ARMOR. THESE ACTIONS. MY STORY?
"THEY'RE A GLOBAL CULT-CONSORTIUM BENT ON DESTABILIZING THE ENTIRE WORLD ECONOMY THROUGH--"
I AM ONLY A SMALL CONTRIBUTOR. BUT THE STORY. THIS ARMOR? IT WILL CONTINUE AFTER I AM GONE.
"SPARE ME THE DETAILS, CAPSHAW."
I AM SIMPLY A STEWARD. I HAVE BEEN GIVEN THE REINS FOR JUST A WHILE.
KERASSHH

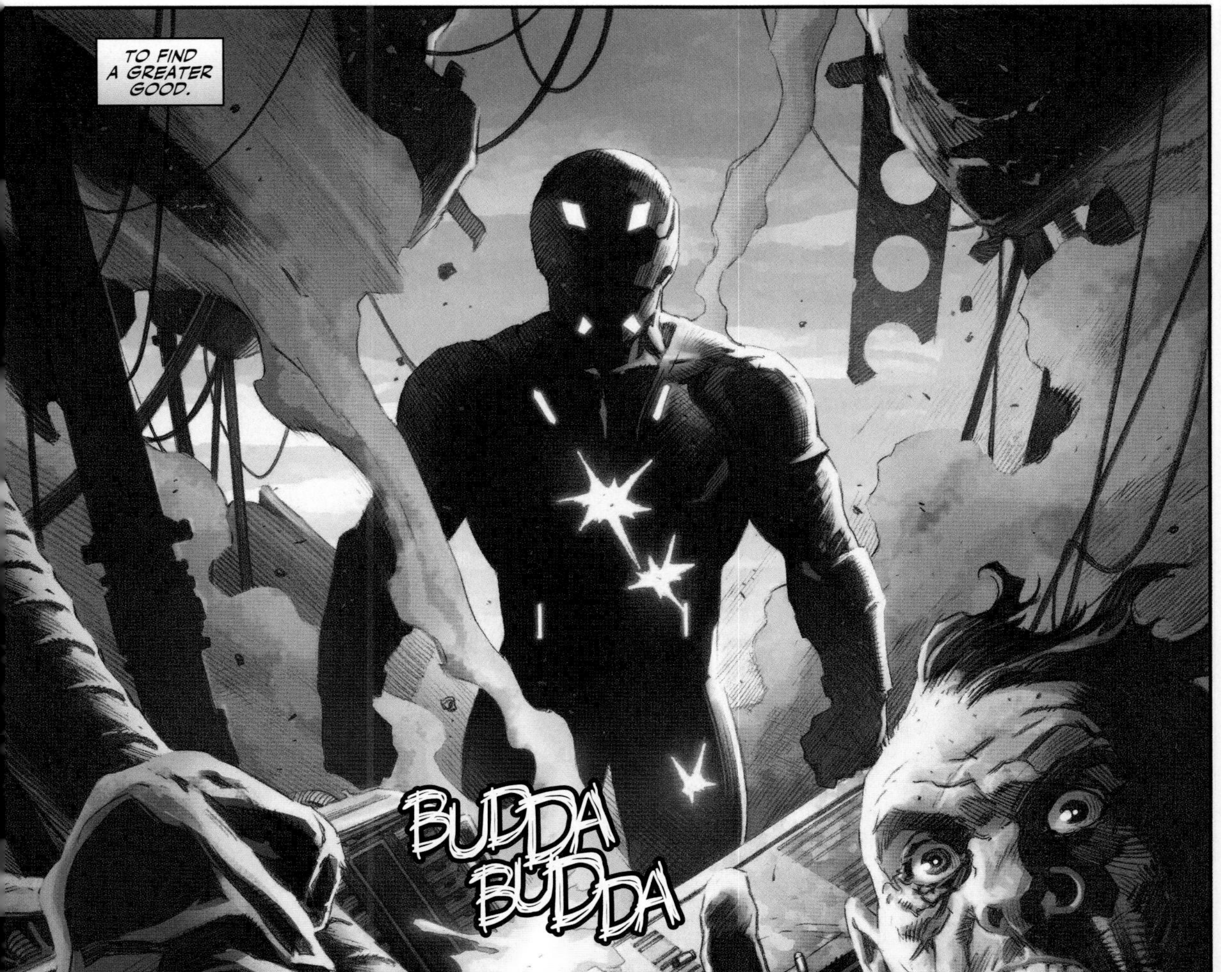
TO FIND A GREATER GOOD.
BUDDA BUDDA
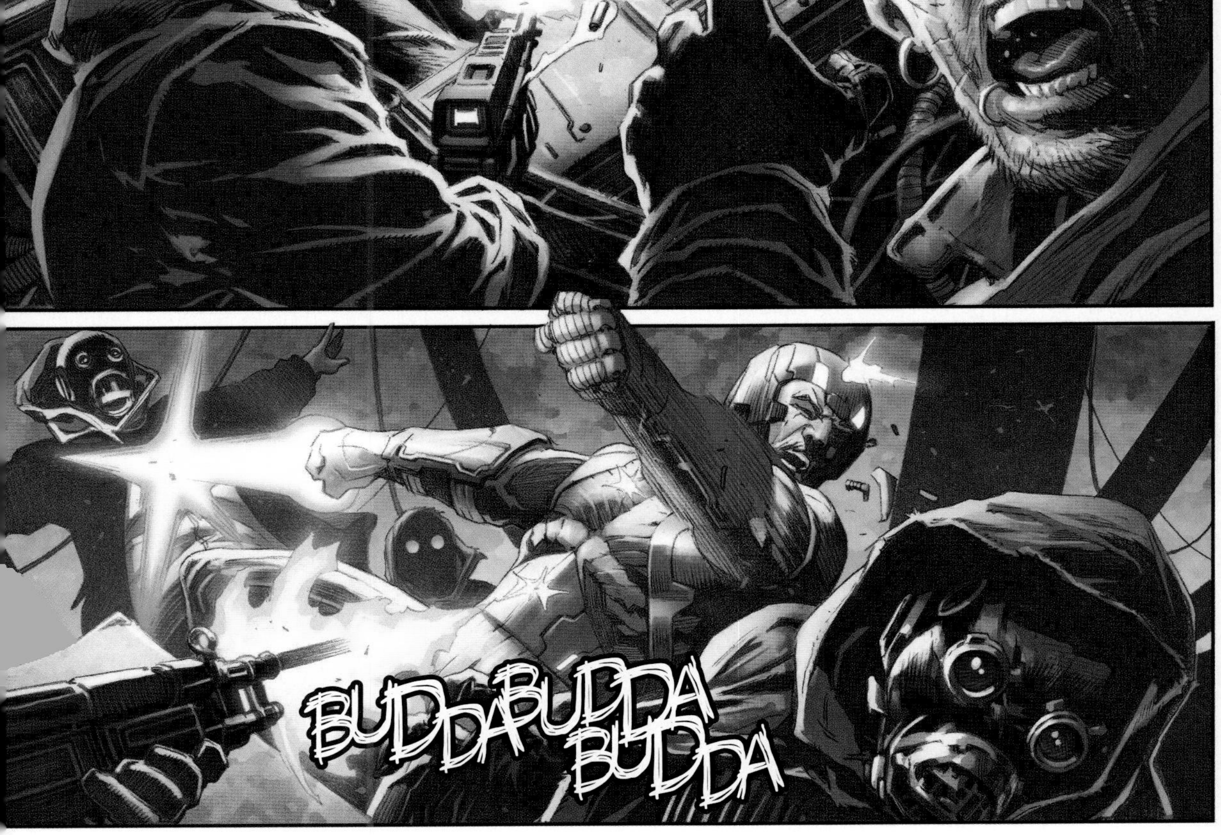
BUDDA BUDDA BUDDA

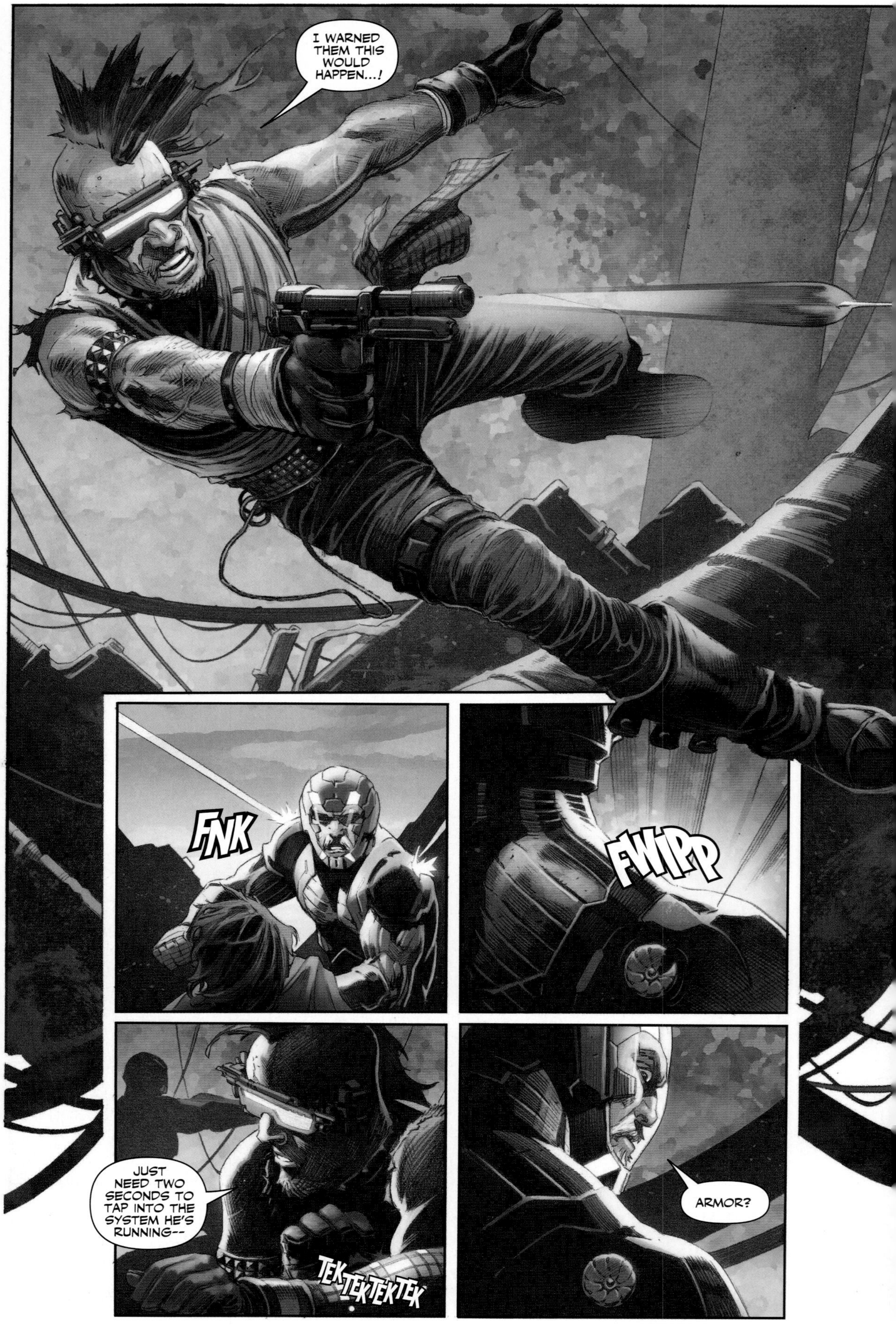
I WARNED THEM THIS WOULD HAPPEN...!
FNK
FWIPP
JUST NEED TWO SECONDS TO TAP INTO THE SYSTEM HE'S RUNNING--
TEKTEKTEKTEK
ARMOR?

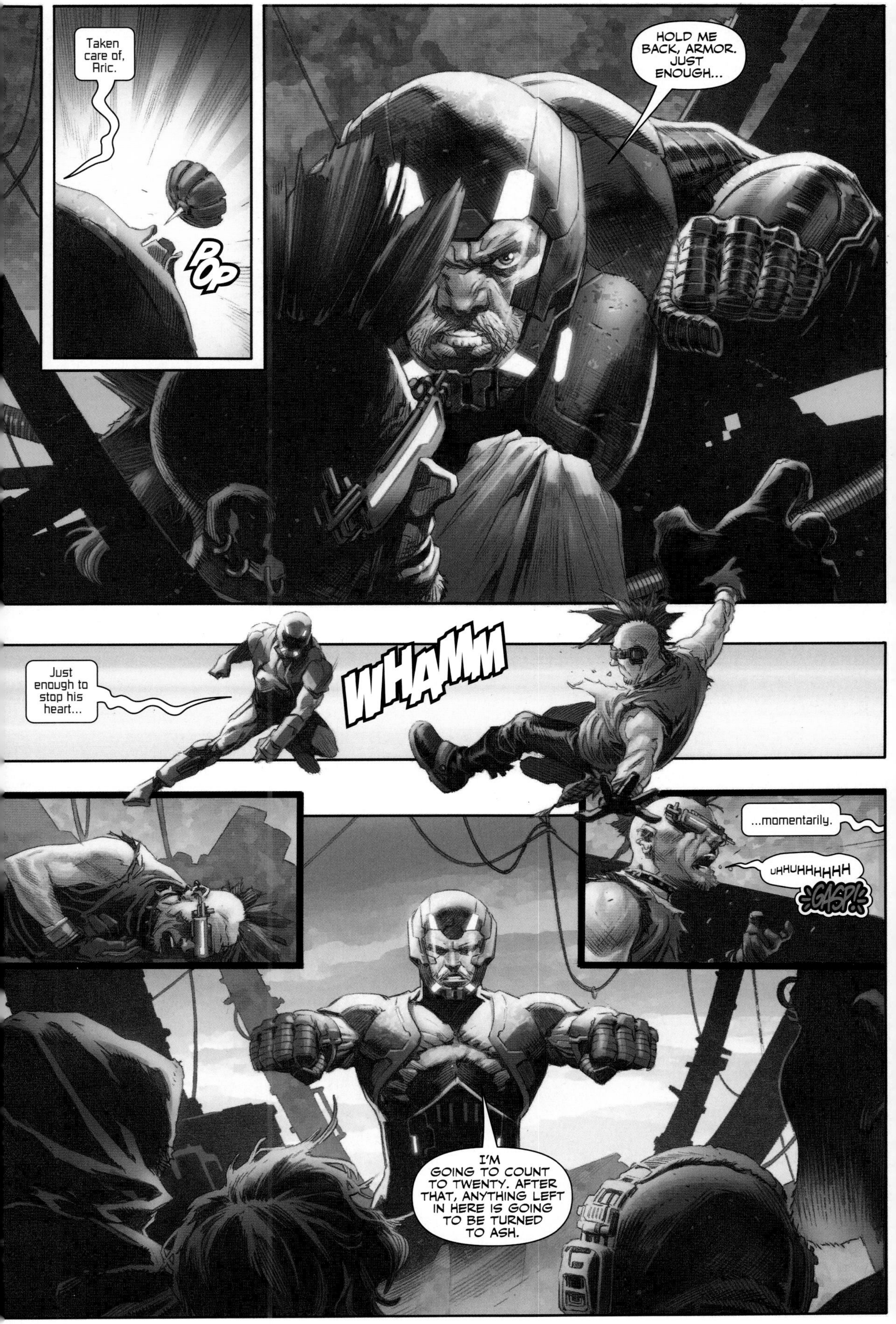
Taken care of, Aric.
POP
HOLD ME BACK, ARMOR. JUST ENOUGH...
Just enough to stop his heart...
WHAMM
...momentarily.
UHHUHHHHHH
GASP!
I'M GOING TO COUNT TO TWENTY. AFTER THAT, ANYTHING LEFT IN HERE IS GOING TO BE TURNED TO ASH.

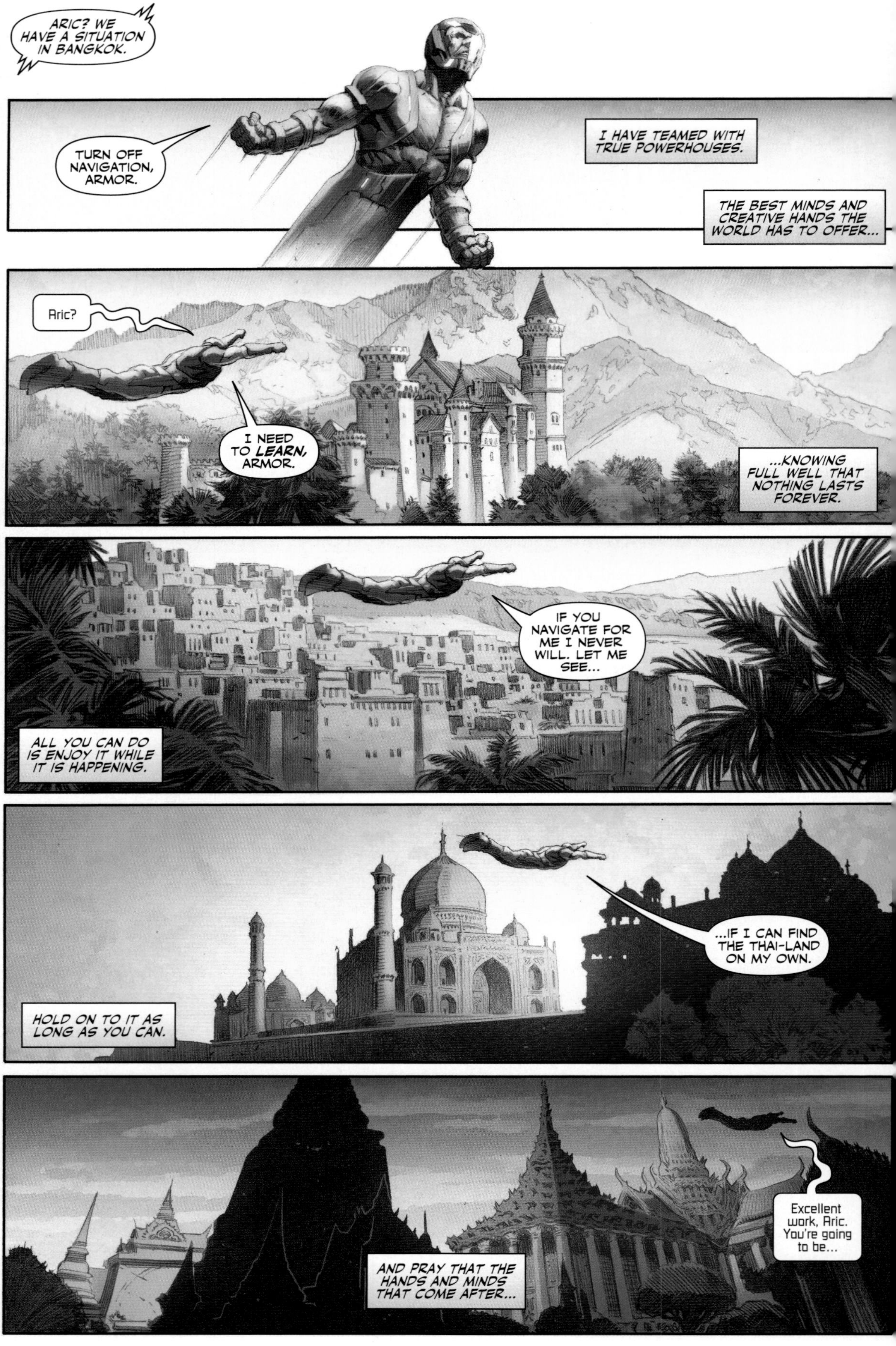
ARIC? WE HAVE A SITUATION IN BANGKOK.
TURN OFF NAVIGATION, ARMOR.
I HAVE TEAMED WITH TRUE POWERHOUSES.
THE BEST MINDS AND CREATIVE HANDS THE WORLD HAS TO OFFER...
Aric?
I NEED TO LEARN, ARMOR.
...KNOWING FULL WELL THAT NOTHING LASTS FOREVER.
IF YOU NAVIGATE FOR ME I NEVER WILL. LET ME SEE...
ALL YOU CAN DO IS ENJOY IT WHILE IT IS HAPPENING.
...IF I CAN FIND THE THAI-LAND ON MY OWN.
HOLD ON TO IT AS LONG AS YOU CAN.
Excellent work, Aric. You're going to be...
AND PRAY THAT THE HANDS AND MINDS THAT COME AFTER...

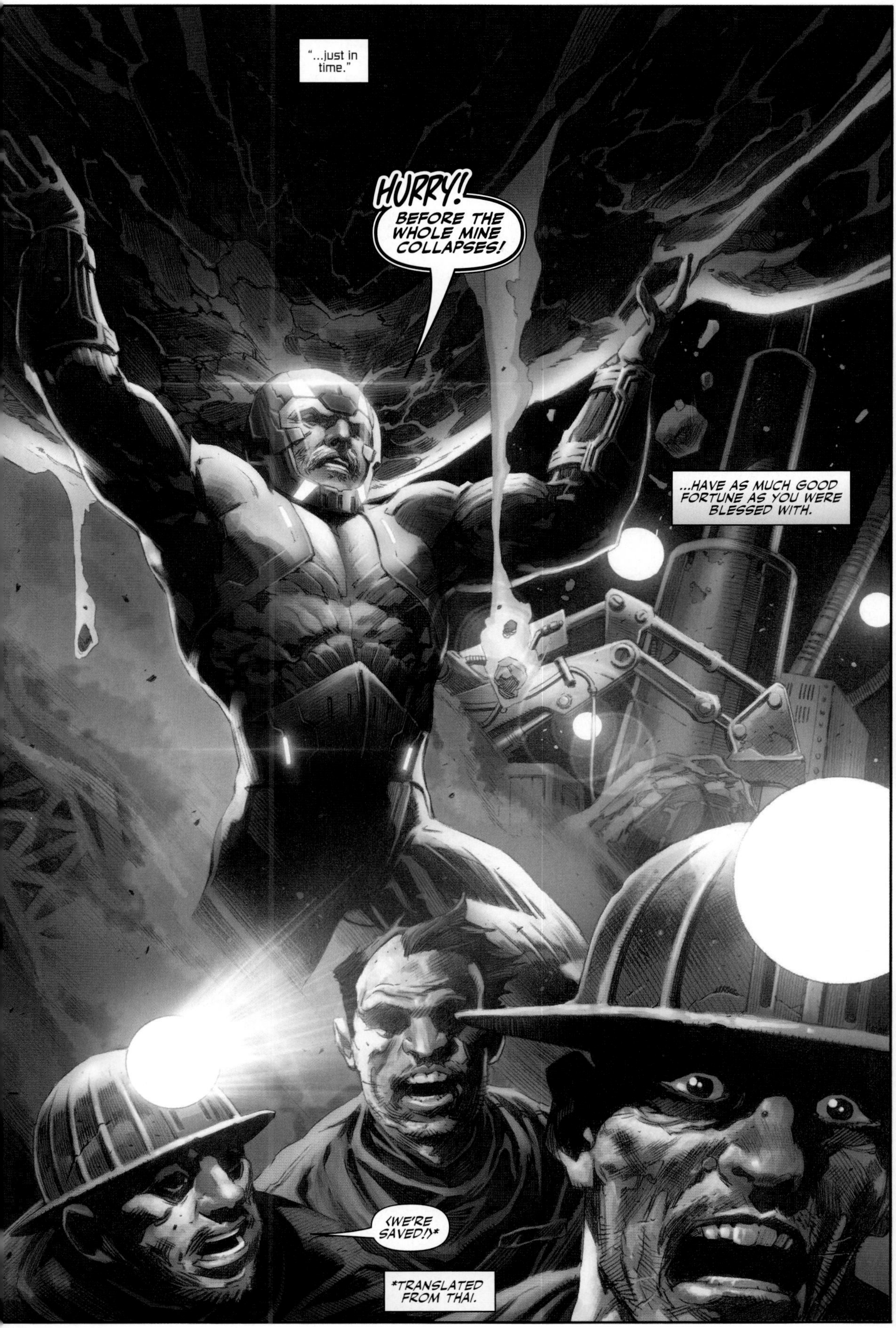
"...just in time."
HURRY! BEFORE THE WHOLE MINE COLLAPSES!
...HAVE AS MUCH GOOD FORTUNE AS YOU WERE BLESSED WITH.
‹WE'RE SAVED!›*
*TRANSLATED FROM THAI.

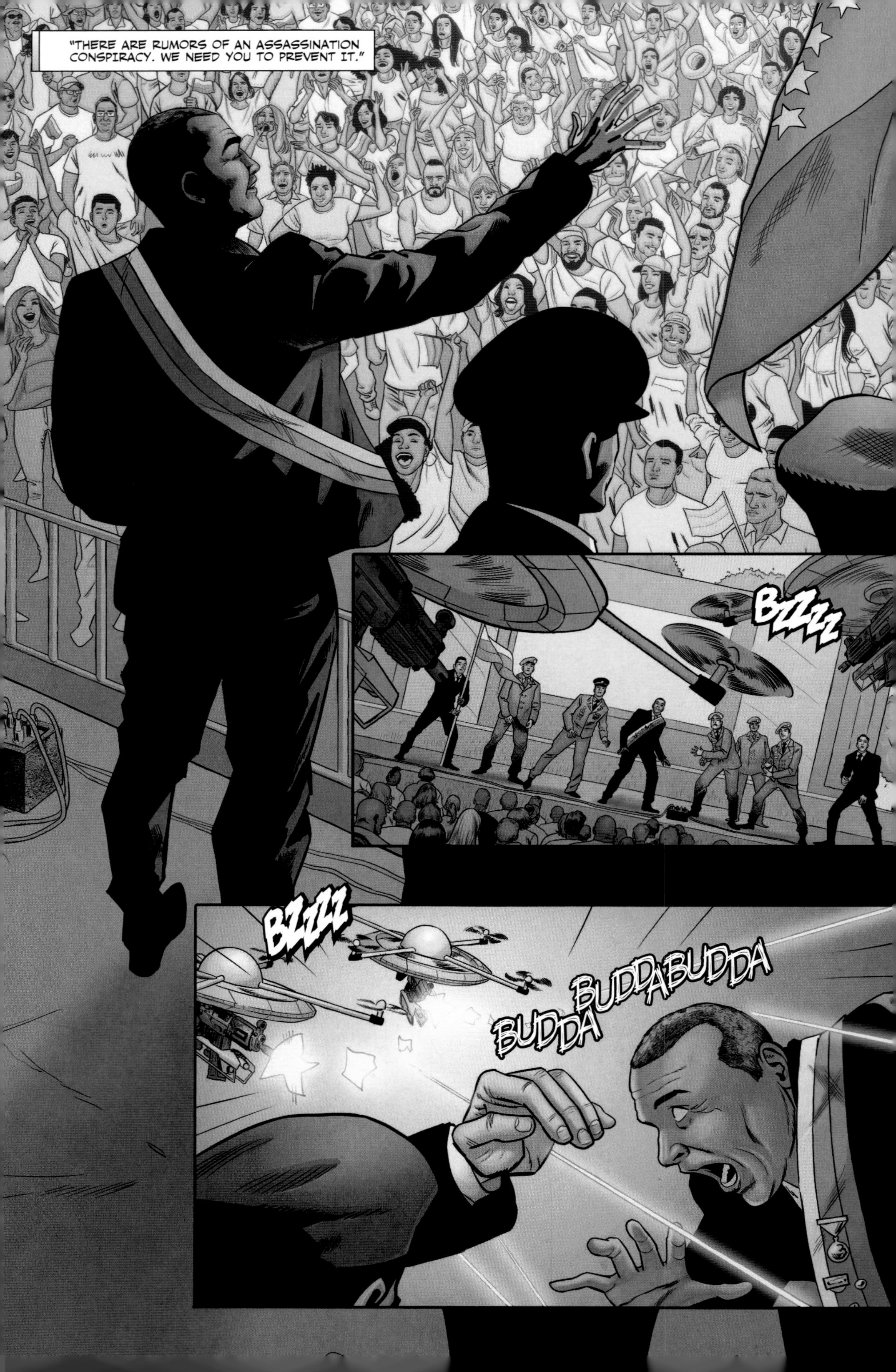
"THERE ARE RUMORS OF AN ASSASSINATION CONSPIRACY. WE NEED YOU TO PREVENT IT."
BZZZZ
BZZZZ
BUDDA BUDDABUDDA

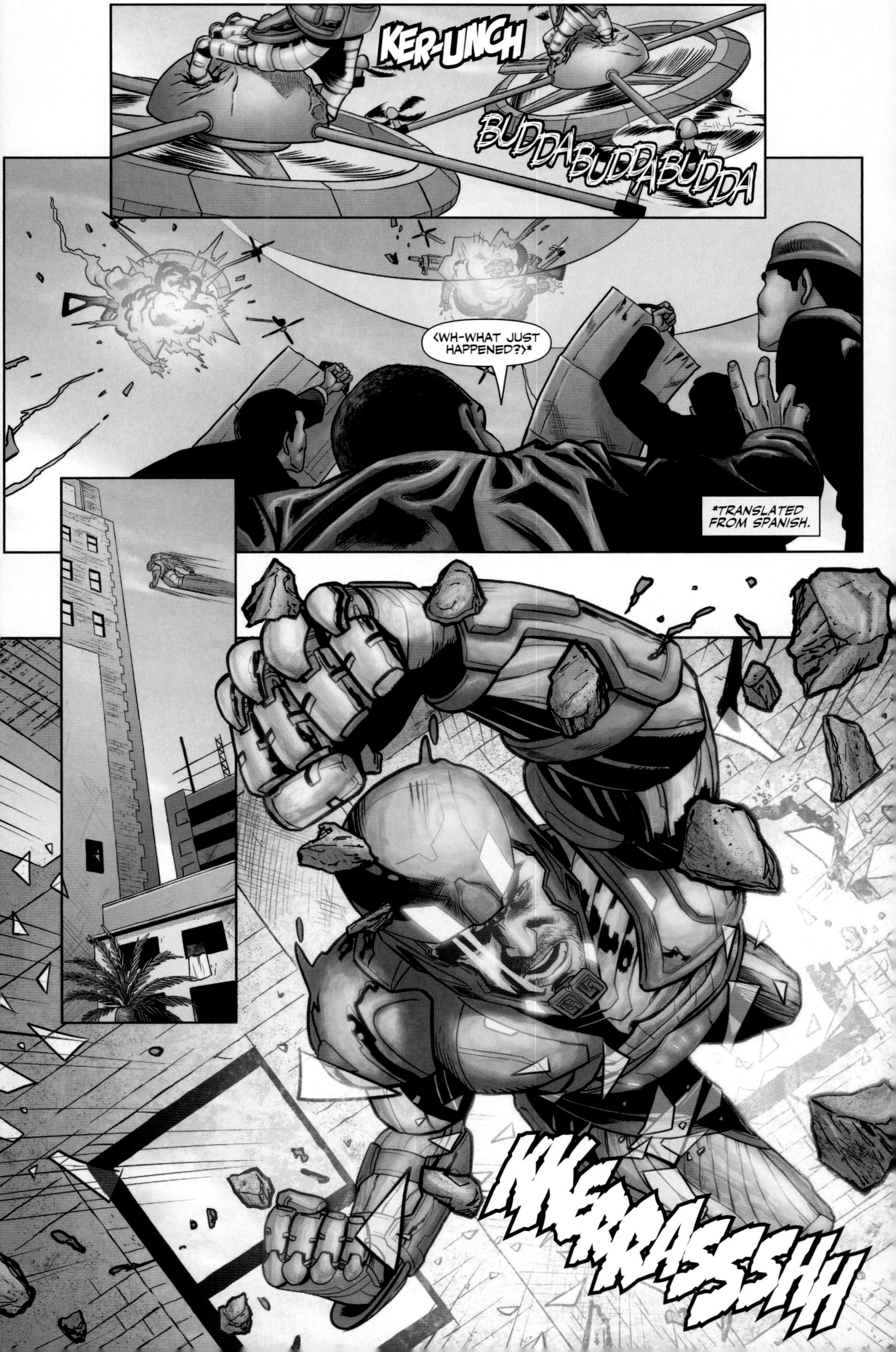
KER-UNCH
BUDDABUDDABUDDA
<WH-WHAT JUST HAPPENED?>*
*TRANSLATED FROM SPANISH.
KKKRRASSSHH

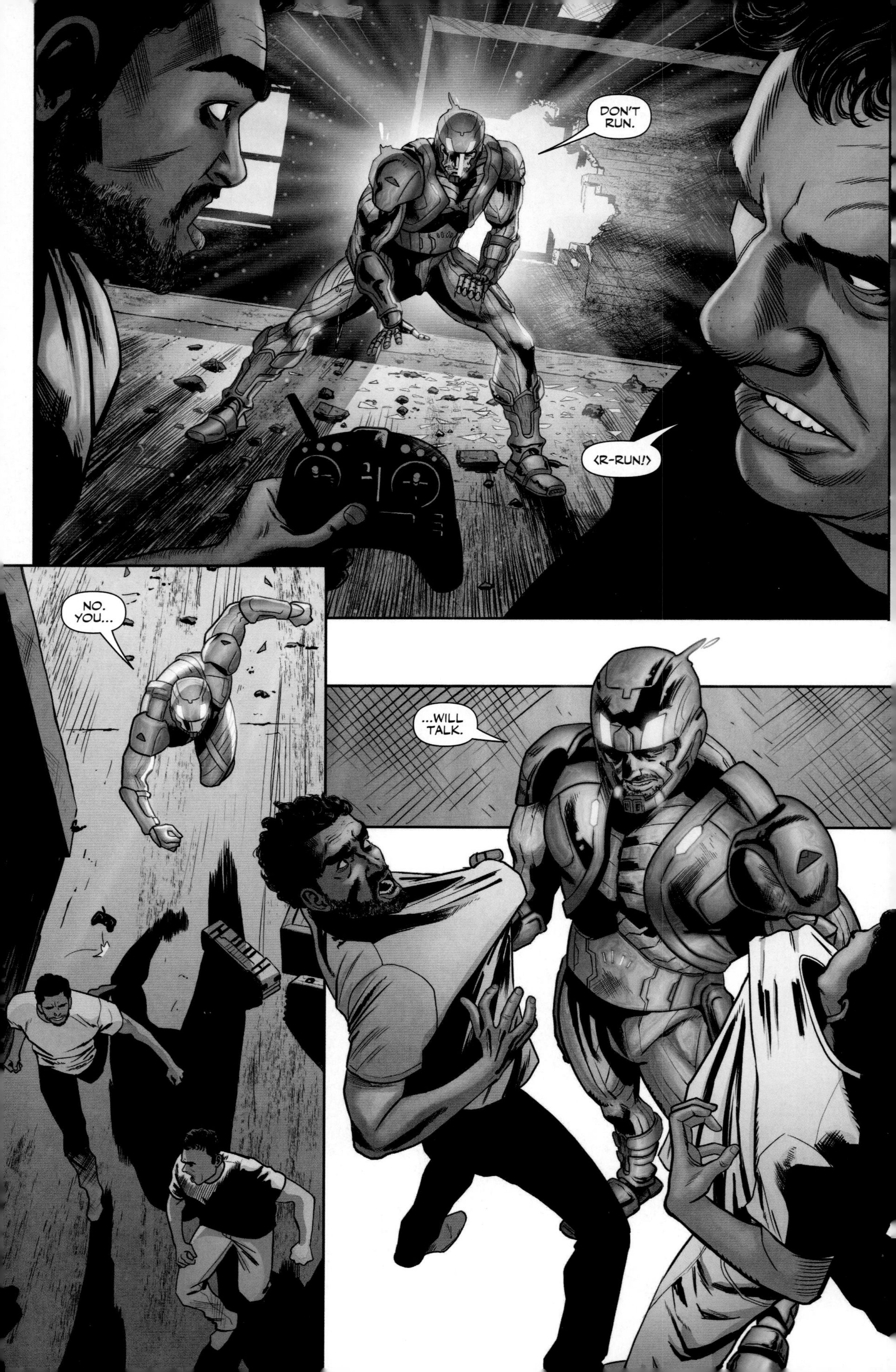
DON'T RUN.
‹R-RUN!›
NO. YOU...
...WILL TALK.

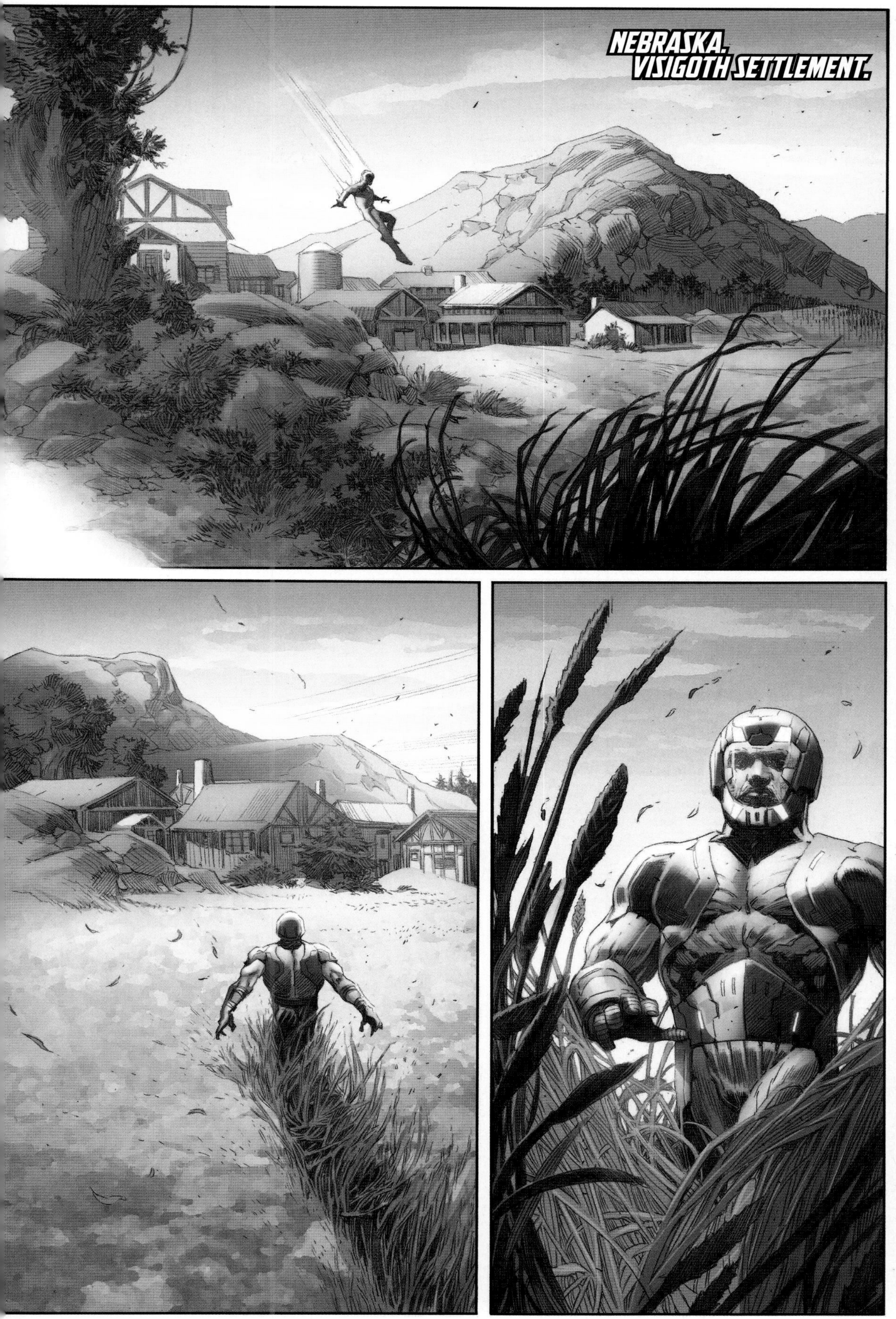
NEBRASKA.
VISIGOTH SETTLEMENT.

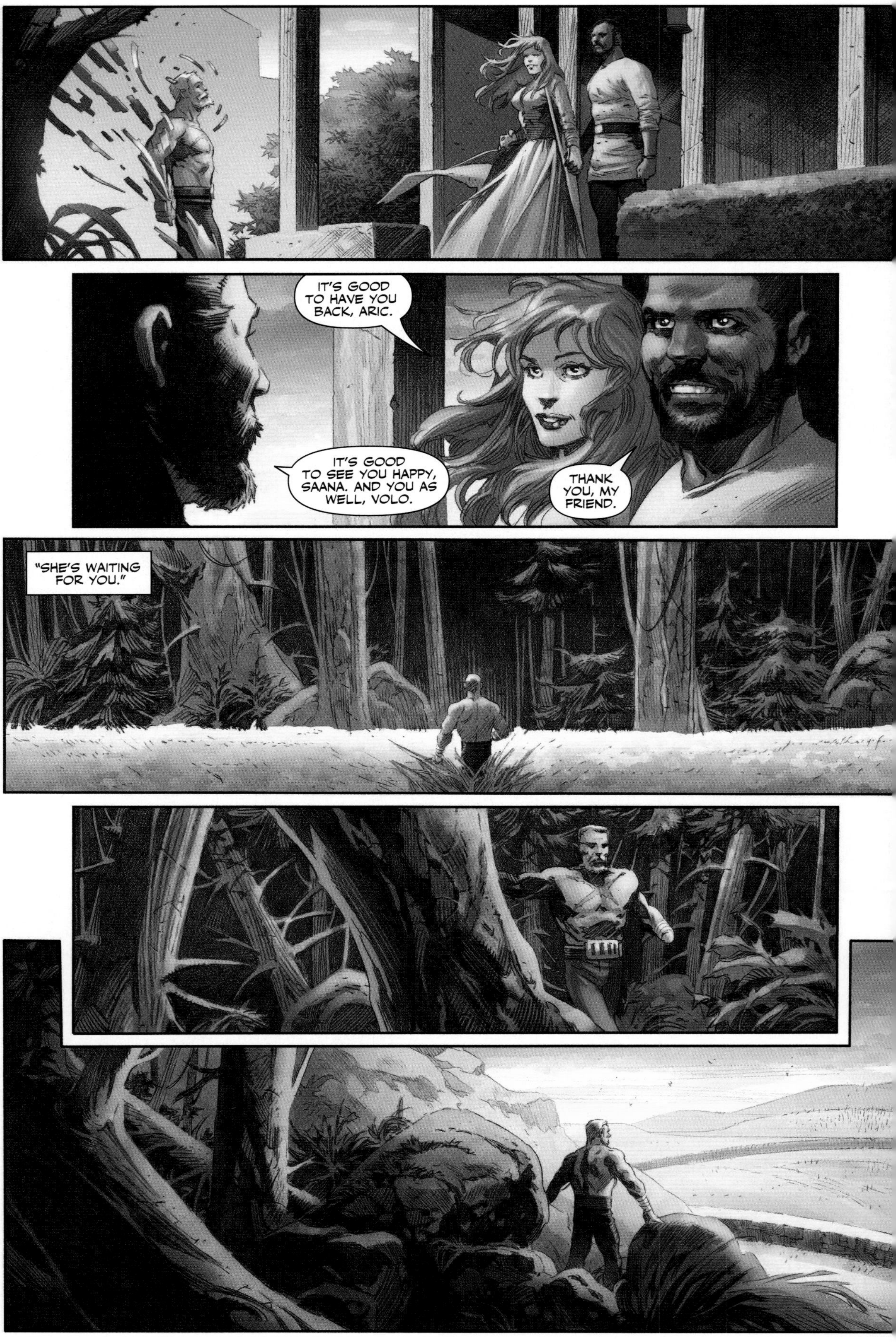
IT'S GOOD TO HAVE YOU BACK, ARIC.
IT'S GOOD TO SEE YOU HAPPY, SAANA. AND YOU AS WELL, VOLO.
THANK YOU, MY FRIEND.
"SHE'S WAITING FOR YOU."

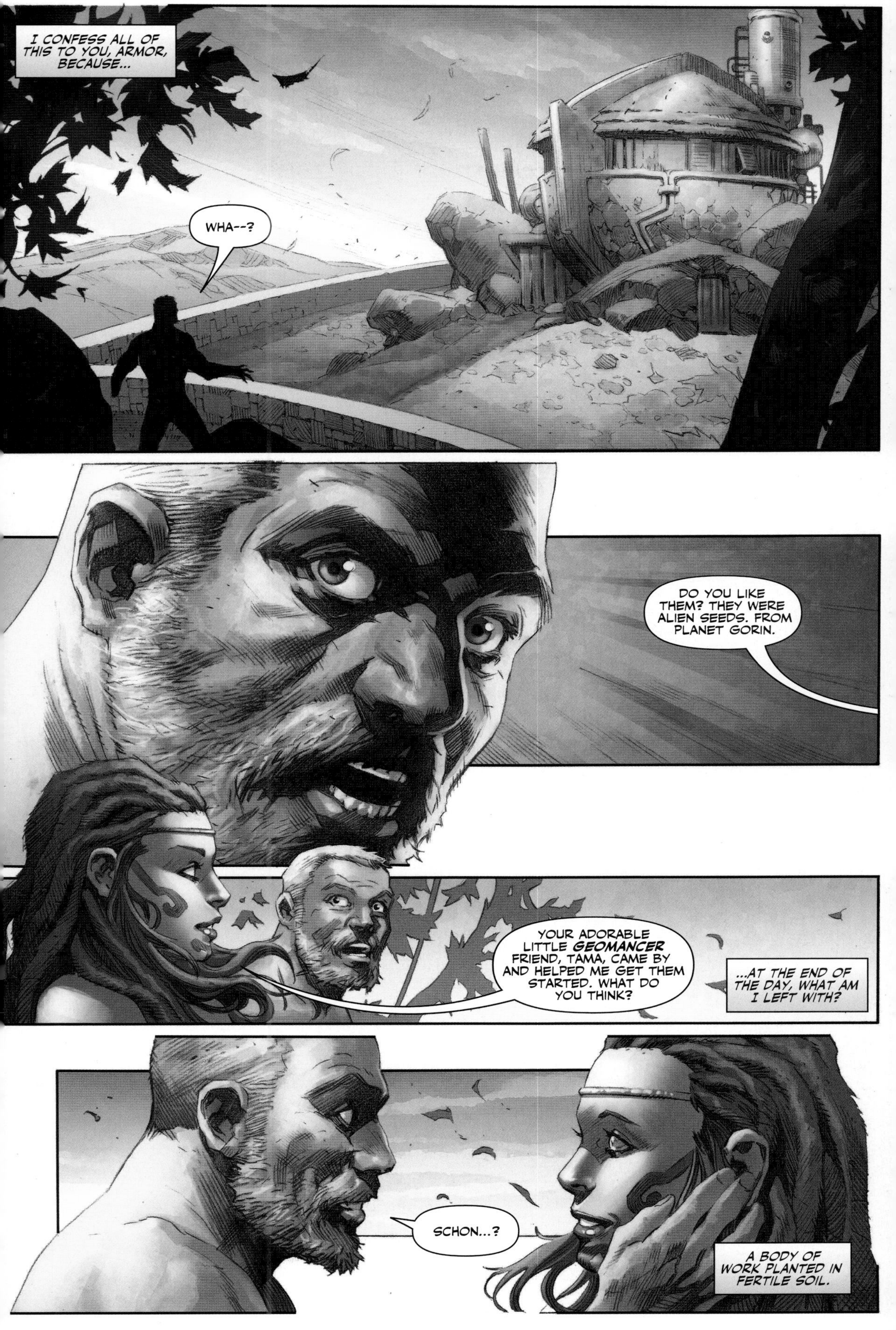
I CONFESS ALL OF THIS TO YOU, ARMOR, BECAUSE...
WHA--?
DO YOU LIKE THEM? THEY WERE ALIEN SEEDS. FROM PLANET GORIN.
YOUR ADORABLE LITTLE GEOMANCER FRIEND, TAMA, CAME BY AND HELPED ME GET THEM STARTED. WHAT DO YOU THINK?
...AT THE END OF THE DAY, WHAT AM I LEFT WITH?
SCHON...?
A BODY OF WORK PLANTED IN FERTILE SOIL.

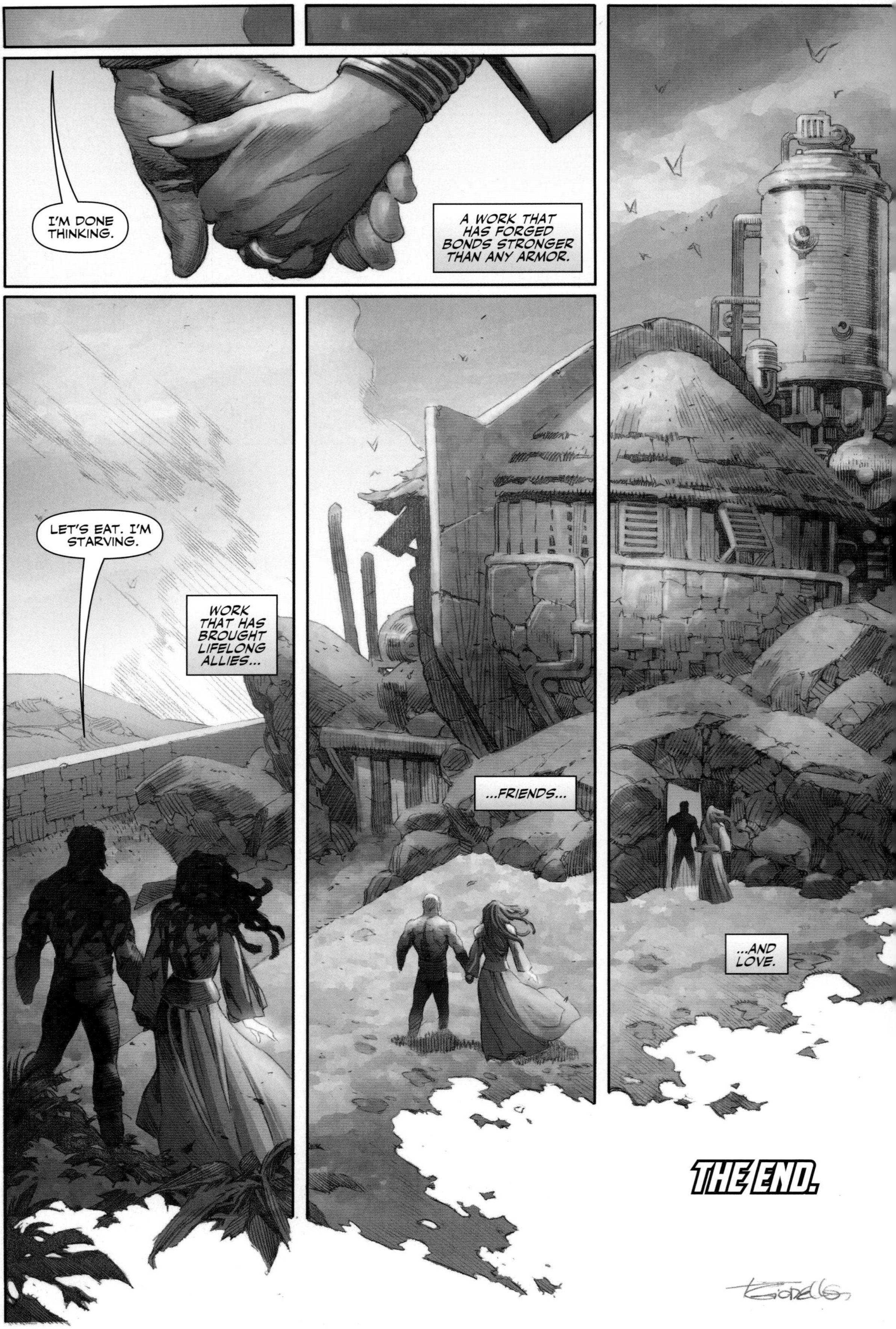
I'M DONE THINKING.
A WORK THAT HAS FORGED BONDS STRONGER THAN ANY ARMOR.
LET'S EAT. I'M STARVING.
WORK THAT HAS BROUGHT LIFELONG ALLIES...
...FRIENDS...
...AND LOVE.
THE END.

GALLERY

X-O MANOWAR #23 PRE-ORDER EDITION COVER
Art by TOMÁS GIORELLO with DIEGO RODRIGUEZ

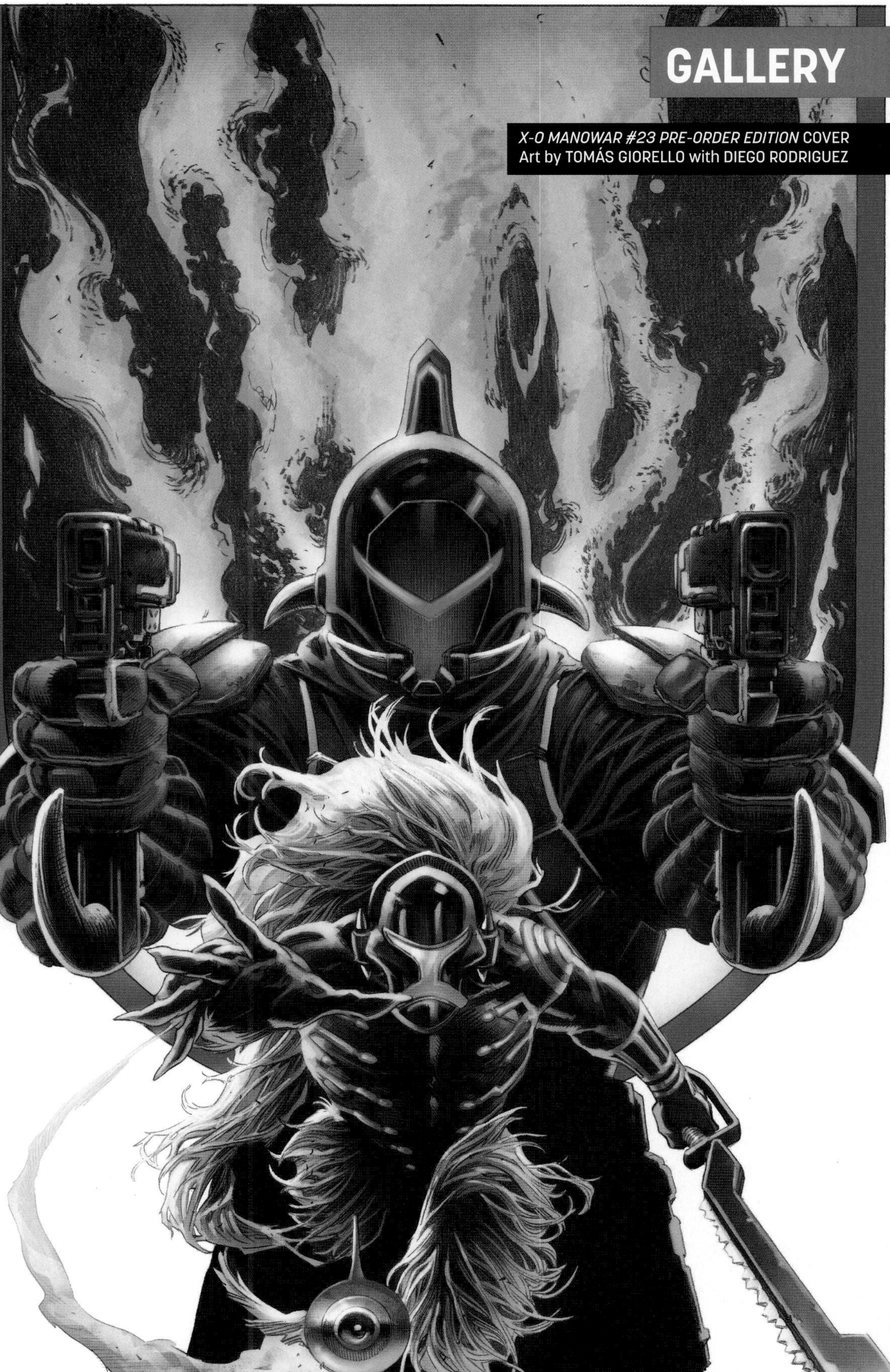

X-O MANOWAR #23 COVER B
Art by DIEGO YAPUR with DIEGO RODRIGUEZ

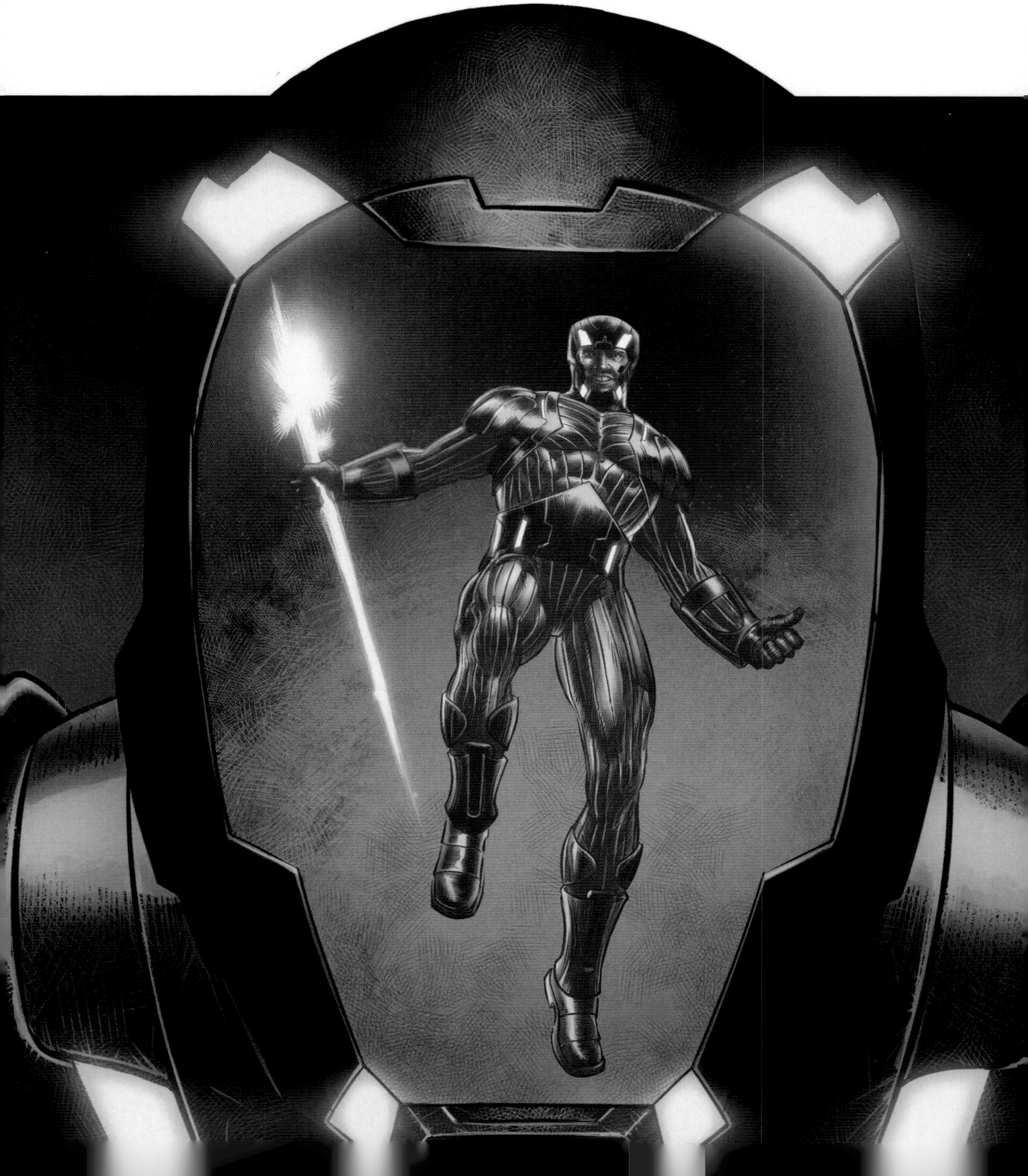

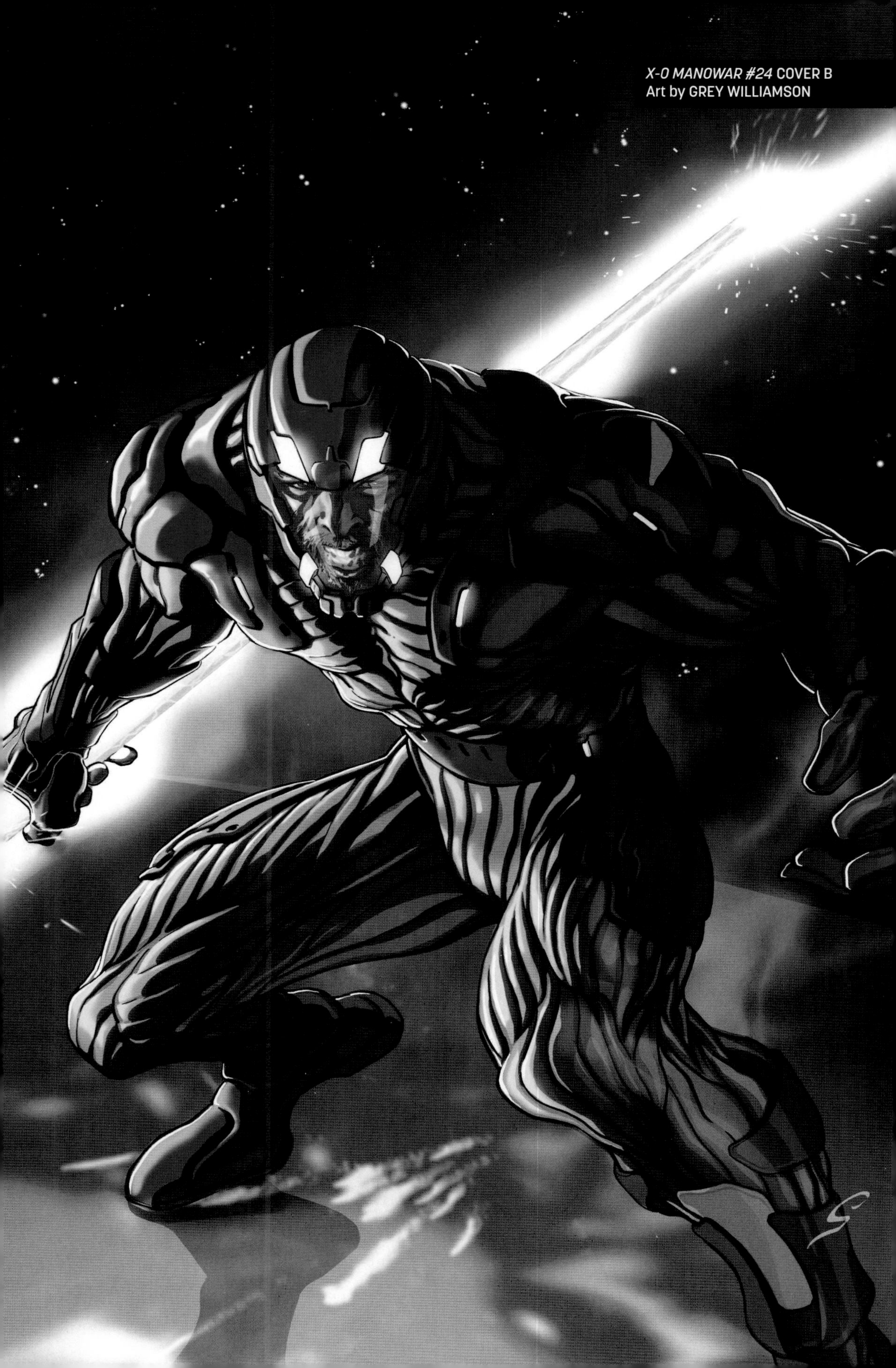

X-O MANOWAR #24 COVER B
Art by GREY WILLIAMSON

X-O MANOWAR #23 COVER C
Art by MICHAEL MANOMIVIBUL

X-O MANOWAR #24 COVER C
Art by MICHAEL MANOMIVIBUL

X-O MANOWAR #25 COVER C (facing)
Art by MICHAEL MANOMIVIBUL

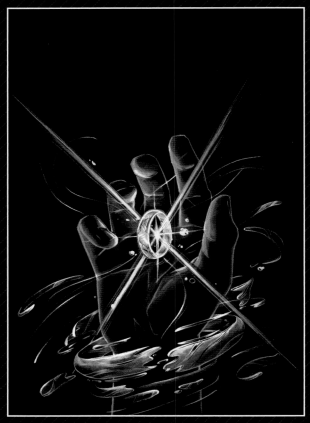

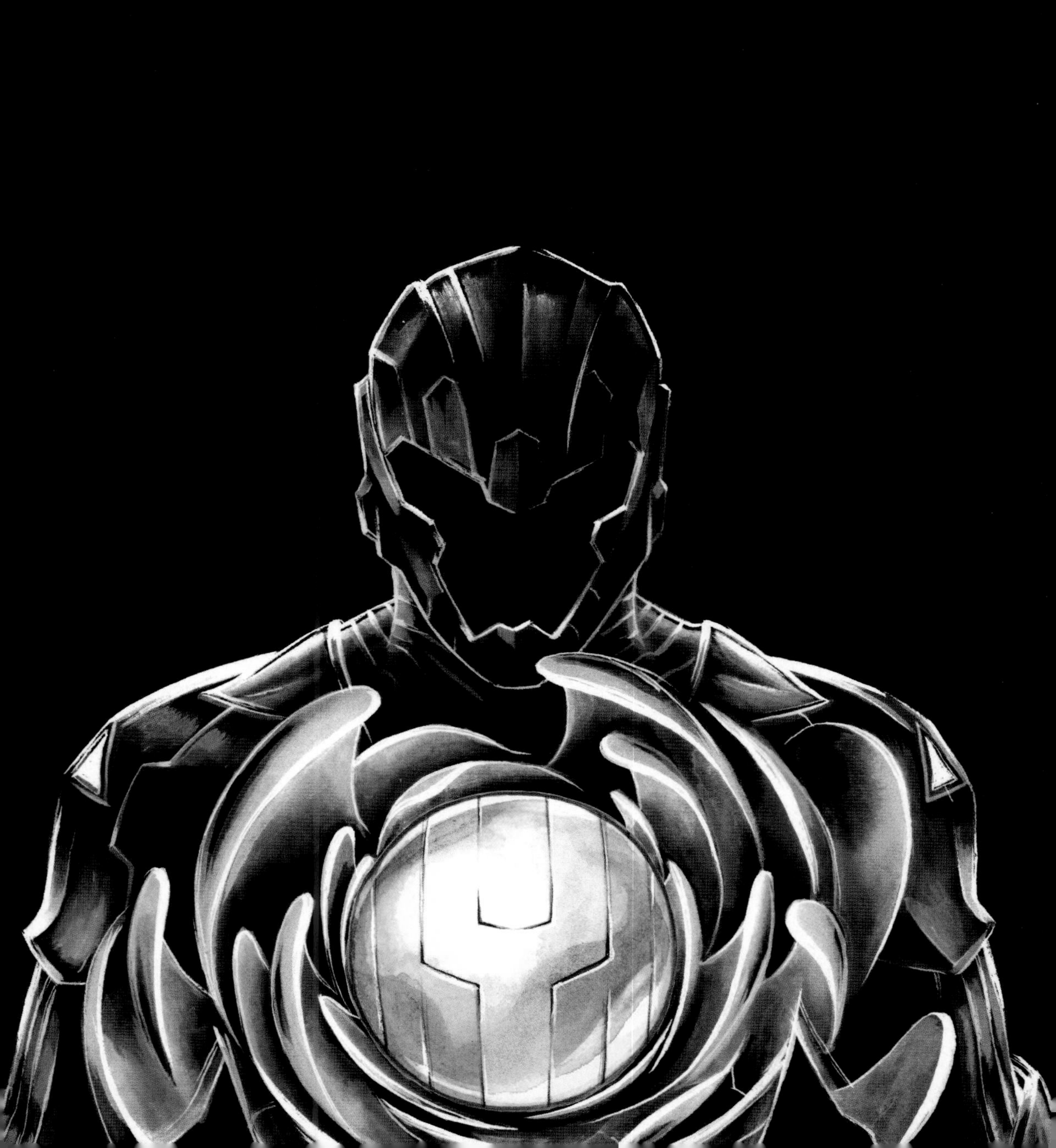

X-O MANOWAR #23-26 INTERLOCKING VARIANT COVERS
Art by FRANCIS PORTELA with LEONARDO PACIAROTTI

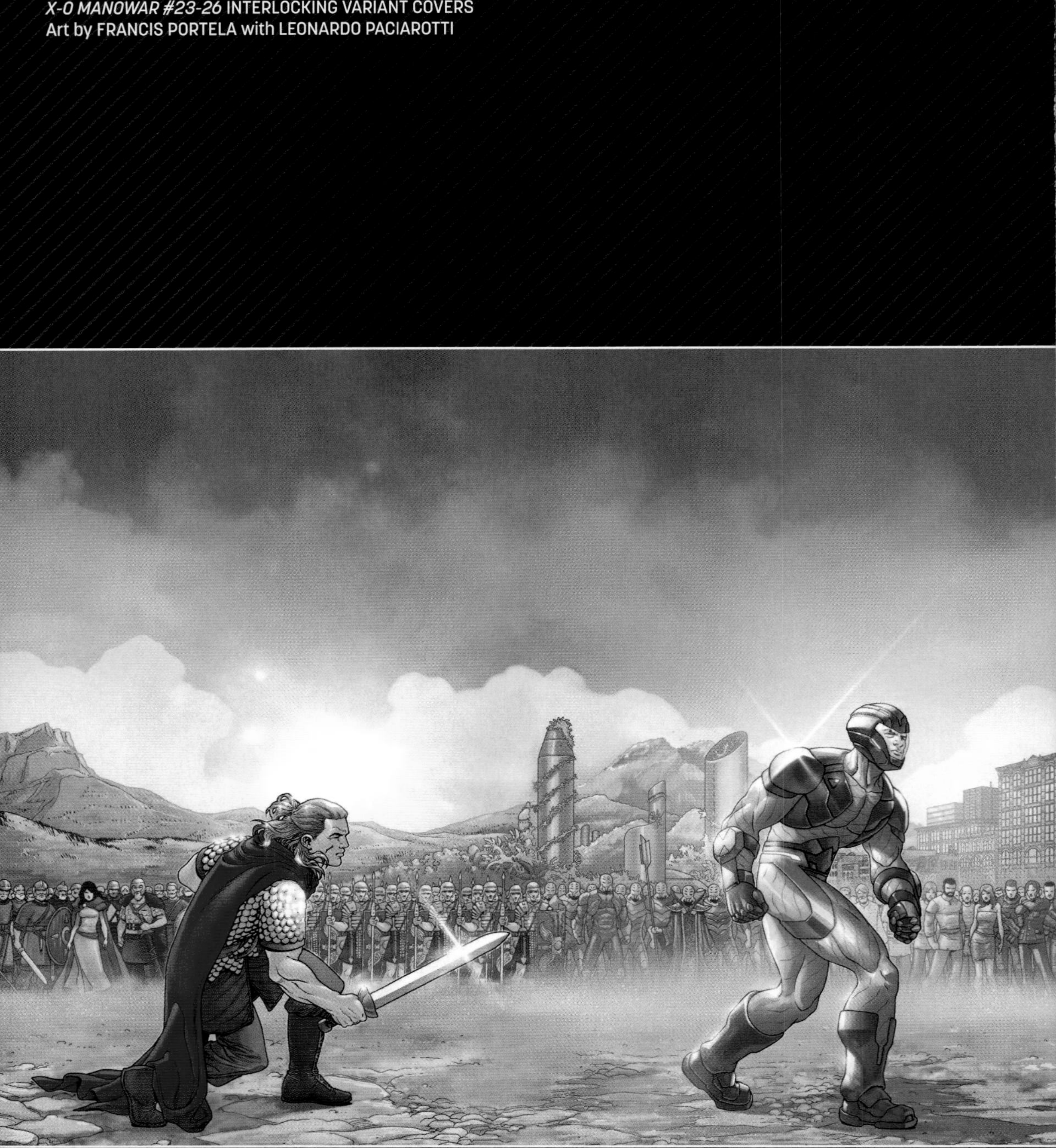

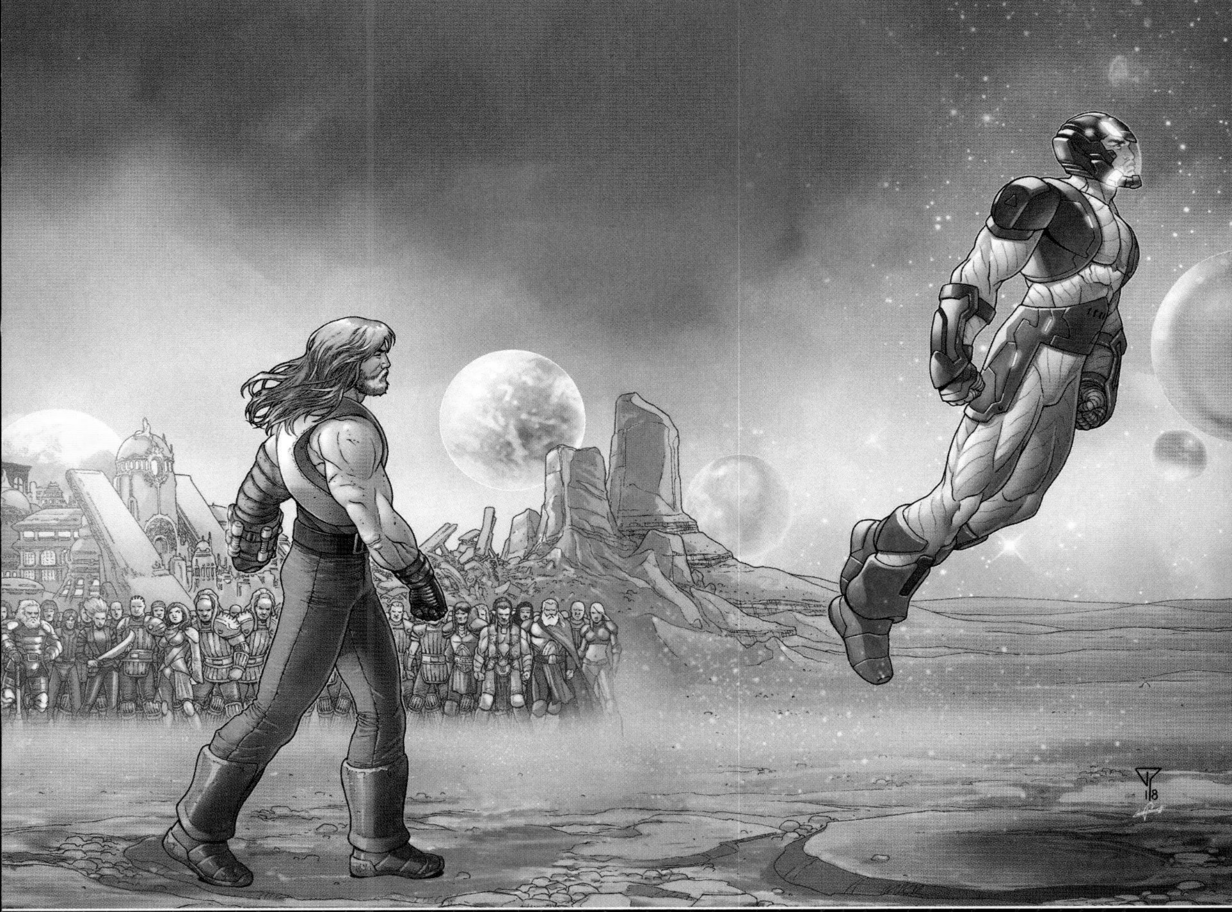

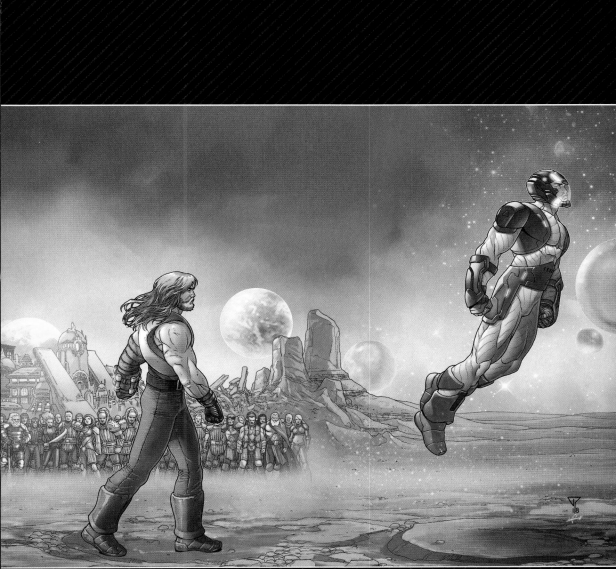

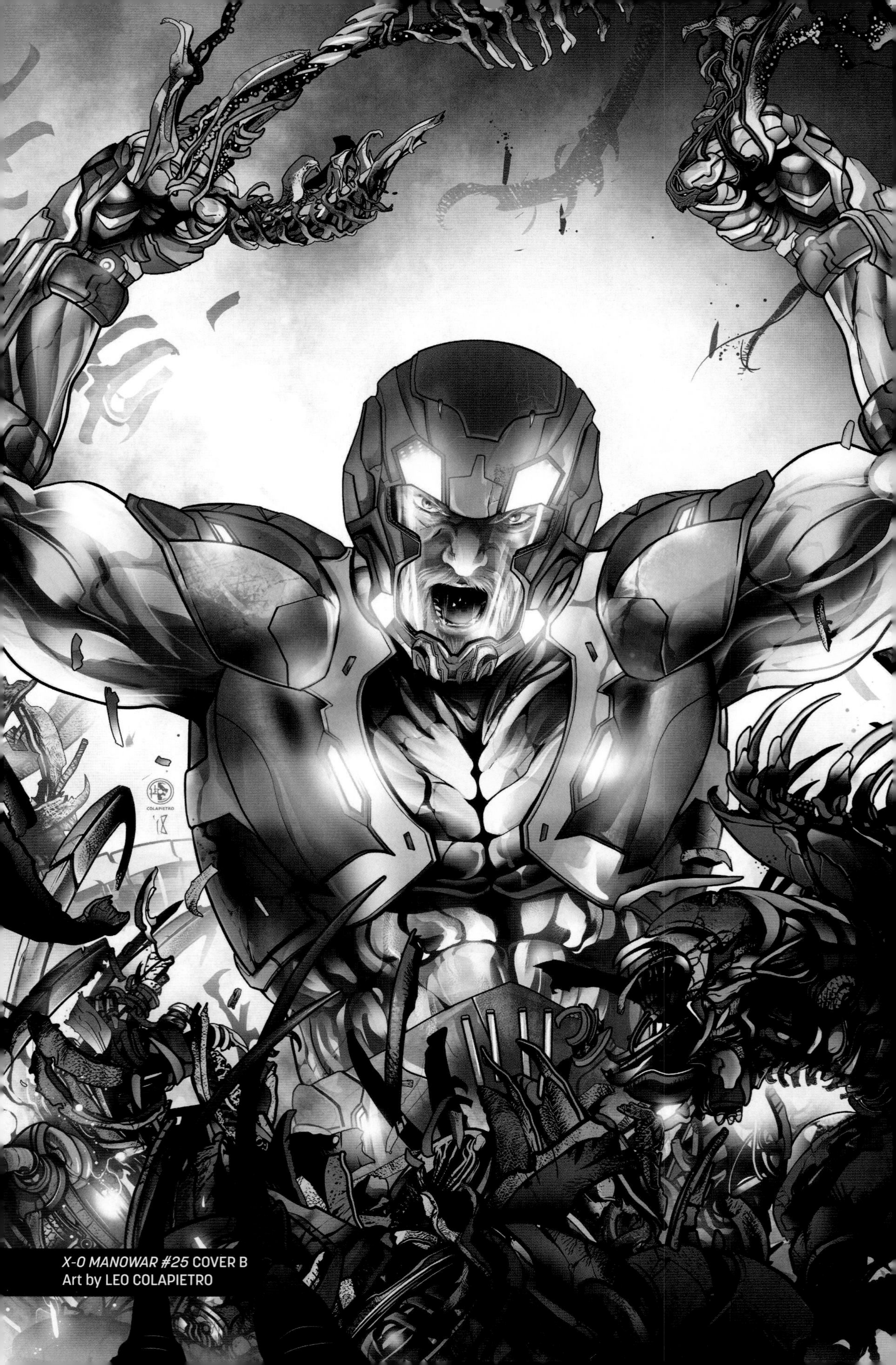
COLAPIETRO
'18

X-O MANOWAR #25 COVER B
Art by LEO COLAPIETRO

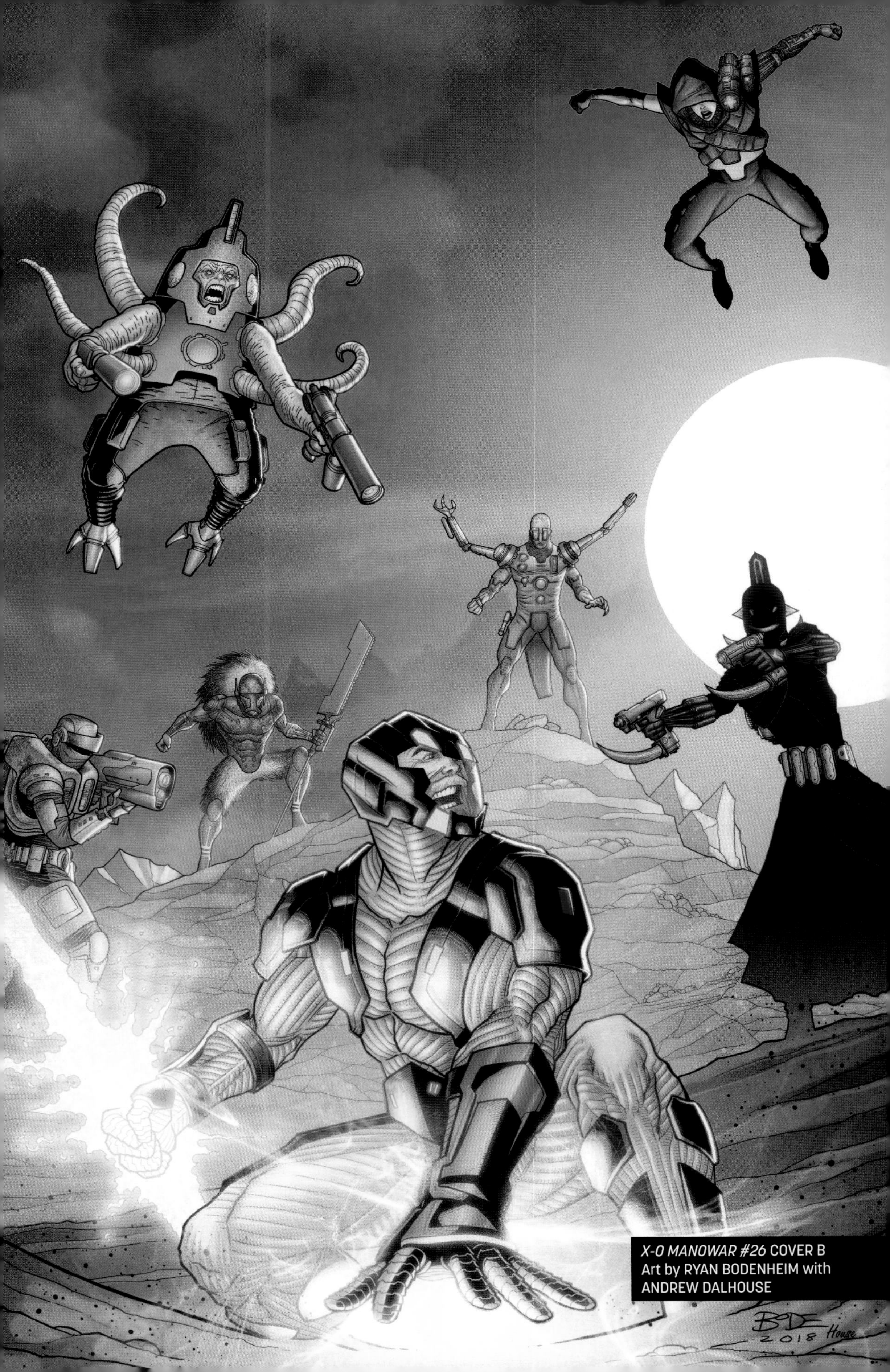
BODE
2018
House

X-O MANOWAR #26 COVER B
Art by RYAN BODENHEIM with
ANDREW DALHOUSE

X-O MANOWAR #23, pages 3, 4, and (facing) 5
Art by TOMÁS GIORELLO

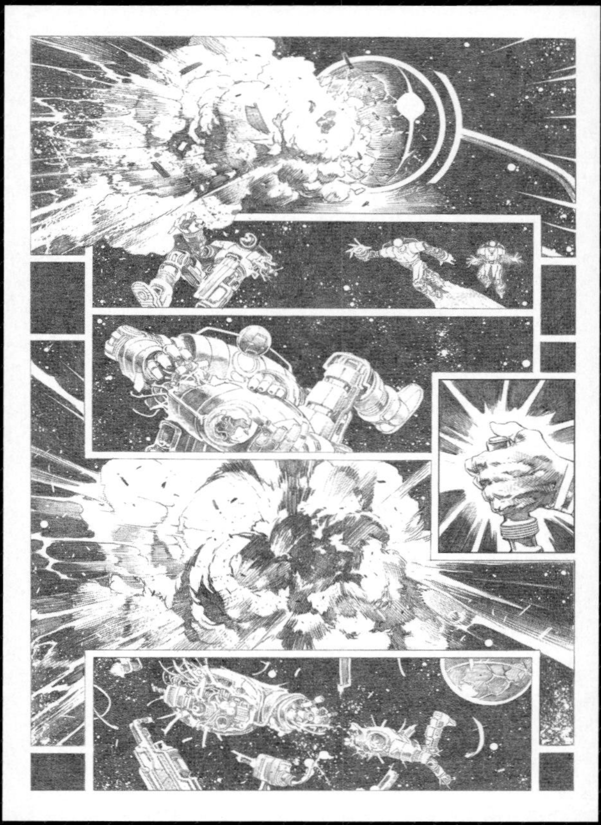

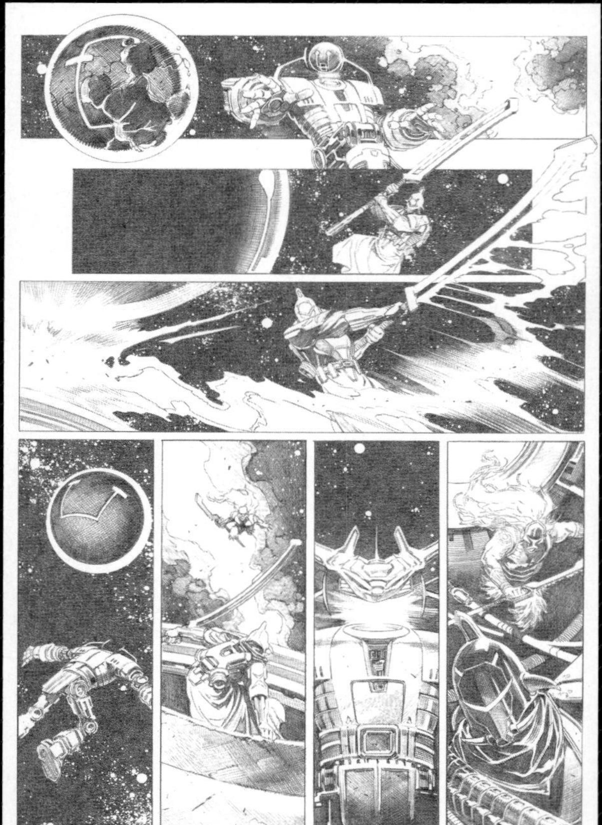

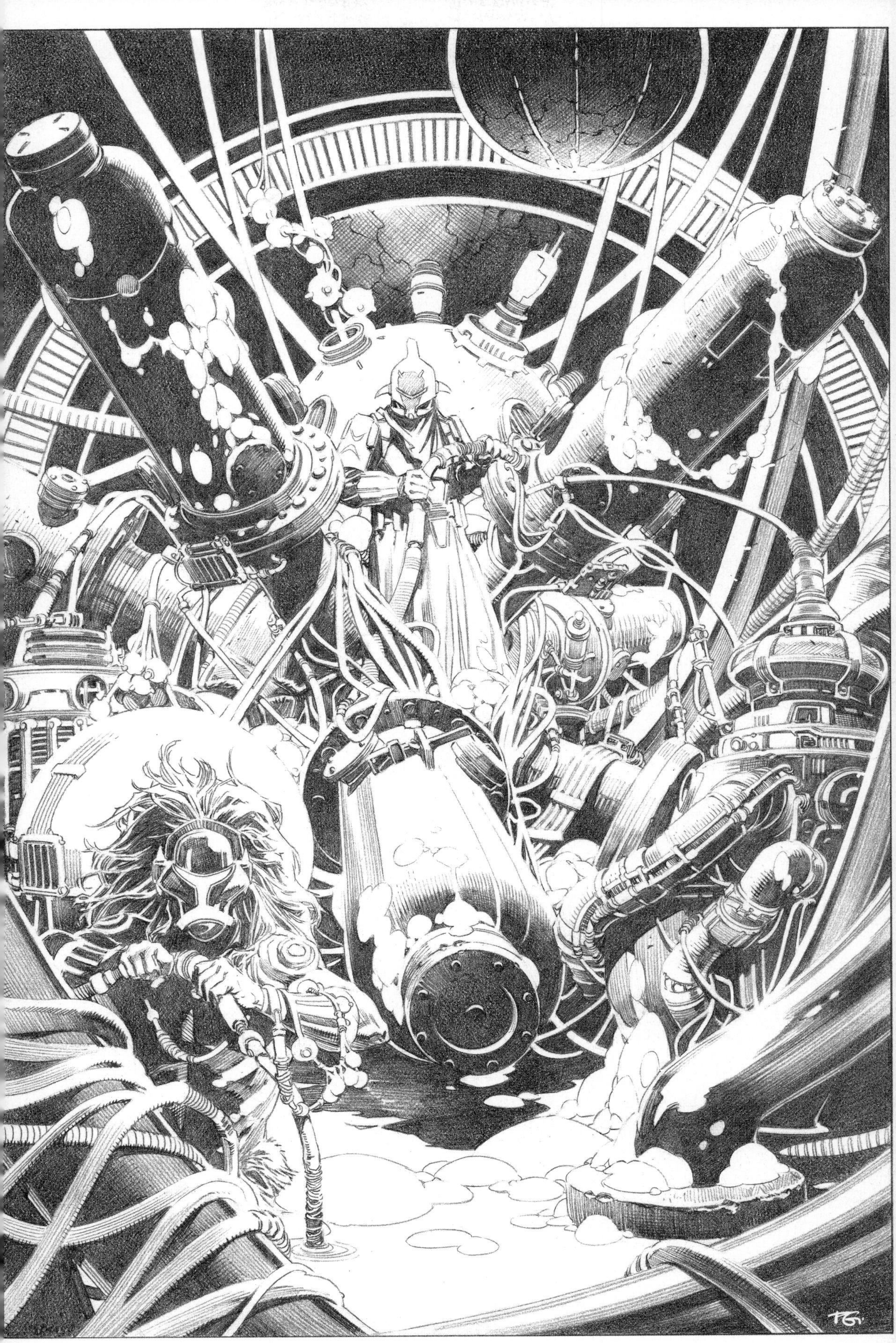

X-O MANOWAR #24, pages 18, 19, and (facing) 20
Art by TOMÁS GIORELLO

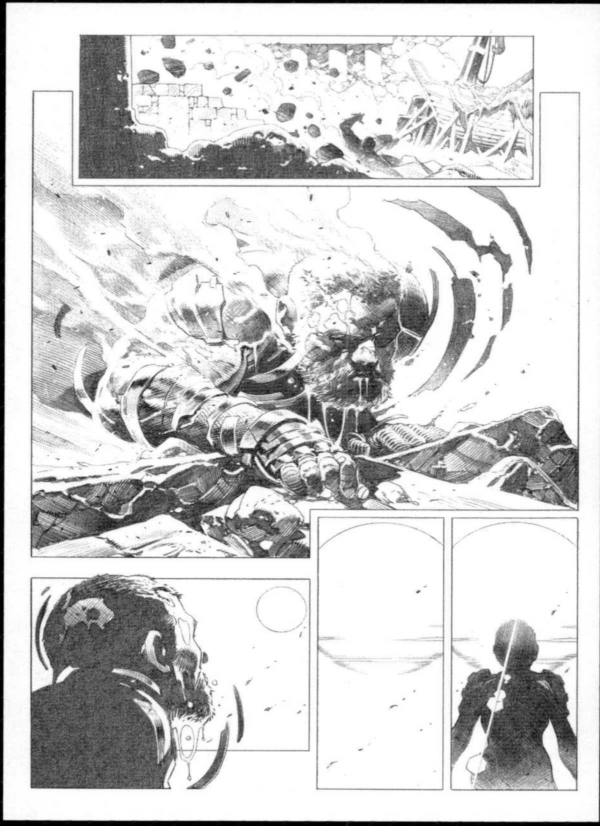

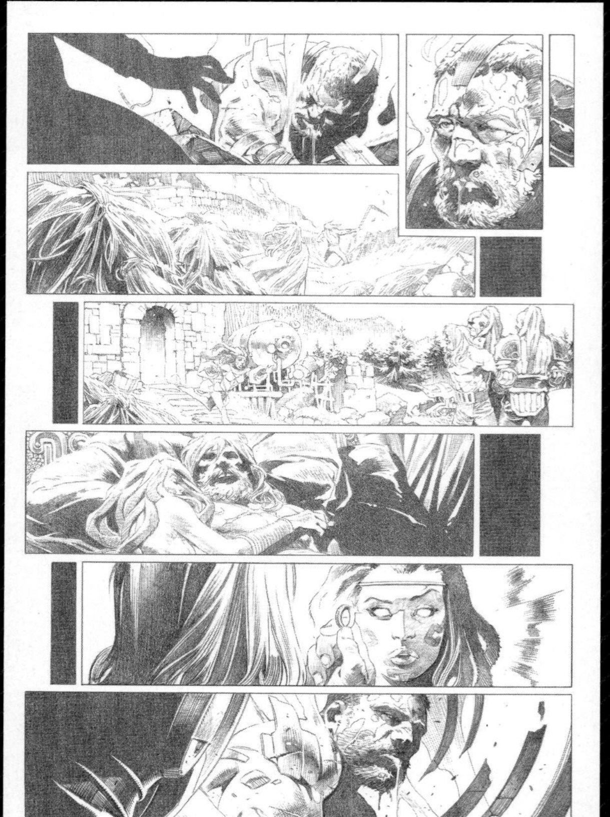

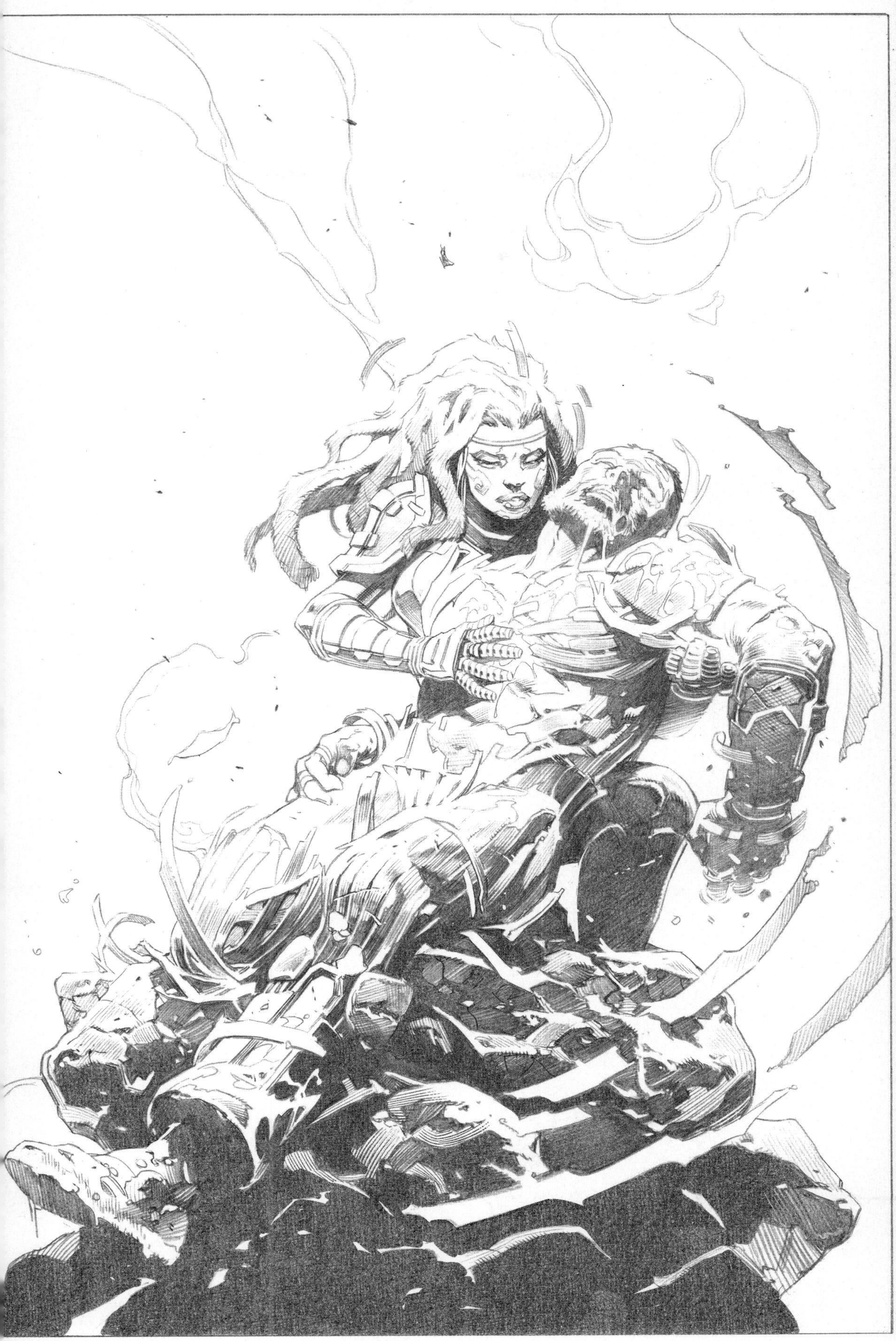

X-O MANOWAR #25, pages 11, 12, and (facing) 13
Art by TOMÁS GIORELLO

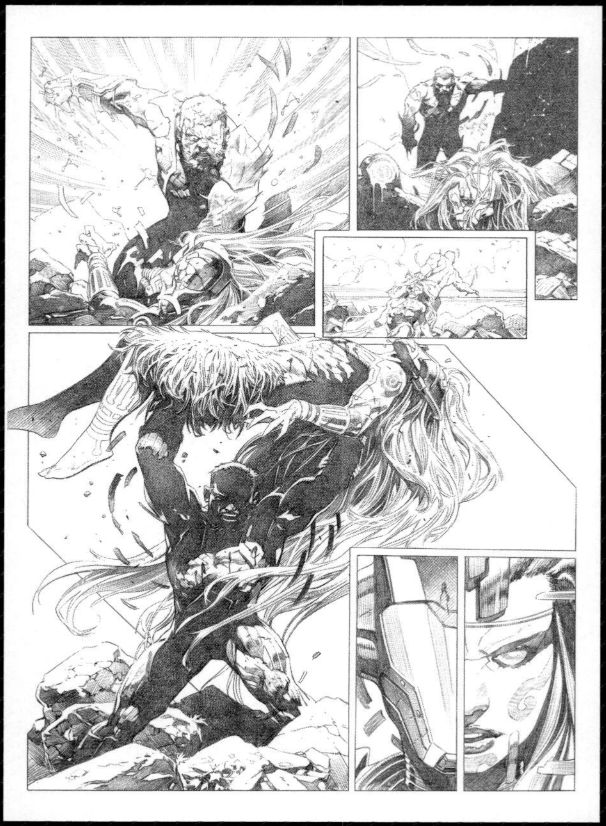

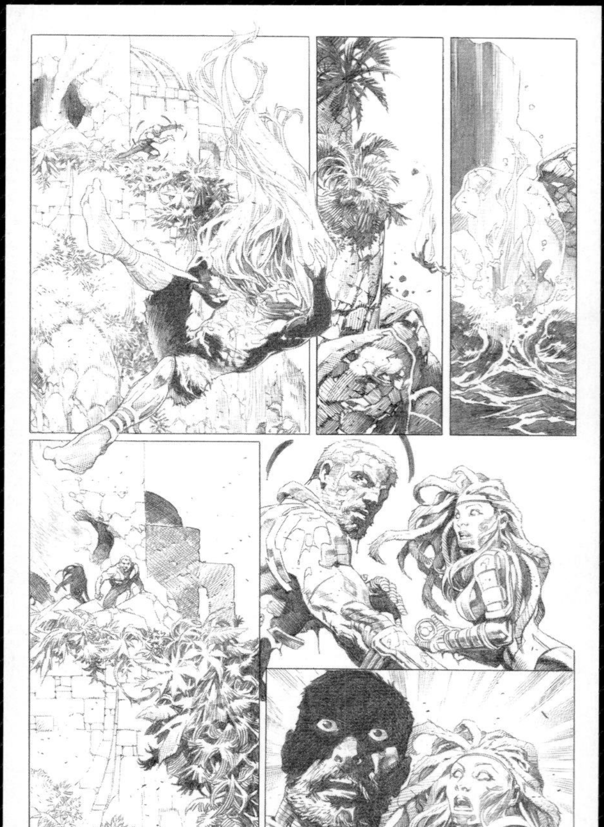

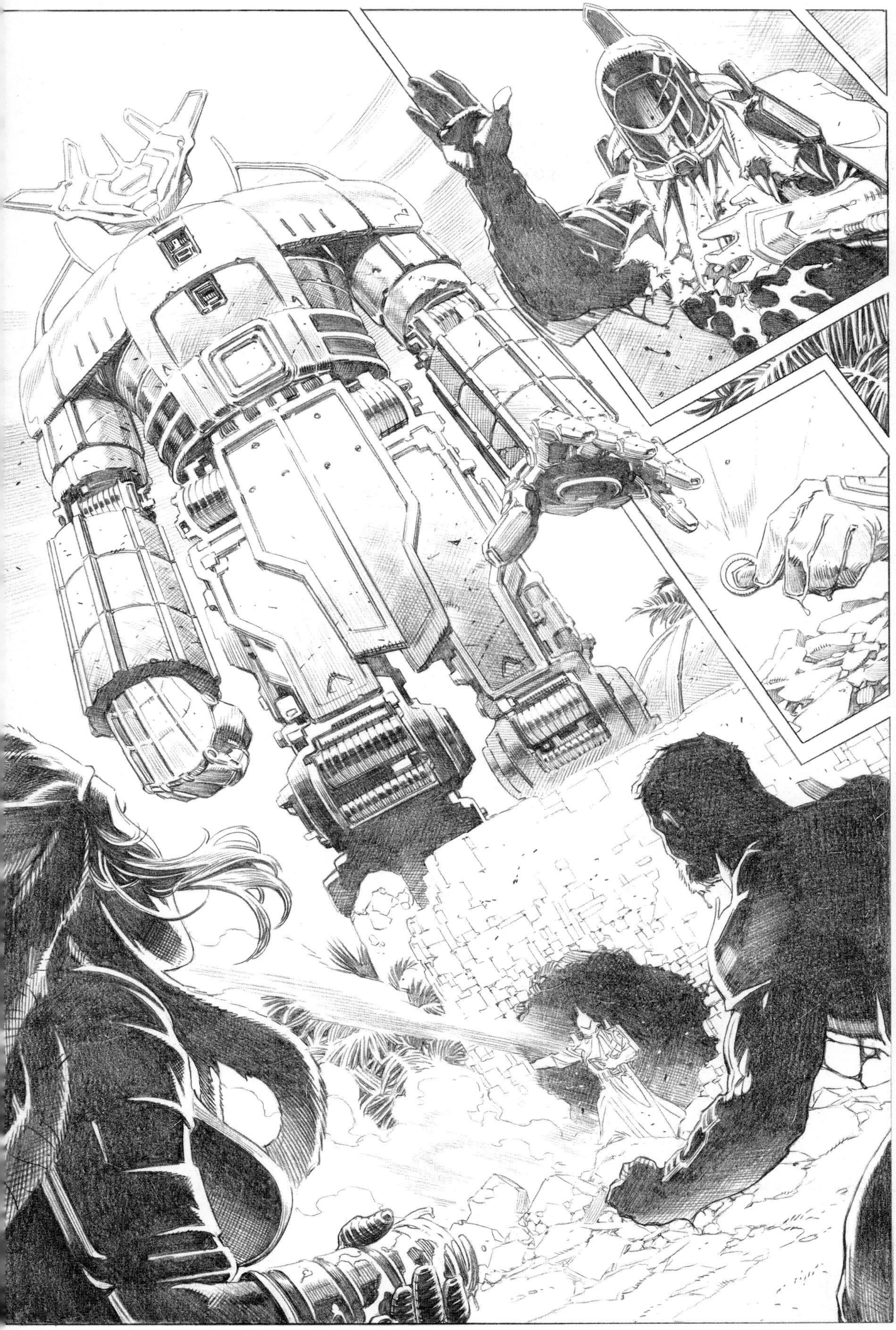

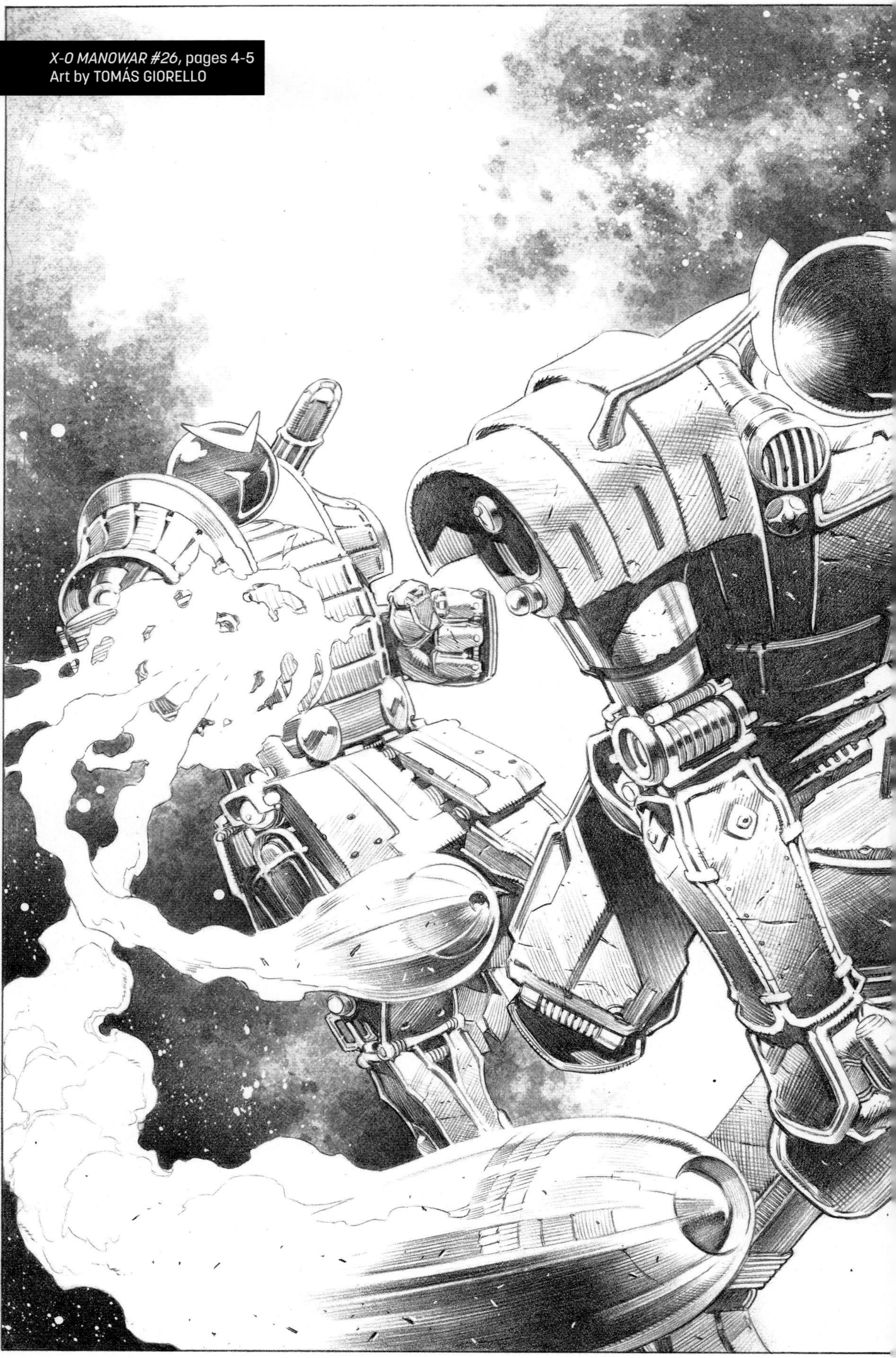

X-O MANOWAR #26, pages 4-5
Art by TOMÁS GIORELLO

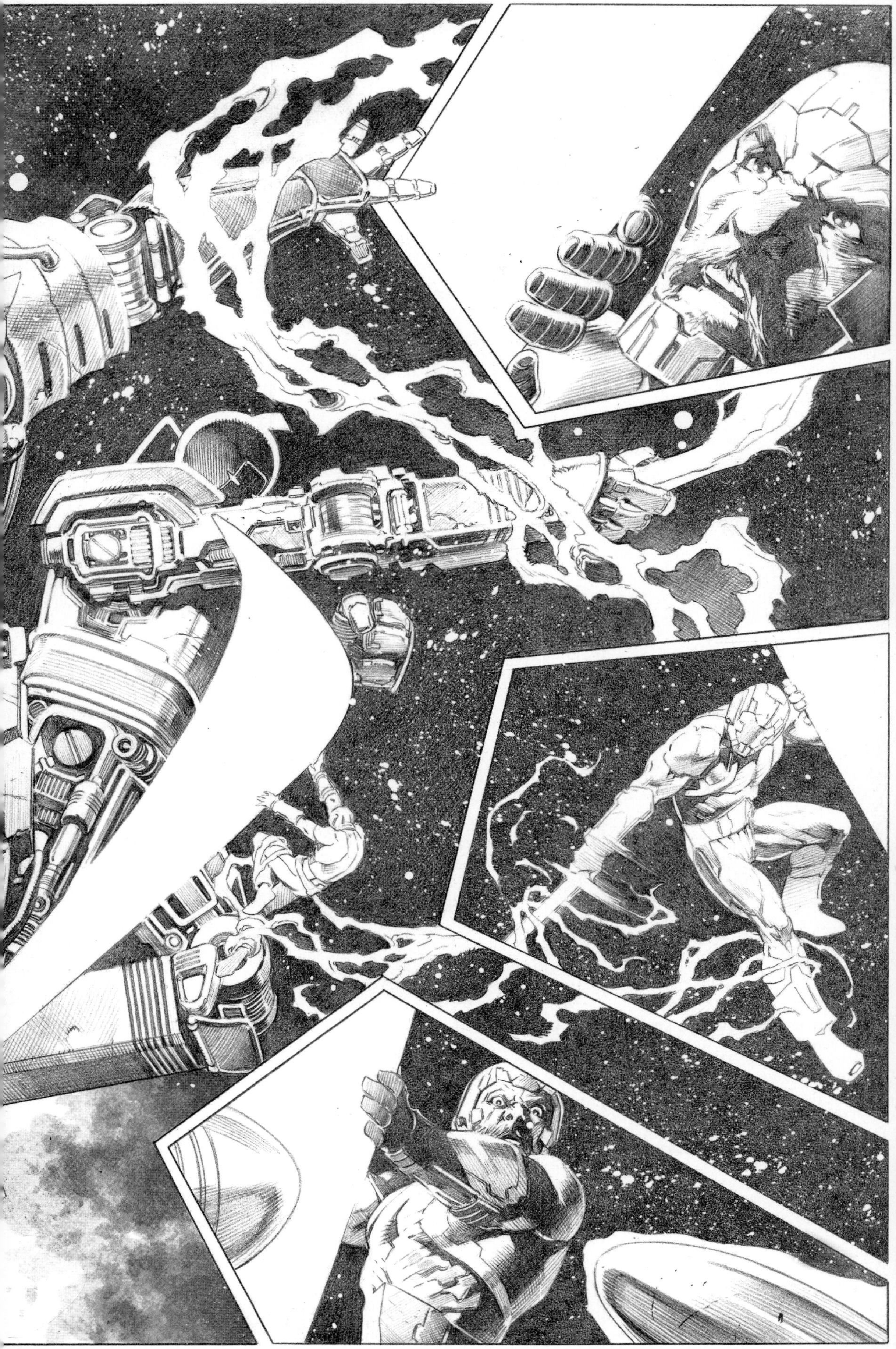

EXPLORE THE VALIANT

ACTION & ADVENTURE

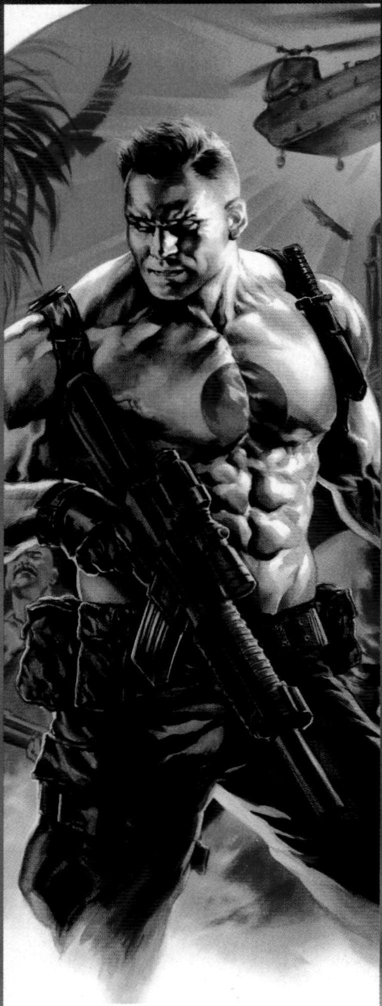

BLOODSHOT SALVATION VOL. 1: THE BOOK OF REVENGE
ISBN: 978-1-68215-255-3
NINJA-K VOL. 1: THE NINJA FILES
ISBN: 978-1-68215-259-1
SAVAGE
ISBN: 978-1-68215-189-1
WRATH OF THE ETERNAL WARRIOR VOL. 1: RISEN
ISBN: 978-1-68215-123-5
X-O MANOWAR (2017) VOL. 1: SOLDIER
ISBN: 978-1-68215-205-8

BLOCKBUSTER ADVENTURE

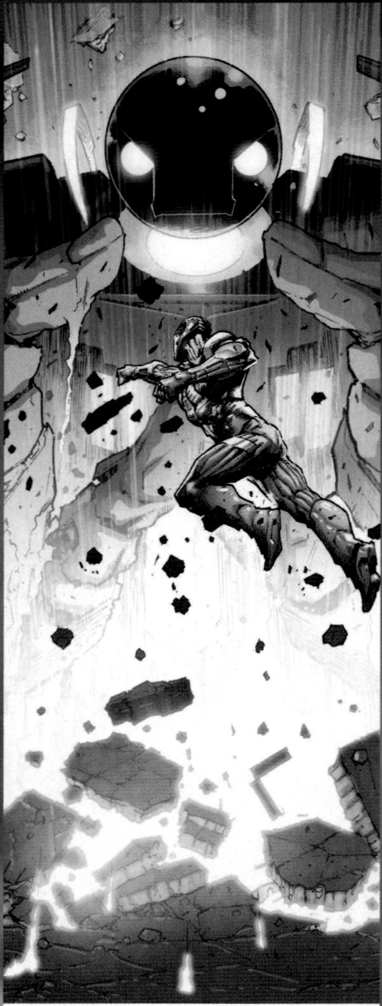

4001 A.D.
ISBN: 978-1-68215-143-3
ARMOR HUNTERS
ISBN: 978-1-939346-45-2
BOOK OF DEATH
ISBN: 978-1-939346-97-1
HARBINGER WARS
ISBN: 978-1-939346-09-4
THE VALIANT
ISBN: 978-1-939346-60-5

COMEDY

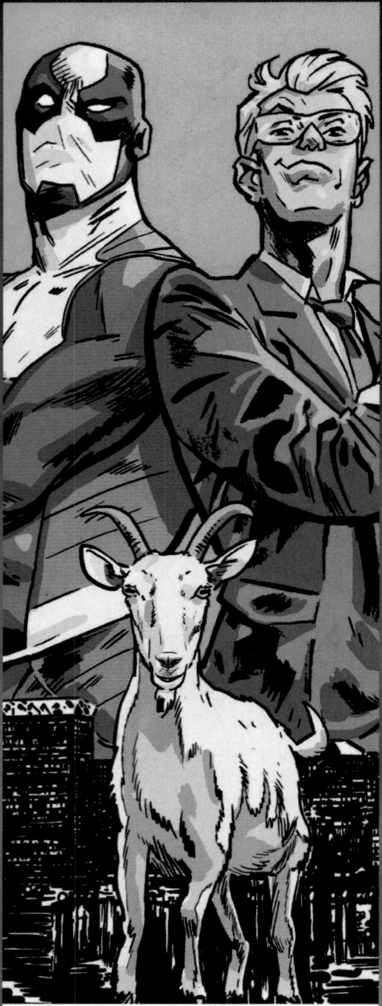

A&A: THE ADVENTURES OF ARCHER & ARMSTRONG VOL. 1: IN THE BAG
ISBN: 978-1-68215-149-5
THE DELINQUENTS
ISBN: 978-1-939346-51-3
QUANTUM AND WOODY! (2017) VOL. 1: KISS KISS, KLANG KLANG
ISBN: 978-1-68215-269-0

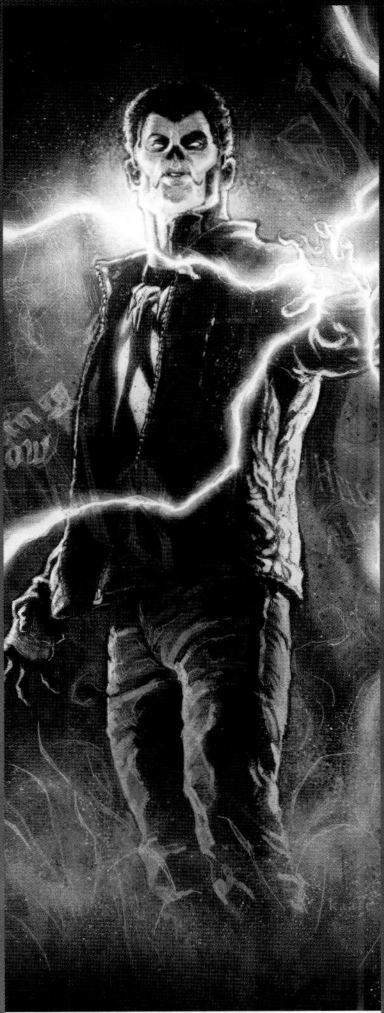

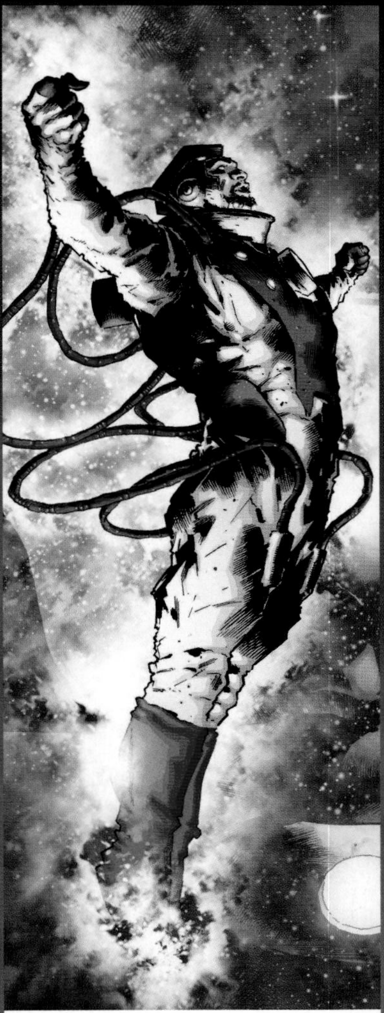

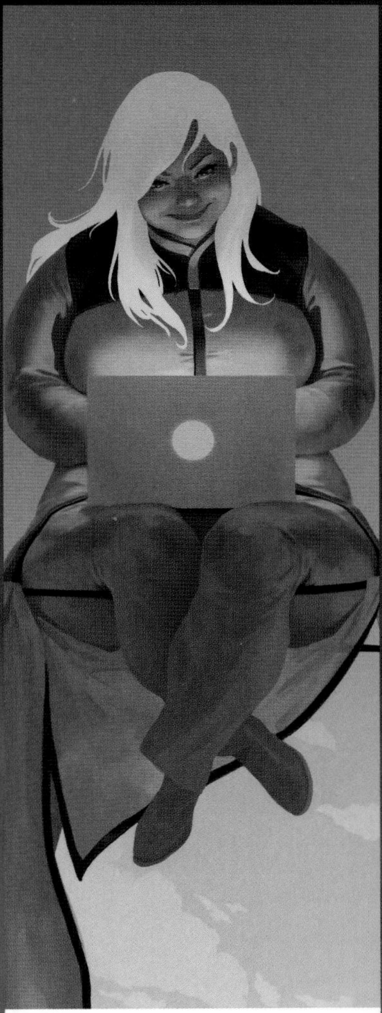

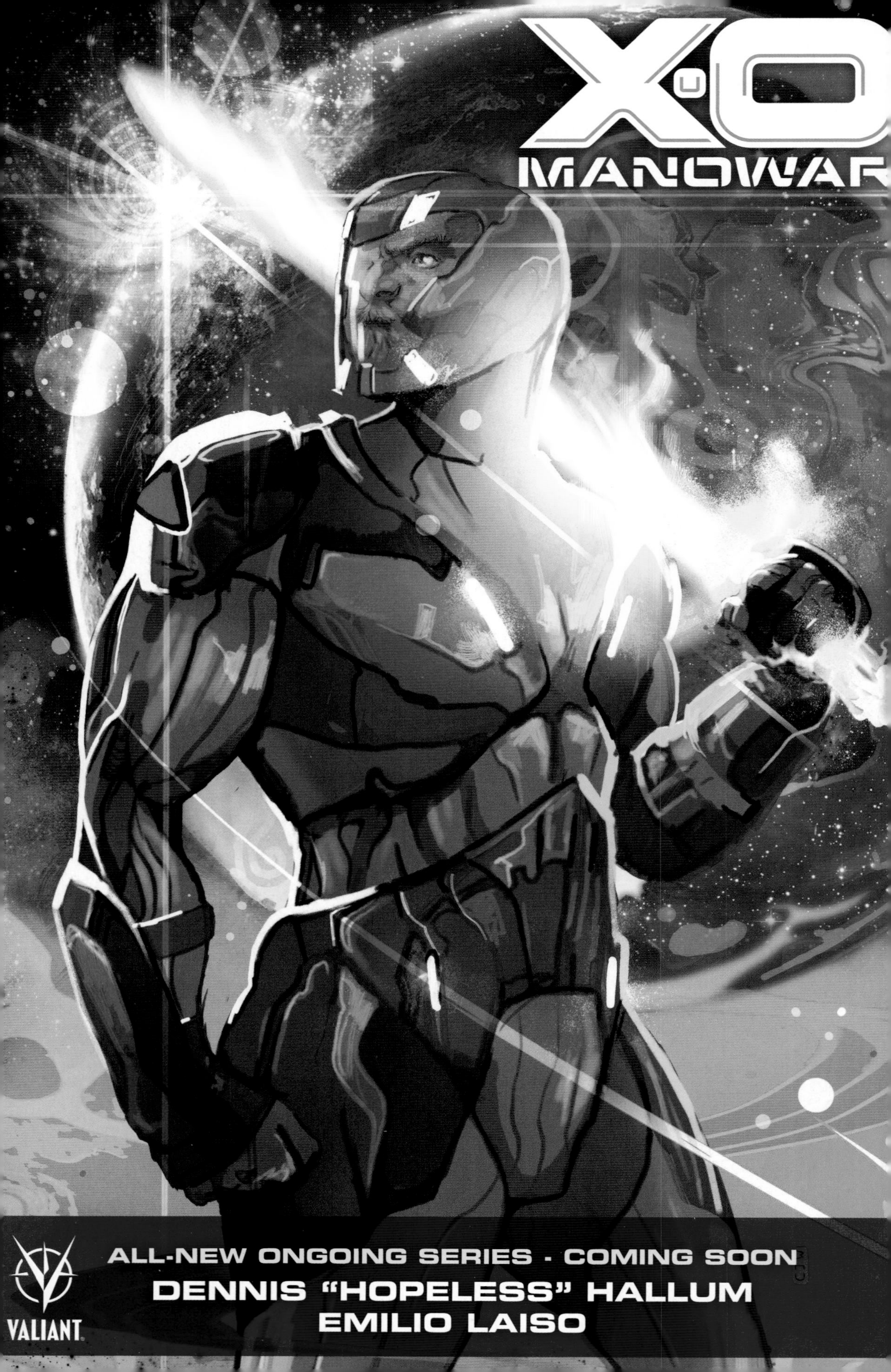
X-O MANOWAR
ALL-NEW ONGOING SERIES · COMING SOON
DENNIS "HOPELESS" HALLUM
EMILIO LAISO
VALIANT